Gospel of Matthew

The Word IN LIFE Study Bible

THOMAS NELSON PUBLISHERS
Nashville

The Word In Life Study Bible,
Gospel of Matthew

Printed in the United States of America

1 2 3 4 5 6 7 8 9 10 11 12 — 98 97 96 95 94 93

Acknowledgments

Matthew 13:34–35: "Ten Myths About Christianity, Myth #1: Jesus Christ Was Only a Great Moral Teacher." Adapted by permission from *Ten Myths About Christianity* by Michael Green and Gordon Carkner, Lion Publishing, 1988. Quotation from C.S. Lewis, *Mere Christianity,* Macmillan, 1978, used by permission of HarperCollins Publishers.

Matthew 20:28: quotation from *Honest To God,* by John A.T. Robinson. © SCM Press Ltd. 1963. Published in the U.S.A. by The Westminster Press. Used by permission of Westminster/John Knox Press.

Matthew 23:1–30: excerpt from letter to Sheldon Vanauken from C.S. Lewis, Jan. 5, 1951, in Sheldon Vanauken, *A Severe Mercy,* Harper & Row, 1977, used by permission of HarperCollins Publishers.

Matthew 28:1–10: "Ten Myths About Christianity, Myth #2: There Is No Evidence That Jesus Rose from the Dead." Adapted by permission from *Ten Myths About Christianity* by Michael Green and Gordon Carkner, Lion Publishing, 1988.

CONTENTS

Acknowledgments ii

Introduction iii

Why This Kind of Publication? iv

A "User-Friendly" Study Bible iv

Features to Look For v

Themes to Consider vii

How to Use the Symbol System ix

New King James Footnotes x

Matthew Introduction 1

Matthew 1 7

Themes to Study 125

Index to Key Passages 129

INTRODUCTION

This edition of Matthew's Gospel is part of *The Word In Life Study Bible,* the beginning of a new generation of study Bibles. Its purpose is to help you discover ways to relate the Word of God to you and the world you live in. This Bible makes it easy to bring the Word into your own world by taking you right into the world of the Bible.

The Word In Life Study Bible helps you get a clear understanding of God's Word by focusing on the surroundings of the biblical narrative. Stimulating articles get you thinking about how to relate the teachings of God's Word to life. The articles raise questions about what it means to live for God in today's world—about what a believer's role in the world is—and about how the Word in one life can touch the lives of others.

Features about the people, places, and customs of Jesus' world make the teachings of the Bible more vivid. You'll find friends in the Word of God. You'll feel at home where they lived. You'll discover that people aren't much different now than they were two thousand years ago. And you'll see that God's Word is more useful than you ever realized.

Explore the following pages and take a closer look at *The Word In Life Study Bible*—what it's meant to do, what it looks like, and how it works.

Why This Kind of Publication?

Someone has well said that Scripture was not written merely to be studied, but to change our lives. Likewise, James exhorts us to be "doers of the word, and not hearers only" (James 1:22). And Jesus said, "By this My Father is glorified, that you bear much fruit; so you will be my disciples" (John 15:8). Clearly, the point of God's Word is not to make us "smarter sinners" but to help us become more like Jesus Christ by making the Word of God part of our lives.

However, applying biblical truth in this day and age is far from easy. In the first place, the fact that the Bible was written thousands of years ago in a different culture can sometimes make it difficult to understand. And even if we grasp what the writers were saying to their original readers, we still must make the connection to our own situation today. In the end, many people wonder: can Scripture really make any difference in our complex, modern world? Yes it can, and this publication helps to show the way. ◆

A "User-Friendly" Study Bible

The Word In Life Study Bible helps you understand the biblical text.

Before you can apply Scripture, you must understand what Scripture means. That's why The Word In Life Study Bible *provides the kind of information you'll need to make sense of what the biblical text is talking about. The articles and other information (see below) provide the "who, what, when, where, how, and why" behind scores of passages, in an interesting, easy-to-understand way. Not only do they offer insight into the text, they also help you to understand the context of those passages, so that you can connect the words and events of biblical times with today.*

The Word In Life Study Bible helps you apply Scripture to everyday life.

"Wow! This is the kind of Bible I need in my life," one reader said. "It just makes Scripture come alive. It's contemporary. It's relevant." As you read The Word In Life Study Bible, *you won't have to search and struggle for ways to apply God's Word; the articles suggest numerous possibilities for how Scripture makes a difference. That's especially helpful if you're one who is strapped for time or likes to quickly get to the point.*

The Word In Life Study Bible challenges you to develop your own thinking.

You won't find pat answers or a "packaged" theology in this study Bible. Instead, the articles are designed to provoke your thinking by relating the text of Scripture to the issues of today, providing information to guide your thinking. Sometimes the commentary will raise a question without answering it; sometimes it will suggest possible answers. Often it will point out things that you may not have considered before. The articles don't pretend to address every issue raised by the biblical text or to solve every theological problem. But they're guaranteed to make you think!

The Word In Life Study Bible introduces you to the people of Scripture.

For too many readers, the Bible can seem dull and lifeless, a book that only scholars and mystics might find interesting. But Scripture comes alive once we discover the people in the text. The Word In Life Study Bible *is designed to help you do that, to "make friends" with some of the fascinating characters that God chose to include in His Word. Almost fifty of them receive special attention through "Personality Profiles" that summarize what we know of them (see below). Even though these people lived long ago, you'll find that you have far more in common with them than you have differences. They experienced many of the same things you do. By learning what God did in their lives, you'll gain insight into what God is doing in yours.*

The Word In Life Study Bible makes the Bible easy to read.

"I know I should read the Bible more, but to be honest, I just don't have time!" Have you ever felt that way? If so, The Word In Life Study Bible *is for you. It was designed for busy people. In the first place, you'll enjoy how easy it is to read the New King James Version. A modern translation that preserves the stylistic beauty of the King James Version, the NKJV presents the eternal Word of God in everyday language that people can understand. You'll also find the material presented in bite-size units, with section headings to mark the text. The Scriptures are accompanied not by long, drawn out treatises, but by straight-to-the-point articles and other information presented in simple, easily grasped terms.* ◆

◆ ◆

Features to Look For

Introductory Articles

At the beginning of a book of the Bible you'll find information that explains why the book is important and what to pay attention to as you read it. You'll learn something of the background behind the book, including who the author and original readers were. You'll also get an idea of the issues the book addresses through a table of contents that describes some of the articles you'll find alongside the text.

Consider This

(symbols enlarged)

As mentioned above, God intended His Word to change people's lives. That's why occasionally you'll find a symbol that refers you to a nearby article relating in some way to the text indicated. These articles help to explain the Scriptural passages and highlight the significance of biblical truths for modern readers. In articles with this symbol, ways are offered for you to consider how *the passage applies to your life and the world around you.*

For Your Info

This symbol indicates articles that primarily offer information *about the text or its cultural context. Knowing the background of a biblical passage will help you understand it more accurately and make it more useful to you.*

Personality Profiles

One of the goals that the editors of The Word In Life Study Bible *had in developing their material was to introduce readers to* the people *of the Scriptures, including those who lived and worked in public places. One of the important ways that this study Bible does that is through personality profiles that highlight various individuals. These are not biographies, but summaries of what the Bible tells us about the person, what can be reasonably inferred from the text, and what other sources report about his or her life and legacy.*

You Are There

One of the most important windows on understanding the text of Scripture is knowing the places *where the events occurred. Unfortunately, ancient localities are unknown to most modern readers. The cities of Acts, for example, are little more than dots on a map for most of us. Yet when we examine the geography of the New Testament, we discover that the first-century Roman world was quite a bit like our own. The articles indicated by the "you are there" symbol will take you to places that you may never have "visited" before. Sometimes there's also information about what life was like for the people who lived there.*

A Closer Look

Sometimes the best way to understand a text of Scripture is to compare the text to a related passage and/or its connected article. That's why you'll find symbols that "advertise" companion passages and articles that provide insight into the passage indicated.

Quote Unquote

Occasionally you might be interested in knowing what someone else besides the writers of Scripture had to say about an idea raised in the biblical text, or about the text itself. That's not to suggest that these quotations *from various authors are on a par with Scripture. But one way to gain perspective on the implications of a passage is to read what someone has written, and then use that to reflect on what God has said.*

Themes to Consider

In designing The Word In Life Study Bible, *the editors wanted to create a resource that would help people deal with the issues of today, not yesterday. To that end, they identified a number of themes to highlight. Articles and other information provide a starting point for thought, study, and discussion of the following important areas:*

Work

For most of us, work is the most dominating area of life. It determines where we'll live, what kind of lifestyle we'll have, even who our friends will be. Yet how many of us are aware of how much the Bible says about work and workplace issues?

Economics

Who can doubt the importance of economic issues in a world increasingly tied together in a giant global marketplace? Of course, Scripture wasn't written to be an economics textbook. Nevertheless, it gives us principles relating to wealth, money, value, service, the environment, and other topics affecting both public policy and personal financial decisions.

Ethics

This is the issue of right and wrong, of integrity and character. In a day when truth and values have become relative, we need to return to God's unchanging Word as our absolute standard for ethical conduct and commitments.

Ethnicity

One has only to glance at a map of our modern world to recognize the impact of racial and ethnic differences. The landscape is strewn with wars, conflicts, and problems tied to long-standing ethnic tensions. How should Christians respond, especially living in an increasingly pluralistic society? As the early church discovered, the gospel has enormous implications for how we relate to others from different backgrounds.

The Church

Enormous opportunities and critical choices face the church today. A fresh look at the church's beginnings and its impact on the first-century world can offer valuable guidelines for the church's impact on the twenty-first-century world.

Laity

Elton Trueblood has pointed out that the first Reformation put the Word of God back into the hands of the people of God; now we face the prospect of a "second reformation" that can put the *work* of God back into the hands of the people of God. This means that "everyday" believers can participate in carrying out God's work and find meaning and value in their efforts.

The Family

Building marriages and families that honor God has perhaps never been harder than today. That's why *The Word In Life Study Bible* highlights passages, principles, and people that show us the fundamental truths—and the honest realities—of building healthy family relationships in a fallen world.

The City

Today for the first time in history, more people live in metropolitan than in rural areas. That has enormous implications for how Christians engage the world. Yet many believers have adopted a negative view of the city; some even see it as an evil. But when we read the Bible, we discover that the gospel "conquered" the Roman world by penetrating its major cities. The same thing can happen today.

Witness

One thing is certain about evangelism: both non-Christians and Christians feel uncomfortable with it. Yet Jesus has sent His followers into the world to communicate His message of salvation. Fortunately, the Bible gives us guidelines for carrying out the task in a way that is winsome, sensitive, and effective.

Women

One of the most significant developments in recent culture has been the growing awareness of and sensitivity to issues and concerns of women—their dignity, their needs, and their rights. *The Word In Life Study Bible* places a special emphasis on the many women of the Scriptures and their significant contribution to the ministry of Jesus and the growth of the church. It also highlights the condition of women in the ancient world and the biblical teaching that pertains to the lives of women both then and now.

The themes mentioned above are just some of the ones that are touched on. It wouldn't be possible to classify them all. But as you use *The Word In Life Study Bible,* it will stir up your thinking and show you other areas in which to apply God's word to life. ◆

How to Use the Symbol System

The section above concerning 'Features to Look For' mentions four symbols that are used to designate various kinds of articles, tables, or related material in The Word In Life Study Bible.

From time to time as you read the biblical text, you will see one of those four symbols along the left side of the text, accompanied by a box containing information that will lead you to a feature that has to do with the biblical passage you are reading.

If the feature you are being sent to is on one of the two pages you are opened to (called a 'spread'), then the box next to the symbol by the text will contain just chapter-and-verse information, designating one verse (for example, 1:10) or a range of verses (1:1–16). No page number is given. Just look on the spread you are opened to for a matching symbol accompanied by a box containing the name of the symbol (such as CONSIDER THIS) and matching chapter-and-verse information.

1:1–16 [1]The
Christ
Abraham:
[2]Abraham begot Isaac,

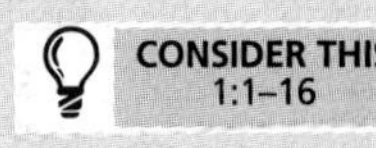

Matt
of Je
Don't skip this genealogy a
includes it for at least three

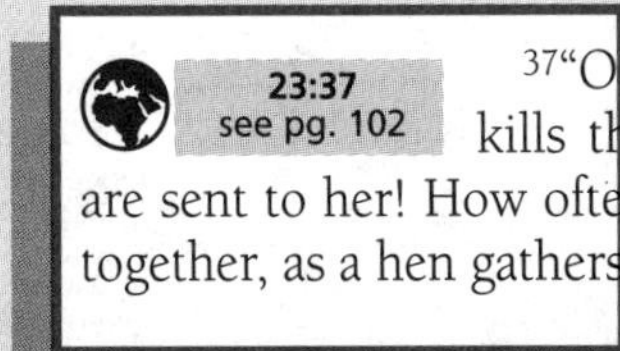

If the feature you are being sent to is someplace other than the spread you are opened to, then the box next to the symbol by the text will contain chapter-and-verse information and a page number. Just look on the designated page for a matching symbol accompanied by a box containing the name of the symbol and matching chapter-and-verse information.

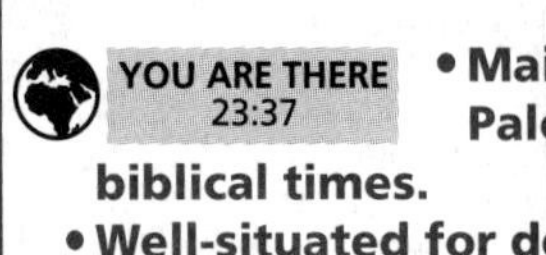

NEW KING JAMES FOOTNOTES

your brethren[a] only, what do you do more *than* not even the tax collectors[b] do so? [48]Therefore

As you read, you will often see a raised letter in the biblical text. Each raised letter designates a New King James footnote, to be found at the foot of the text. Each footnote is designated by the chapter and verse in which its raised letter is contained. Then you will see the raised letter, followed by the footnote. (The letter *a* is used for the first footnote connected to each verse. If a verse has more than one footnote connected to it, then the second footnote receives the letter *b*. The chapter and verse are not repeated in such cases.)

New King James footnotes contain helpful information about significant textual variations and alternate translations, as well as some explanations and references to other passages of Scripture.

Footnotes concerning textual variations make no evaluation of readings, but do clearly indicate the manuscript sources of readings. They objectively present the facts without such remarks as 'the best manuscripts omit' or 'the most reliable manuscripts read,' which are value judgments that differ according to varying viewpoints on the text.

Where significant variations occur in the New Testament Greek manuscripts, textual notes are classified as followed:

These variations from the traditional text represent the text as published in the twenty-sixth edition of the Nestle-Aland Greek New Testament (N) and in the United Bible Societies' third edition (U), hence the abbreviation, 'NU-Text.'

Example:

As we forgive our debtors.

6:4 [a]NU-Text omits *openly.* *6:6* [a]NU-Text omits *openly.*

These variations from the traditional text represent the Majority Text, which is based on the majority of surviving manuscripts. It should be noted that M stands for whatever reading is printed in the first edition of *The Greek New Testament According to the Majority Text,* whether supported by overwhelming, strong, or only a divided majority textual tradition.

Example:

be baptized by him. [14]And John *tried to* prevent

3:11 [a]M-Text omits *and fire.*

The textual notes reflect the scholarship of the past 150 years and will assist the reader to observe the variations between the different manuscript traditions of the New Testament. Such information is generally not available in English translations of the New Testament.

Maps

Many maps appear throughout The Word In Life Study Bible. *They are designed to provide relevant geographical information in an accessible and easy-to-read format, on the same pages with the biblical text and related features.*

A number of locator maps *show you quickly where a certain place is with regard to its surrounding area.*

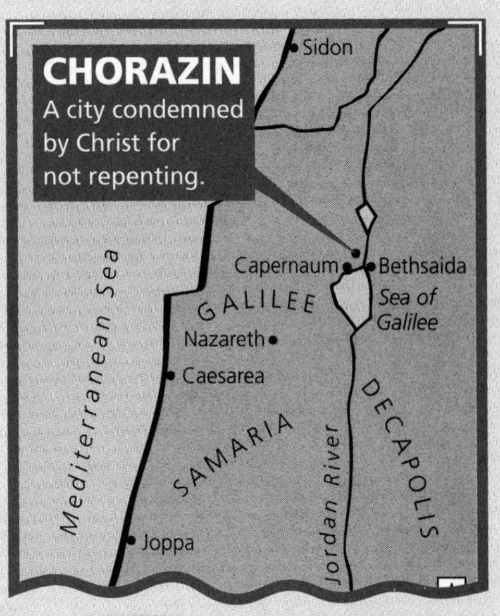

CHORAZIN
A city condemned by Christ for not repenting.

Tables

Information is often presented in the form of tables or lists, showing at a glance how various facts and ideas relate to each other.

THE TWELVE

Apostle	Description
Simon (Peter) (Mark 1:16)	Fisherman from Galilee, Andrew's brother
Andrew (John 1:40)	Fisherman from Galilee, Peter's brother
James	Son of Zebedee, brother to John; from Capernaum
John (Introduction to John)	Son of Zebedee, brother to James; from Capernaum
Philip	From Bethsaida
Bartholomew	From [illegible] in [illegible]

In the back of this edition of Matthew's Gospel are two handy indexes:

Themes to Study (p. 125)

A list of *themes to study* includes information about articles and their related texts, arranged by subject. Using this feature, you can read in connected fashion the material that relates to certain themes or issues.

Index to Key Passages (p. 129)

This index directs you to passages in Matthew that pertain to a variety of practical and spiritual topics. Passages are listed alphabetically within each topic by brief content summaries.

Together the two indexes allow you to reference quickly those passages that speak to particular life concerns.

Marching Orders!

No other person has ever touched the world in quite the way Jesus did. And no other book of the New Testament records Jesus' teaching in quite the way Matthew does. Built around five major addresses that Jesus gave to His followers, Matthew records the essence of Christ's message, the core commands that He not only wanted His people to live by, but to spread to "all the nations . . . teaching them to observe all things that I have commanded you" (Matt. 28:19–20).

Thus Matthew contains marching orders for Christ's followers today. He sends us into the world to have impact—not the impact of coercion or force, but the irresistible influence of lives that reflect His ways, His love, and His values.

How appropriate, then, that Matthew leads off the New Testament. All of the books that follow are God's Word, but Matthew sets the pace. It highlights the agenda of our Lord: "all things that I have commanded you."

Matthew

Christ sends us into the world to have impact.

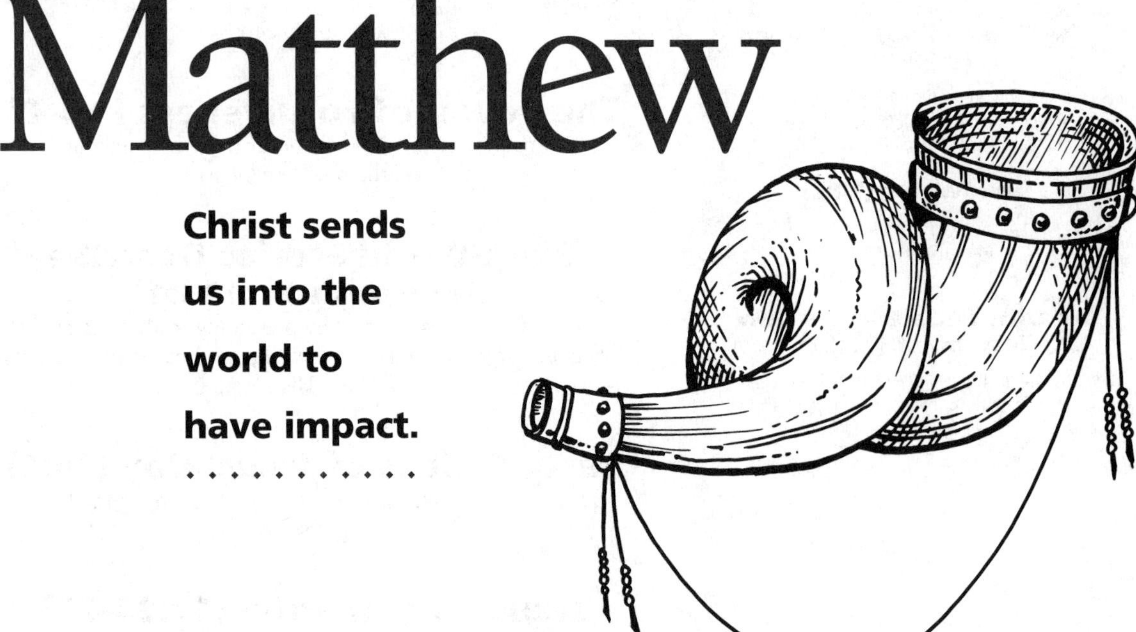

C O N T E N T S

People You'll Meet in Matthew

The Women in Jesus' Genealogy (1:3–6)

Four women feature significantly in Jesus' family tree. All had unusual lives.

John the Street Preacher (3:4)

Jesus' forerunner looked anything but successful.

A Man under Authority (8:5–13)

Jesus encounters a centurion who demonstrates some important lessons in faith and leadership.

Jesus' Global Connections (8:10)

Jesus is an international Savior.

A Rich Man Enters the Kingdom (9:9–13)

Jesus said it would be hard for the rich to enter the kingdom of heaven—hard, but not impossible.

The Hemorrhaging Woman (9:20–22)

A desperate woman grasps at Jesus and comes away healed of a chronic illness.

The Twelve (10:2)

Who were the twelve men that Jesus chose to be His inner circle?

Wealthy People in the New Testament (27:57)

We can learn much from the wealthy people of the New Testament about the dangers and the disciplines of money.

A R T I C L E S

Jesus' Roots (1:1–16)

Matthew opens with a fascinating list of Jesus' ancestors. Whatever you do, don't skip this section!

A Poor Family Comes into Wealth (2:11)

Gifts to Jesus' parents made them extraordinarily wealthy for a brief time—and may have provided a means of escape from danger.

The King Declares His Kingdom (4:17)

Jesus came with a message about something He called "the kingdom." What is the kingdom, and what difference does it make for people today?

The Power of Forgiveness (9:4–8)

With a dramatic display of power, Jesus healed a paralytic. But He also had the power to *forgive sins*.

Work-World Stories Describe the Kingdom (13:1)

Jesus captivated His listeners by presenting truth in terms that they could understand. He used workplace images and analogies to talk about His kingdom.

Party Politics of Jesus' Day (16:1)

There were at least five major political parties among the Hebrews of Jesus' day.

Jesus and Taxation (17:24–27)

A curious episode shows that Jesus claimed to be God. It's also a lesson in the proper exercise of liberty.

Servant-Leaders (20:25–28)

Jesus revealed a unique style of authority—that whoever wishes to be great should become a "slave."

Whitewashed Tombs (23:27–28)

Jesus used a grim, arresting image to denounce His self-righteous enemies.

A Global Gospel with a Jewish Accent

For centuries, Jews had waited for a Messiah. They based their expectations on numerous Old Testament promises. For example, God told Abraham, the father of the nation, that through him "all the families of the earth [would] be blessed" (Gen. 12:3). To David, God's choice for Israel's king, God promised an enduring kingdom (2 Sam. 7:16). Through the prophets God renewed His pledge and provided details about the One who would fulfill it (Is. 7:14; 9:6–7; Dan. 2:44; 7:13–14).

Over the years, various figures came and went, some claiming to be the Messiah, others regarded by the people as likely candidates. But none proved convincing. None quite fulfilled the expectations of either the religious scholars who carefully studied the Scriptures, or the people who developed popular conceptions of what the Chosen One would accomplish.

What about the rabbi Jesus? He claimed to be God's Son. He performed extraordinary miracles that seemed to indicate divine power. He also taught with unprecedented authority and attracted a devoted band of followers. Yet hadn't He been rejected by the nation's leaders? Didn't He die a criminal's death? How, then, did He fulfill the promises of God? Was He really Israel's Messiah?

Matthew's Gospel answers with a resounding yes! He fills his account with Old Testament prophecies that point to Jesus as God's Chosen One (Matt. 1:23; 2:6, 15, 18, 23 to mention just a few). He wants his fellow Jews to study their Scriptures and find Jesus to be the Christ, the son of David, the son of Abraham, and the Son of God.

However, Matthew is not so much a Jewish Gospel as a global Gospel with a Jewish accent. In Jesus, all of us can find hope, no matter what our ethnic background. We don't have to be Jewish to be eligible for God's blessing and salvation. ◆

MATTHEW, THE SOCIAL OUTCAST

As a tax collector, Matthew was a member of a group that other Jews detested. Tax collectors were perceived not only as cheats, but mercenaries working for the Romans. Condemned by the religious leaders as unrighteous and ostracized by the general public as frauds and traitors, they found friends only among prostitutes, criminals, and other outcasts.

Yet Jesus selected Matthew to follow Him (Matt. 9:9). Scripture gives no indication why, but it does record the Lord's comment, "Go and learn what this means: 'I desire mercy and not sacrifice' [Hos. 6:6]. I did not come to call the righteous, but sinners to repentance" (v. 13). Apparently the call of Matthew was an act of pure mercy on the Lord's part—a choice that outraged self-satisfied religionists like the Pharisees.

They also criticized Jesus' willingness to attend a dinner that Matthew threw for Him (vv. 10–11). But Jesus knew whom He had come to help and where to find them. In Matthew, He had a direct entrée into the underworld of Jewish society, a class of people untouched by the religious legalists but deeply in need of a Savior. As the Great Physician (v. 12), Jesus was neither condoning nor glorifying lifestyles of sin, but merely reaching out to people who knew that they were sick and, as matters stood, completely lost. Matthew showed that Jesus can save anyone—that is, anyone who admits he needs saving. ◆

It's no wonder that Jews at the time of Jesus despised anyone associated with taxation: they were probably paying no less than 30 or 40 percent of their income on taxes and religious dues. *See "Taxes," Mark 12:14.*

Another tax collector who responded to Jesus was Zacchaeus of Jericho. *See Luke 19:1–10.*

PERSONALITY PROFILE: MATTHEW

Also known as: Levi. His given name, Matthew, meant "gift of Yahweh [the Hebrew term indicating God]."

Home: Capernaum (headquarters of Jesus' ministry); later Damascus, Syria.

Family: His father was Alphaeus.

Occupation: Tax collector; later an author, and pastor of a church in Damascus.

Special interests: Collecting Jesus' sermons and stories. He preserved them in a book that some call a new Torah because Jesus fulfilled so much Old Testament prophecy and restated much of the Mosaic Law.

Best known today as: The author of one of the Gospels.

HE SAW A MAN NAMED MATTHEW SITTING AT THE TAX OFFICE.
—Matthew 9:9

A Christian Torah

Tradition holds that after Jesus' departure, Matthew established a mostly Jewish church in or near Damascus of Syria and became its pastor. If so, his Gospel may have been a manual for Christian discipleship organized in a way that resembles the Pentateuch, the five books of Moses—Genesis, Exodus, Leviticus, Numbers, and Deuteronomy.

In Jesus' day, the Pentateuch was known as the Torah, which means "instruction" or "law." Moses warned the people to carefully observe all the words of the Law, the commandments of God (Deut. 32:46). The English word "law" does not convey all that Moses intended. Both the hearing and *the doing of the Law made the Torah. It was a manner of life, a way to live based on the covenant that God made with His people.*

In the same way, Matthew balances the teaching of Christ with the application of that truth in day-to-day life. He builds his material around five major speeches that Jesus gave, producing a sort of five-volume "Christian Torah":

5:1—7:27	*The Sermon on the Mount, given to a large crowd*
9:35—10:42	*Instructions to the Twelve, chosen by Christ*
13:1–52	*Parables of the kingdom, given on a crowded beach*
18:1–35	*Instructions on community, given to the disciples*
24:1—25:46	*The Olivet Discourse, also given to the disciples*

Before and after each of these teaching sections are action sections in which Jesus and His followers carry out God's Word. The book climaxes with what has been called the Great Commission, where Jesus instructs the Twelve to go throughout the world and make disciples, "teaching them to observe *all things that I have* commanded *you" (28:16–20, emphasis added). Discipleship involves not only truth believed, but truth applied.*

It's interesting how Matthew ties Jesus' earthly life to the history of Israel. For example, Jesus fled to Egypt as an infant (Matt. 2:13–15) just as Israel dwelt in Egypt beginning with Joseph (Gen. 39:1). Jesus was tempted by the devil in a wilderness (Matt. 4:1–11) just as Israel was tested in the wilderness (Ex. 15:22—32:35). The point is that Jesus was not some detached, heaven-sent Savior untouched by the pain that Israel experienced. On the contrary, Jesus was a full-fledged Hebrew who fulfilled the name Immanuel, "God with us" (Matt. 1:23).

Yet Matthew also shows Jesus reaching out to non-Jews and other "undesirables." In fact, Jesus' own ancestry was laced with "sinners" and "foreigners" (see "The Women in Jesus' Genealogy," Matt. 1:3–6). As a former tax collector, Matthew knew better than most that Jesus "did not come to call the righteous, but sinners to repentance" (9:13). The pastor/author wanted his congregation to understand that people don't have to be Jewish to be saved. ◆

THE LAND OF THE GOSPELS

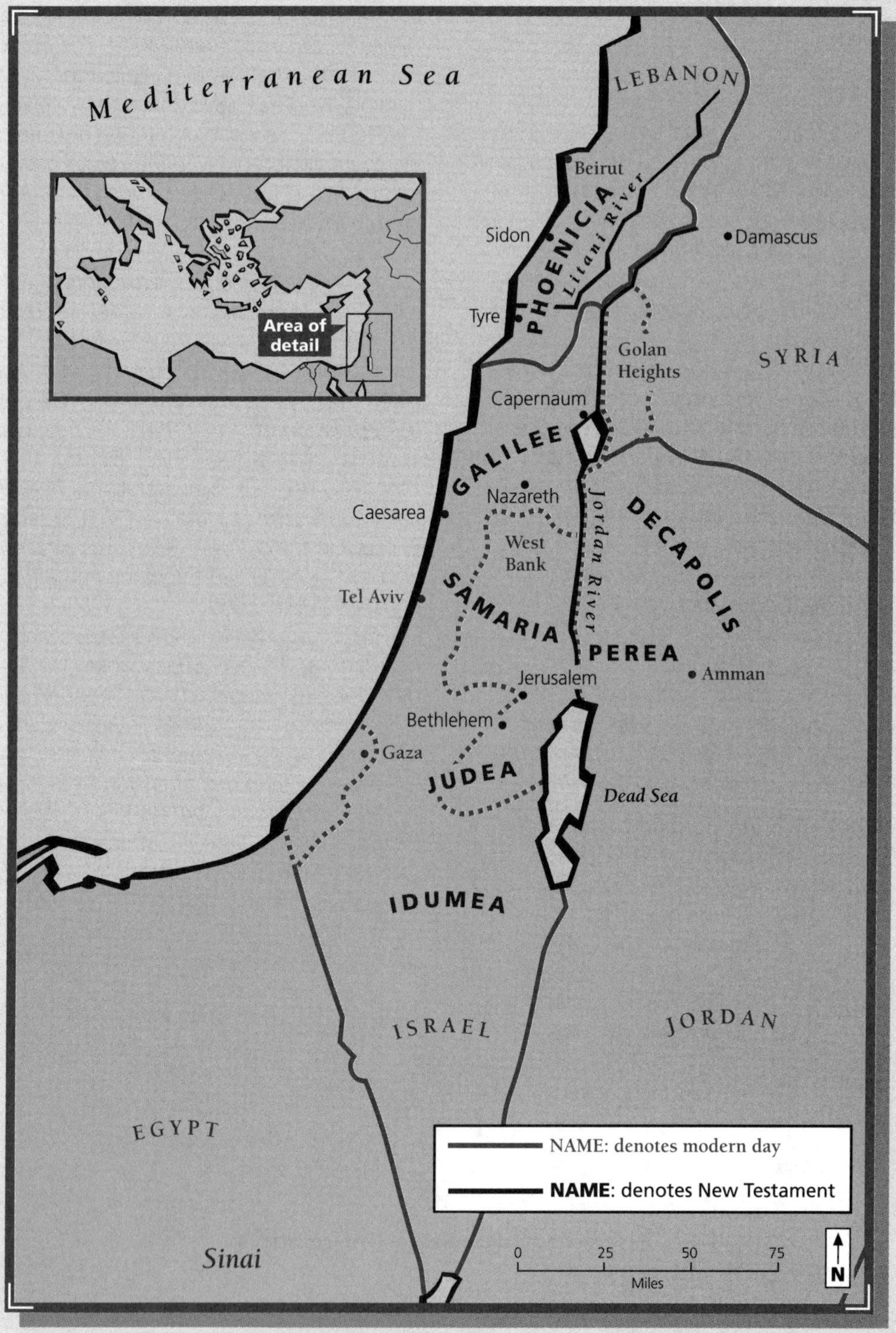

CHAPTER 1

The Background of Christ

1:1–16 1 The book of the genealogy of Jesus
Christ, the Son of David, the Son of
Abraham:
2 Abraham begot Isaac, Isaac begot Jacob, and Jacob begot
1:3–6 see pg. 8 Judah and his brothers. 3 Judah begot
Perez and Zerah by Tamar, Perez begot
Hezron, and Hezron begot Ram. 4 Ram begot Amminadab,
Amminadab begot Nahshon, and Nahshon begot Salmon.
5 Salmon begot Boaz by Rahab, Boaz begot Obed by Ruth,
Obed begot Jesse, 6 and Jesse begot David the king.
David the king begot Solomon by her *who had been the*
wife[a] of Uriah. 7 Solomon begot Rehoboam, Rehoboam begot
Abijah, and Abijah begot Asa.[a] 8 Asa begot Jehoshaphat, Je-
hoshaphat begot Joram, and Joram begot Uzziah. 9 Uzziah

(Bible text continued on page 9)

1:6 [a]Words in italic type have been added for clarity. They are not found in the original Greek. *1:7* [a]NU-Text reads *Asaph.*

JESUS' ROOTS

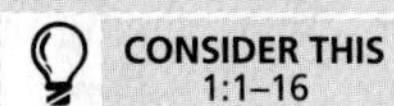

CONSIDER THIS 1:1–16 *Matthew opens with a family tree of Jesus' ancestors (vv. 1–16). Don't skip this genealogy and begin at v. 18! Matthew includes it for at least three important reasons:*

(1) To show that God's Son was also a real, flesh-and-blood human. This was a crucial concept for Matthew's first-century readers (see "Jesus, the Son of . . . ," Luke 3:23–38).

(2) To show that Jesus was the long-awaited Messiah of Israel. Notice the prominence of David and Abraham.

(3) To show that Jesus is also the international Christ, the Savior of the whole world. His genealogy reaches beyond Jews to include several ethnic groups that populated the Middle East during Israel's Old Testament history (see the accompanying article, "The Women In Jesus' Genealogy"). Jesus came to "make disciples of all the nations" (Matt. 28:19).

WHAT IT MEANS TO BE LIKE JESUS

CONSIDER THIS 1:1–17 *Jesus indicated that those who follow Him will become like Him (10:25). What does it mean to* **"be like Jesus"** *in today's complex world? Matthew paints eight portraits of what Christlikeness looks like, including:*

#1: To Be Like Jesus Means TO ACCEPT OUR ROOTS

Jesus' family tree hides nothing. His heritage was multiethnic and included several unattractive or embarrassing individuals. Indeed, the circumstances surrounding His own birth might have raised questions in the minds of some. But Jesus never denied His ancestry or allowed others to shame Him. If we want to be like Him, we need to understand and accept our roots in terms of culture, race, gender, and reputation. Moreover, like Jesus we want to avoid demeaning anyone else's heritage.

For a summary of all eight portraits of Christlikeness, see "What It Means to Be Like Jesus" at 10:25. The next item in the series can be found at 1:18—2:23.

CONSIDER THIS
1:3–6

THE WOMEN IN JESUS' GENEALOGY

Much has been made of the virgin Mary, but Matthew's genealogy (vv. 1–16) highlights four other women in Jesus' family. They were touched by scandal and remembered as "sinners" and "foreigners." Their inclusion can be an encouragement to us.

Tamar (v. 3; Gen. 38:1–30)

- Left a widow by Er, the firstborn son of Judah.
- Married Onan, Judah's second son, who refused to consummate the marriage and also died, leaving her childless—and therefore without means of support.
- Sent away to her home village by her father-in-law, Judah, who avoided responsibility to provide another husband.
- Eventually resorted to trickery, acting as a prostitute to cause Judah to father an heir and thereby provide economic security. The child also continued the line that eventually led to Jesus. Exposed as the father, irresponsible Judah acknowledged that Tamar was "more righteous than I" (Gen. 38:26).

Rahab (v. 5; Josh. 2:1–24; 6:22–25)

- A Canaanite harlot in Jericho.
- Protected two Hebrew spies in exchange for her own protection from the Israelites, who surrounded the city.
- Later married a Hebrew and gave birth to Boaz, David's great-grandfather.
- Praised in the New Testament as a person of faith (Heb. 11:31) and faithful action (James 2:25).

Ruth (v. 5; Ruth 1:1—4:22)

- A woman of Moab, a nation that began after the fall of Sodom when Lot committed incest with his daughters (Gen. 19:30–38). The Moabites became bitter enemies of Israel.
- Widowed when her Jewish husband died, and left without sons.
- Migrated to Israel with her mother-in-law, Naomi.
- Married Boaz (Rahab's son) and became the mother of Obed, making her David's great-grandmother. In effect, hostile Israel joined hated Moab to bring about God's will.

The Wife of Uriah (v. 6; 2 Sam. 11:1—12:25)

- Unnamed by Matthew, but known to be Bathsheba, wife of Uriah the Hittite.
- Attracted the eye of King David while bathing in ritual obedience on her roof, cleansing herself from her monthly flow.
- Summoned by the king, who committed adultery with her.
- Suffered the murder of her husband by David and the loss of the child that David had fathered.
- Married David, giving birth to a second child, Solomon, who became David's successor. (If Bathsheba was a Hittite like her first husband, then Solomon was half-Jew, half-Gentile. However, she was likely a Hebrew who married a Hittite sojourner.)

Jesus is the Messiah for women as well as men—even for women with (supposedly) checkered pasts and tainted bloodlines. He is the Messiah for all people, regardless of gender, race, or background. ◆

Matthew offers plenty of evidence to show Jesus' global connections. See Matt. 8:10.

begot Jotham, Jotham begot Ahaz, and Ahaz begot Heze-
kiah. 10Hezekiah begot Manasseh, Manasseh begot Amon,[a]
and Amon begot Josiah. 11Josiah begot Jeconiah and his
brothers about the time they were carried away to Babylon.

12And after they were brought to Babylon, Jeconiah begot
Shealtiel, and Shealtiel begot Zerubbabel. 13Zerubbabel begot Abiud, Abiud begot Eliakim, and Eliakim begot Azor.
14Azor begot Zadok, Zadok begot Achim, and Achim begot
Eliud. 15Eliud begot Eleazar, Eleazar begot Matthan, and
Matthan begot Jacob. 16And Jacob begot Joseph the husband of Mary, of whom was born Jesus who is called Christ.

1:1–17 see pg. 7

17So all the generations from Abraham
to David *are* fourteen generations, from
David until the captivity in Babylon *are* fourteen generations, and from the captivity in Babylon until the Christ *are*
fourteen generations.

The Birth of Christ

1:18—2:23 see pg. 10

18Now the birth of Jesus Christ was as
follows: After His mother Mary was be-
trothed to Joseph, before they came together, she was found
with child of the Holy Spirit. 19Then Joseph her husband,
being a just *man,* and not wanting to make her a public example, was minded to put her away secretly. 20But while he
thought about these things, behold, an angel of the Lord
appeared to him in a dream, saying, "Joseph, son of David,
do not be afraid to take to you Mary your wife, for that
which is conceived in her is of the Holy Spirit. 21And she
will bring forth a Son, and you shall call His name JESUS, for
He will save His people from their sins."

22So all this was done that it might be fulfilled which was
spoken by the Lord through the prophet,
saying: 23"Behold, the virgin shall be with
child, and bear a Son, and they shall call His name Immanuel,"[a] which is translated, "God with us."

1:23

24Then Joseph, being aroused from sleep, did as the angel
of the Lord commanded him and took to him his wife,
25and did not know her till she had brought forth her firstborn Son.[a] And he called His name JESUS.

CHAPTER 2

Wise Men Visit

1Now after Jesus was born in Bethlehem of Judea in the
days of Herod the king, behold, wise men from the East
came to Jerusalem, 2saying, "Where is He who has been
born King of the Jews? For we have seen His star in the East
and have come to worship Him."

1:10 [a]NU-Text reads *Amos.* *1:23* [a]Isaiah 7:14 *1:25* [a]NU-Text reads *a Son.*

What's in a Name?

CONSIDER THIS 1:23 **Jesus was and is Immanuel, "God with us" (v. 23). God comes to us as people and lives in our world, rather than having us try the impossible of going to Him. Jesus does not take us out of the turmoil and pain of daily life, but rather walks *with us* as we live life.**

It's a mistake to think of salvation as escape from the world instead of engagement with the world. God has a job for us to do right where we live and work. That's where Jesus is *with us;* that's where He gives us power (see Acts 1:8).

The name of Jesus played a powerful role in a five-act drama of which early Christians were a part. See "Jesus—The Name You Can Trust," Acts 3:1.

A Poor Family Comes into Wealth

CONSIDER THIS 2:11 **What happened to the gifts presented to Jesus by the wise men (v. 11)? Scripture doesn't say. Clearly they reflected the Magi's worship of Christ at His birth. Yet we can speculate that they may have provided the means for His family's flight to Egypt (vv. 13–15).**

The angel's warning and instructions to Joseph were sudden and unexpected. There was no time to save enough money for such a long journey—if saving was even an option. The family, after all, was poor (see "A Poor Family's Sacrifice," Luke 2:22–24). In fact, the costly gifts probably represented more wealth than either spouse had seen in a lifetime.

God promises to provide what is necessary for His children and to care for their needs (Matt. 6:19–34). In this instance, offerings of worship may have paid for a journey to Egypt and a new life in a strange land.

What It Means To Be Like Jesus

CONSIDER THIS 1:18—2:23 *Jesus indicated that those who follow Him will become like Him (10:25). What does it mean to* **"be like Jesus"** *in today's complex world? Matthew paints eight portraits of what Christlikeness looks like, including:*

#2: To Be Like Jesus Means TO ENGAGE THE WORLD'S PAIN

Jesus' entry into human life was fraught with awkward tensions and human dilemmas: a miraculous but nevertheless embarrassing conception, an earthly father who was considering a quiet divorce, an outraged king resorting to infanticide, an early childhood in a strange culture, and a return to a homeland that remained hostile and dangerous. We, too, are all born into some troubles and circumstances. If we want to be like Jesus, we need to face up to the world and remain very much in it, despite all its troubles.

For a summary of all eight portraits of Christlikeness, see "What It Means to Be Like Jesus" at 10:25. The next item in the series can be found at 3:1–17.

2:3

3 When Herod the king heard *this,* he
was troubled, and all Jerusalem with him.
4 And when he had gathered all the chief priests and scribes
of the people together, he inquired of them where the
Christ was to be born.
5 So they said to him, "In Bethlehem of Judea, for thus it is
written by the prophet:

6 'But you, Bethlehem, *in* the land of Judah,
Are not the least among the rulers of Judah;
For out of you shall come a Ruler
Who will shepherd My people Israel.' "[a]

7 Then Herod, when he had secretly called the wise men,
determined from them what time the star appeared. 8 And
he sent them to Bethlehem and said, "Go and search carefully for the young Child, and when you have found *Him,*
bring back word to me, that I may come and worship Him
also."
9 When they heard the king, they departed; and behold,
the star which they had seen in the East went before them,
till it came and stood over where the young Child was.
10 When they saw the star, they rejoiced with exceedingly
2:11 see pg. 9
great joy. 11 And when they had come into
the house, they saw the young Child with
Mary His mother, and fell down and worshiped Him. And
when they had opened their treasures, they presented gifts
to Him: gold, frankincense, and myrrh.
12 Then, being divinely warned in a dream that they
should not return to Herod, they departed for their own
country another way.

The Family Flees to Egypt

2:13–15

13 Now when they had departed, behold, an angel of the Lord appeared to
Joseph in a dream, saying, "Arise, take the young Child and

2:6 [a]Micah 5:2

Herod the Great

A CLOSER LOOK 2:3 *Herod the Great (v. 3) was a highly ambitious leader who would stop at nothing to advance or protect his position. He routinely disposed of his enemies—even one of his wives and three of his sons. So it was no surprise that his immediate thought upon hearing the wise men's question—"Where is He who has been born King of the Jews?" (v. 2)—was to plan the infant's extermination. Read more about this ruler's infamy and the bloody family he came from in "The Herods," Acts 12:1–2.*

His mother, flee to Egypt, and stay there until I bring you word; for Herod will seek the young Child to destroy Him."
14When he arose, he took the young Child and His mother by night and departed for Egypt, 15and was there until the death of Herod, that it might be fulfilled which was spoken by the Lord through the prophet, saying, "Out of Egypt I called My Son."[a]

Herod Slaughters Infants

2:16–18
see pg. 12

16Then Herod, when he saw that he was deceived by the wise men, was exceedingly angry; and he sent forth and put to death all the male children who were in Bethlehem and in all its districts, from two years old and under, according to the time which he had determined from the wise men. 17Then was fulfilled what was spoken by Jeremiah the prophet, saying:

18 "A voice was heard in Ramah,
Lamentation, weeping, and great mourning,
Rachel weeping *for* her children,
Refusing to be comforted,
Because they are no more."[a]

The Family Returns to Nazareth

19Now when Herod was dead, behold, an angel of the Lord appeared in a dream to Joseph in Egypt, 20saying,

2:15 [a]Hosea 11:1 *2:18* [a]Jeremiah 31:15

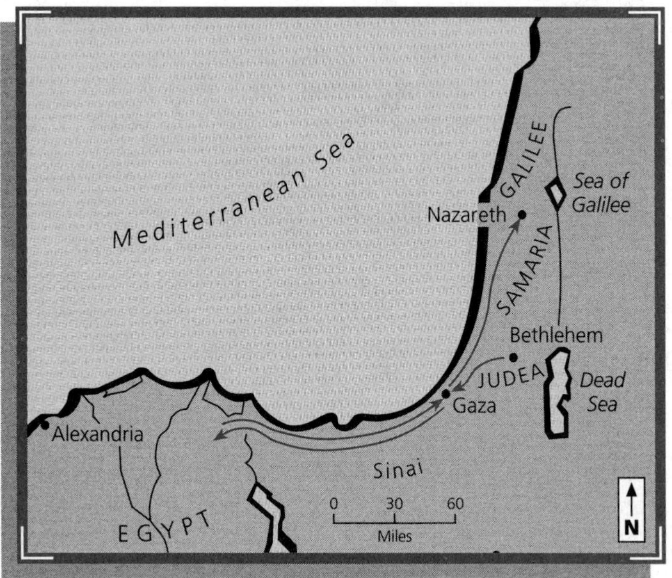

TO EGYPT AND BACK

"OUT OF EGYPT I CALLED MY SON."
—Matthew 2:15

ASIAN-BORN JESUS BECOMES A REFUGEE IN AFRICA

YOU ARE THERE 2:13–15 **Have you ever thought of Jesus as an intercontinental political refugee? He was, according to the Christmas story in vv. 13–15. Through His parents, the Asian-born Jesus sought political asylum in Africa, avoiding the infanticide ordered by King Herod, the ruthless ruler of Palestine.**

The text doesn't say where the family stayed. Perhaps they were absorbed into the one million Jews estimated to have lived in Alexandria at that time. Wherever they ended up, we know that Jesus, perhaps close to two years old at the start of the journey (2:16), spent at least some of His formative years in Egypt, displaced from His homeland. And when the family migrated back to Palestine (2:22–23), they did not settle in a privileged neighborhood, but in Nazareth in rural Galilee.

Jesus can identify with the many migrating peoples of the world today. He is an international Savior who knows the pain of forced migration. That is indeed good news for those who have been displaced by natural disasters, famine, or political unrest.

Herod shared a reputation for villainy with others in his family. See "The Herods," Acts 12:1–2.

JOHN THE STREET PREACHER

CONSIDER THIS 3:4 **Would John the Baptist (v. 4) have been comfortable using today's media to proclaim his startling message? Probably not. Even for his own day he reflected none of the outward trappings of a successful ministry. He was not the head rabbi of a large city synagogue. He was not dressed in fine clothes. He did not sport a fine chariot. Nor did he enjoy sumptuous meals with leading citizens.**

Nevertheless, news about him spread far and wide, and people from throughout the region around Jerusalem and the Jordan came to hear him.

John illustrates the truth of Paul's words that "God has chosen the weak things of the world to put to shame the things which are mighty" (1 Cor. 1:27).

For the follower of Christ, how does success relate to wealth? See "Christians and Money," 1 Tim. 6:6–19.

"Arise, take the young Child and His mother, and go to the
land of Israel, for those who sought the young Child's life
are dead." 21 Then he arose, took the young Child and His
mother, and came into the land of Israel.
22 But when he heard that Archelaus was reigning over
Judea instead of his father Herod, he was afraid to go there.
And being warned by God in a dream, he turned aside into
the region of Galilee. 23 And he came and dwelt in a city
called Nazareth, that it might be fulfilled which was spoken
by the prophets, "He shall be called a Nazarene."

CHAPTER 3

The Ministry of John the Baptist

3:1–17 1 In those days John the Baptist came
preaching in the wilderness of Judea,
2 and saying, "Repent, for the kingdom of heaven is at
hand!" 3 For this is he who was spoken of by the prophet
Isaiah, saying:

"The voice of one crying in the wilderness:
'Prepare the way of the LORD;
Make His paths straight.' "[a]

3:4 4 Now John himself was clothed in
camel's hair, with a leather belt around

3:3 [a]Isaiah 40:3

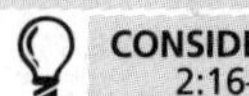

CONSIDER THIS 2:16–18

CITY KIDS DIE OVER ADULT MATTERS

In the tragic account in vv. 16–18, we read of an entire village of baby boys being slaughtered, due to the insane rage of a jealous king. The story reminds us that growing numbers of children today die needlessly for the sins of adults.

Like Rachel (v. 18), mothers all over the world, particularly in urban ghettos and developing nations, weep over their dead children. Rachel had lots of experience with tears. Her father tricked her fiancé into marrying her sister and she remained childless for years (Gen. 29:1—30:24). Later, Jeremiah the prophet described her as wailing over the exiled tribes (Jer. 31:15, the passage quoted by Matthew).

The weeping and wailing in Bethlehem must have gone on for days. It could not have been quickly silenced, nor could Rachel's wailing be comforted. The babies of Bethlehem and the people in exile had a common bond: in both cases, innocent people suffered as a result of the proud, ungodly acts of powerful leaders.

his waist; and his food was locusts and wild honey. 5Then Jerusalem, all Judea, and all the region around the Jordan went out to him 6and were baptized by him in the Jordan, confessing their sins.

7But when he saw many of the Pharisees and Sadducees coming to his baptism, he said to them, "Brood of vipers! Who warned you to flee from the wrath to come? 8Therefore bear fruits worthy of repentance, 9and do not think to say to yourselves, 'We have Abraham as *our* father.' For I say to you that God is able to raise up children to Abraham from these stones. 10And even now the ax is laid to the root of the trees. Therefore every tree which does not bear good fruit is cut down and thrown into the fire. 11I indeed baptize you with water unto repentance, but He who is coming after me is mightier than I, whose sandals I am not worthy to carry. He will baptize you with the Holy Spirit and fire.[a] 12His winnowing fan *is* in His hand, and He will thoroughly clean out His threshing floor, and gather His wheat into the barn; but He will burn up the chaff with unquenchable fire."

3:11 see pg. 14

John Baptizes Jesus

13Then Jesus came from Galilee to John at the Jordan to be baptized by him. 14And John *tried to* prevent Him, say-

3:11 [a]M-Text omits *and fire.*

◆ ◆ ◆ ◆ ◆ ◆ ◆ ◆ ◆ ◆ ◆ ◆ ◆ ◆ ◆ ◆

Jesus can offer particular comfort to those who grieve the loss of a child. In effect, the babies of Bethlehem died for Him. He must have carried the pain of that throughout His life and onto the cross. It doubtless shaped His special concern for children (compare Matt. 18:6–7). And His concerned activity toward them beckons us to find ways to serve children today.

Matthew's retelling of this slaughter is a very significant part of the Christmas story. In a powerful way, it reminds city kids today that they need not die in vain: Jesus lived and died for them, too. ◆

What It Means To Be Like Jesus

CONSIDER THIS 3:1–17 *Jesus indicated that those who follow Him will become like Him (10:25). What does it mean to* **"be like Jesus"** *in today's complex world? Matthew paints eight portraits of what Christlikeness looks like, including:*

#3: To Be Like Jesus Means TO COMMIT OURSELVES TO OTHER BELIEVERS

John the Baptist was not your average individual. He was an unexpected child. He lived in the wilderness—the "other side of the tracks" for that day. He wore strange clothing and ate strange food. He was pugnacious, even offensive at times. Yet he helped launch Jesus' career. In return, Jesus had nothing but praise for him (11:7–15). If we want to be like Jesus, we must not pick and choose our brothers and sisters in God's family. We need to embrace other believers and demonstrate our unity in Christ, no matter how awkward or inconvenient.

For a summary of all eight portraits of Christlikeness, see "What It Means to Be Like Jesus" at 10:25. The next item in the series can be found at 4:1–11.

The Power of Humility

CONSIDER THIS 3:11 **How difficult is it for you to accept and admit that others are mightier than you? If you regard strength as the power to dominate, you'll always be intimidated by those who seem to have more than you—more expertise, more experience, more energy, more intelligence.**

John held a different understanding of strength (v. 11). He saw it as a gift from God to be used for divine purposes. That gave him tremendous power in his community (v. 5). His humility gave him the capacity to serve and to welcome others—in this case, Jesus—as valuable associates.

Like John, Paul challenged believers to cultivate humility. Not a groveling, abject demeanor, but rather an acknowledgment of what one is. See "Humility—The Scandalous Virtue," Phil. 2:3.

ing, "I need to be baptized by You, and are You coming to
me?"
15But Jesus answered and said to him, "Permit *it to be so*
now, for thus it is fitting for us to fulfill all righteousness."
Then he allowed Him.
16When He had been baptized, Jesus came up immediately from the water; and behold, the heavens were opened
to Him, and He[a] saw the Spirit of God descending like a
dove and alighting upon Him. 17And suddenly a voice *came*
from heaven, saying, "This is My beloved Son, in whom I
am well pleased."

CHAPTER 4

The Temptation of Jesus

4:1–11 see pg. 16

1Then Jesus was led up by the Spirit
into the wilderness to be tempted by the
devil. 2And when He had fasted forty days and forty nights,
afterward He was hungry. 3Now when the
tempter came to Him, he said, "If You are
the Son of God, command that these stones become
bread."
4But He answered and said, "It is written, 'Man shall not

4:3

3:16 [a]Or he

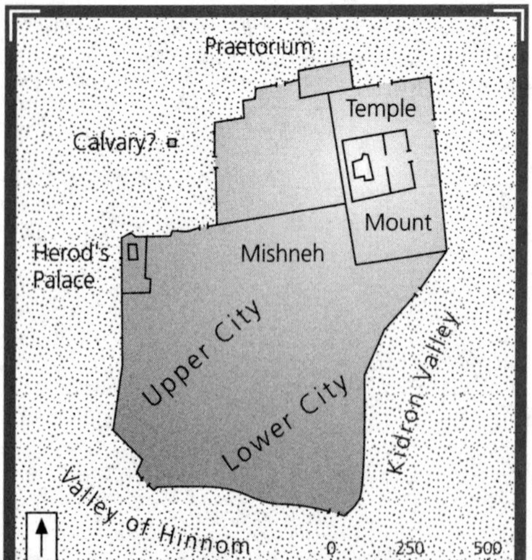

JERUSALEM

Can a Noisy, Dirty, Smelly City Also Be Holy?

YOU ARE THERE 4:5 *Matthew called Jerusalem "the holy city" (v. 5), but it was also noisy, dirty, and smelly. Gehenna, the town garbage dump and home to countless lepers, lay just outside the gates in a deep, narrow ravine, the Valley of Hinnom. Refuse, waste materials, and dead animals were burned there. Fires continually smouldered, and with the right wind, rank smells drifted north, blanketing the city and the temple mount with noxious odors.*

How could such a city be considered "holy"? Because God's presence was there, in the temple. That made it "sacred space" to the Hebrews (see John 1:51).

live by bread alone, but by every word that proceeds from the mouth of God.' "[a]

4:5

5Then the devil took Him up into the holy city, set Him on the pinnacle of the temple, 6and said to Him, "If You are the Son of God, throw Yourself down. For it is written:

'He shall give His angels charge over you,'

and,

'In *their* hands they shall bear you up,
Lest you dash your foot against a stone.' "[a]

7Jesus said to him, "It is written again, 'You shall not tempt the LORD your God.' "[a]

4:8–10 see pg. 16

8Again, the devil took Him up on an exceedingly high mountain, and showed Him all the kingdoms of the world and their glory. 9And he said to Him, "All these things I will give You if You will fall down and worship me."

10Then Jesus said to him, "Away with you,[a] Satan! For it is written, 'You shall worship the LORD your God, and Him only you shall serve.' "[b]

11Then the devil left Him, and behold, angels came and ministered to Him.

Jesus Begins His Ministry

4:12–25 see pg. 17

12Now when Jesus heard that John had been put in prison, He departed to Galilee. 13And leaving Nazareth, He came and dwelt in Capernaum, which is by the sea, in the regions of Zebulun and Naphtali, 14that it might be fulfilled which was spoken by Isaiah the prophet, saying:

15 "The land of Zebulun and the land of Naphtali,
By the way of the sea, beyond the Jordan,
Galilee of the Gentiles:
16 The people who sat in darkness have seen a great light,
And upon those who sat in the region and shadow of death
Light has dawned."[a]

4:17 see pg. 18

17From that time Jesus began to preach and to say, "Repent, for the kingdom of heaven is at hand."

(Bible text continued on page 17)

4:4 [a]Deuteronomy 8:3 *4:6* [a]Psalm 91:11, 12 *4:7* [a]Deuteronomy 6:16 *4:10* [a]M-Text reads *Get behind Me.* [b]Deuteronomy 6:13 *4:16* [a]Isaiah 9:1, 2

"You Don't Understand!"

CONSIDER THIS 4:3 **How often we hear someone dismiss the implications of faith for day-to-day life with the retort, "You don't understand! I live in the real world, where things are tough. They play by a different set of rules there. Christianity is all well and good, but isn't it a bit simplistic when it comes to real life?"**

The account of the temptation in vv. 1–11 offers a response to that sort of thinking. It shows that Jesus *does* understand real life. He faced real temptations—the same temptations that show up every day in the "real world."

Some people think that because He did not give in to what was offered, He must not have been "really" tempted; therefore, He can't "really" understand our situation. But that won't do. Scripture affirms that Satan's devices were real temptations that really tempted Him. And because He was able to resist them, He is able to help us do the same (Heb. 2:18). He completely understands our feelings—and how to do what is right in spite of them.

Temptation is not sin, but giving in is. See "Tired of Praying?" Luke 11:5–13.

Few teachings in Scripture have more practical, day-to-day implications than the truth that people are fallen, temptable, and subject to thinking and doing wrong. "Pay Attention to Temptation!" at 1 Cor. 10:12–13, explores the importance of that for Christians in today's workplace.

What It Means To Be Like Jesus

CONSIDER THIS 4:1–11 *Jesus indicated that those who follow Him will become like Him (10:25). What does it mean to* **"be like Jesus"** *in today's complex world? Matthew paints eight portraits of what Christlikeness looks like, including:*

#4: To Be Like Jesus Means TO ADMIT OUR VULNERABILITY TO TEMPTATION

Matthew's inclusion of the temptation is remarkable. It shows that the sinless Lord of the universe was tempted, just as we are (Heb. 4:15–16). If we want to be like Jesus, we must accept that temptation is real—as is the possibility of overcoming temptation. But we need to be open about our struggles. In doing so we honor God, recognize the power of sin, and encourage others to do likewise.

For a summary of all eight portraits of Christlikeness, see "What It Means to Be Like Jesus" at 10:25. The next item in the series can be found at 4:12–25.

Opportunities for temptation sometimes seem endless. Yet Scripture offers several alternatives for dealing with temptation as we find it. See "Pay Attention to Temptation," 1 Cor. 10:12–13.

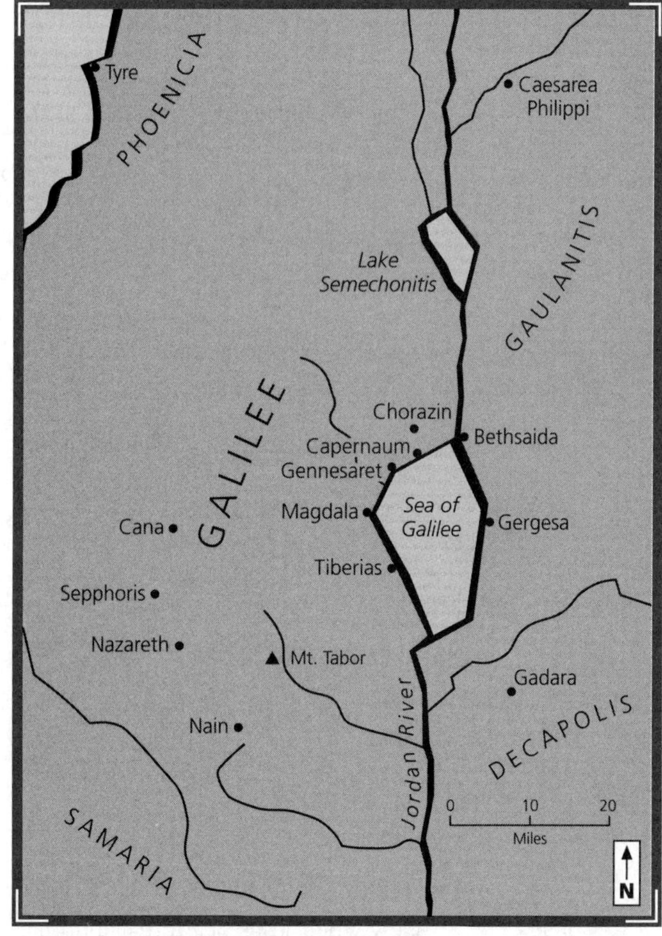

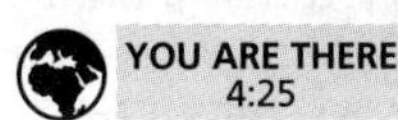

YOU ARE THERE 4:25 **JESUS' GALILEAN MINISTRY**

Wealth's Temptation

CONSIDER THIS 4:8–10 **For us who live in a materialistic culture, it's good to recognize that the desire for wealth and all that it symbolizes—prestige, power, luxury, authority—can be a powerful tool in Satan's hands. It was one of three strategies that the devil used to try to draw Christ away from His mission (vv. 8–10).**

Are you tempted by desires that are closely tied to wealth? If so, Christ's response in v. 10 challenges you to ask: Who or what are you going to worship and serve?

Most of Jesus' followers were not wealthy, but a few notable ones were. From them we can learn a great deal about the dangers and the disciplines of money. See the survey, "Wealthy People in the New Testament," Matt. 27:57.

Jesus Calls the Twelve

4:18–22 18And Jesus, walking by the Sea of
Galilee, saw two brothers, Simon called
Peter, and Andrew his brother, casting a net into the sea; for
they were fishermen. 19Then He said to them, "Follow Me,
and I will make you fishers of men." 20They immediately
left *their* nets and followed Him.
21Going on from there, He saw two other brothers, James
the son of Zebedee, and John his brother, in the boat with
Zebedee their father, mending their nets. He called them,
22and immediately they left the boat and their father, and
followed Him.

Galilean Ministry

4:23 23And Jesus went about all Galilee,
teaching in their synagogues, preaching
the gospel of the kingdom, and healing all kinds of sickness
and all kinds of disease among the people. 24Then His fame
went throughout all Syria; and they brought to Him all sick
people who were afflicted with various diseases and tor-
ments, and those who were demon-possessed, epileptics,
4:25 and paralytics; and He healed them.
25Great multitudes followed Him—from
Galilee, and *from* Decapolis, Jerusalem, Judea, and beyond
the Jordan.

CHAPTER 5

The Sermon on the Mount

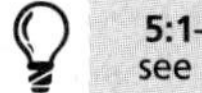

5:1—7:27 see pg. 20 1And seeing the multitudes, He went
up on a mountain, and when He was

(Bible text continued on page 20)

WHAT IT MEANS TO BE LIKE JESUS

CONSIDER THIS 4:12–25 *Jesus indicated that those who follow Him will become like Him (10:25). What does it mean to* **"be like Jesus"** *in today's complex world? Matthew paints eight portraits of what Christlikeness looks like, including:*

#5: To Be Like Jesus Means TO PROCLAIM THE MESSAGE OF CHRIST

Jesus' life was *not* an open book, readable by all. To be sure, He lived a perfect, model life. But even that could not stand alone as an undeniable witness. His actions needed interpretation. So He supplemented His good *deeds* with good *news*. In the same way, we need to verbally declare our faith if we want to be like Christ. Certainly we need to back up our words with a Christlike lifestyle. But what we tell others gives meaning to our quiet walk and good deeds.

For a summary of all eight portraits of Christlikeness, see "What It Means to Be Like Jesus" at 10:25. The next item in the series can be found at 5:1—7:27.

The Fishermen

A CLOSER LOOK 4:18–22 *The fishermen Jesus called (vv. 18–22) eventually became members of an inner circle of Jesus' followers. See "The Twelve," Matt. 10:2.*

Galilee

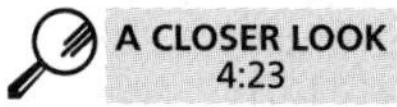

A CLOSER LOOK 4:23 *Though Jesus launched His ministry in Galilee (v. 23) with great energy, there is little evidence that His message ever took firm root there after He left. See "Galilee," Mark 1:14.*

"I WILL MAKE YOU FISHERS OF MEN."
—Matthew 4:19

The King Declares His Kingdom

Jesus initiated His public life with a simple but stiff challenge to repentance (v. 17). It was actually a familiar message—identical, in fact, to the message of John the Baptist, Jesus' forerunner (Matt. 3:2). Both urged their listeners to repent, to change their minds and hearts, not merely for the sake of change, but in light of what they called "the kingdom."

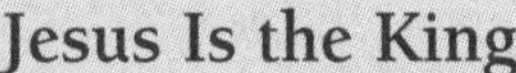

Jesus Is the King

The most important thing to notice is that a kingdom exists because Jesus is the King. He is the Messiah, the Savior promised by God in the Old Testament (1:22–23; 2:6; Is. 7:14; Mic. 5:2). He is not only Israel's King, but the international Christ for all the nations (see "Jesus' Roots," Matt. 1:1–16, and "Jesus' Global Connections," 8:10). At the beginning of His life, magi came to Herod, asking where they could find the King of the Jews (2:2). At the end of His life, Pilate asked Him, "Are you the King of the Jews?" He affirmed that He was (27:11–12), and Pilate sanctioned His crucifixion on that basis (27:37).

So in 4:17–25, the King was declaring His kingdom. Foretold by Scripture and announced by John, Jesus had come to establish His rule. However, He disappointed the expectations of many people—both then and now.

Where Is the Kingdom?

For a few brief decades, Israel had enjoyed a relatively prosperous, peaceful monarchy under David and his son, Solomon. Some Old Testament passages prophesied that the Messiah would reestablish that sort of kingdom. Was now the time? Would Jesus overthrow the iron rule of the Romans and set up a political state? He did not. In fact, He told the Roman governor Pilate that His kingdom was not of this world, that He did not have an army fighting on His behalf (John 18:36). And He told the Pharisees that the kingdom was not something tangible and observable, but was "within" them (Luke 17:20).

Then is Christ's kingdom simply a spiritual concept, a powerful but abstract ideal? No, because He made a definite promise to His disciples that they would rule the tribes of Israel in His kingdom (Matt. 19:23, 28). They apparently took Him literally (Acts 1:6).

When Is the Kingdom?

No less puzzling is the question of when the kingdom has or will come. As they began their ministries, John the Baptist and Jesus declared that the kingdom was "at hand." But a few years later, when Jesus' followers asked whether He was ready to restore Israel's kingdom, He put them off; that was something that only His Father could know, He told them (Acts 1:6–7). Sometimes the kingdom seemed to be a present reality (Matt. 12:28; 13:18–23; 21:43). At other times, it seemed to be a hope for the future (16:28; 20:20–23; 26:29).

Even today, theologians stridently debate over whether and in what form the kingdom has already been established, is currently in the process of being formed, is coming in the future, or is not coming at all. Like most questions that cannot be answered definitively to everyone's satisfaction, agreements are few and positions strongly defended.

What Is the Kingdom?

Is there any simple way to understand this puzzling doctrine of the kingdom? Probably not. Jesus' followers have not ceased to puzzle over His statements about it since the moment they were made. But most would generally agree that Christ's kingdom began in some way with His first coming. It continues to advance as His people live the gospel message throughout the world. However, it will not realize its ultimate completion until He returns.

What Difference Does It Make?

Whatever else we can say, the kingdom has to do with whatever Christ the King rules. That's why Jesus began His ministry with a call to repentance. Repentance means to change one's mind or purpose. In terms of the kingdom, it involves:

(1) A change in one's allegiance. If Christ is the King, He deserves our honor, loyalty, and obedience. We put ourselves under His authority and power. Whatever He says, we determine to do. That's the point of the oft-repeated lines in the Lord's Prayer, "Your kingdom come, Your will be done on earth as it is in heaven" (Matt. 6:10). Kingdom people submit their own will to the will of the King.

(2) A change in one's expectations. One of the difficulties people have with the idea of a kingdom is that it doesn't appear to be in place yet. The world seems to grow farther away from God by the day. As a result, it's easy to live for the here and now, as if this present life is all that matters. But the hope of the kingdom is that there is far more to life than what we see right now. Jesus made extraordinary promises in regard to a future kingdom, not only for Israel, but for all who follow Him as King. The kingdom may not yet be fulfilled completely, but it has been established and will last forever (6:13).

(3) A change in one's values. Our culture values achievement, success, independence, and image. Other cultures value other qualities. But the values of the kingdom reflect what matters to the King. Jesus described a number of His values in Matthew 5:3–10, a section of the Sermon on the Mount known as the Beatitudes (or, as some call them, the "beautiful attitudes"). Kingdom people adopt the King's values and make choices that reflect those values—in their jobs, families, and communities.

(4) A change in one's priorities. The real test of people's values is how they spend their time and money. Jesus spoke directly to that issue in terms of the kingdom (6:24–34). He did not demean the value of work or diminish the need for material goods. But He challenged His followers to bring kingdom values into their day-to-day lives. "Seeking first the kingdom" (6:33) puts a Christlike perspective on one's work and its outcomes.

(5) A change in one's lifelong mission. Some people are driven to accomplish great tasks with their lives. Others live aimlessly from day to day, lacking purpose or direction. Either way, Jesus affects the outlook of a person's life. He gives His followers purpose and a mission—to live as subjects of the kingdom and promote kingdom values in everyday life and work. Ultimately, He wants His followers to extend His message to the ends of the earth, so that all people have the opportunity to give their allegiance to Him as their Savior and King (28:18–20). ◆

WHAT IT MEANS TO BE LIKE JESUS

CONSIDER THIS 5:1—7:27 *Jesus indicated that those who follow Him will become like Him (10:25). What does it mean to* **"be like Jesus"** *in today's complex world? Matthew paints eight portraits of what Christlikeness looks like, including:*

#6: To Be Like Jesus Means TO COMMIT TO CHANGED THINKING AND BEHAVIOR

In His Sermon on the Mount, Jesus explained the values of the kingdom. Money, prayer, relationships, possessions, information, and power were a few of the categories He redefined from God's perspective. He showed that following Him will involve radical change for most of us. It may mean undoing the way we've always done things and rethinking traditional sources of wisdom from our parents and culture. To become like Jesus involves a tough-minded review of our values and a thorough change in our behavior.

For a summary of all eight portraits of Christlikeness, see "What It Means to Be Like Jesus" at 10:25. The next item in the series can be found at 8:1—9:38.

5:2

seated His disciples came to Him. [2]Then
He opened His mouth and taught them,
saying:

The Beatitudes

5:3 see pg. 22

3 "Blessed *are* the poor in spirit,
For theirs is the kingdom of heaven.
4 Blessed *are* those who mourn,
For they shall be comforted.

5:5

5 Blessed *are* the meek,
For they shall inherit the earth.
6 Blessed *are* those who hunger and thirst for righteousness,
For they shall be filled.
7 Blessed *are* the merciful,
For they shall obtain mercy.
8 Blessed *are* the pure in heart,
For they shall see God.
9 Blessed *are* the peacemakers,
For they shall be called sons of God.
10 Blessed are those who are persecuted for righteousness' sake,
For theirs is the kingdom of heaven.

[11]"Blessed are you when they revile and persecute you, and
say all kinds of evil against you falsely for My sake. [12]Re-
joice and be exceedingly glad, for great *is* your reward in
heaven, for so they persecuted the prophets who were before you.

"You Are Salt and Light"

5:13–16 see pg. 24

[13]"You are the salt of the earth; but if
the salt loses its flavor, how shall it be
seasoned? It is then good for nothing but to be thrown out
and trampled underfoot by men.
[14]"You are the light of the world. A city that is set on a hill
cannot be hidden. [15]Nor do they light a lamp and put it under a basket, but on a lampstand, and it gives light to all
who are in the house. [16]Let your light so shine before men,

(Bible text continued on page 22)

The Meek

A CLOSER LOOK 5:5

Nearly every society and every city in biblical times had a large underclass, people scraping by on the margins of society (v. 5). Jesus intentionally directed much of His life and ministry to that disadvantaged group. See Luke 7:22.

The Sermon on the Mount

"Repent, for the kingdom of heaven is at hand," Jesus warned as He began His public ministry in Galilee (Matt. 4:17). His message quickly spread and huge crowds came to hear Him from Galilee, from nearby Syria and the Decapolis, and from as far away as Jerusalem, Judea, and east of the Jordan River (vv. 24–25).

They came to hear about a kingdom. Instead, Jesus talked about a lifestyle—the lifestyle of those who intend to live in the kingdom. As perhaps thousands gathered on a hillside (or "mountain," 5:1; the exact location is unknown), Jesus began to fill out the implications of His appeal for repentance. It would mean far more than an outward show of piety. Indeed, Jesus urged His listeners to make such a complete change of heart and life that they would "be perfect, just as your Father in heaven is perfect" (v. 48).

Jesus may have spoken the contents of Matthew 5–7, known as the Sermon on the Mount, on more than one occasion. It is possible that the address lasted for some time as He described the new lifestyle of the kingdom, holding it up like a jewel with many facets, to be examined from many different angles. On the other hand, bits and pieces of the sermon can be found throughout the gospels. Like any good teacher, Jesus probably repeated much of His teaching at other times and places in order to drive home the message.

The Sermon on the Mount contains the core of Jesus' moral and ethical teaching:

The Beatitudes (5:3–12). True happiness comes from looking at life from God's perspective, which is often the reverse of the human point of view.

Salt and Light (5:13–16). Jesus wants His followers to influence the moral and spiritual climate of the world.

The Morality of the Kingdom (5:17–48). Jesus' listeners were familiar with the Old Testament Law and with the many traditions that generations of rabbis had added to it. But Jesus revealed a morality that went beyond the letter of the Law to its spirit.

Spiritual Disciplines (6:1–18). Practicing religion certainly involves behavior, but it goes beyond an outward show of spirituality to the hidden quality of one's character.

Treasures on Earth (6:19–34). Our relationship to money and material possessions reveals much about our relationship to God. Jesus does not denounce worldly goods, but He urges His listeners to place ultimate value on the treasures of heaven.

Judging Right and Wrong (7:1–6). Most of us are quick to point out the moral flaws of others. Jesus warns us to pay more attention to our own.

Asking and Receiving (7:7–12). When we approach God with a request, we can expect Him to deal with us as a loving father deals with his child. And just as God deals with us in love, He expects us to deal with others in love.

A Challenge to Obedience (7:13–29). Jesus wraps up His message with a challenge to change. The alternatives are clear: living a lifestyle that is worthy of the kingdom, resulting in life and joy; or ignoring the way of Christ, resulting in death and disaster.

In this manner, Jesus described the lifestyle of the kingdom. When He was finished, Matthew says that the people were "astonished" at His teaching (7:28; literally "overwhelmed" or "stunned"). They had come to hear a new teacher, but this one exceeded their expectations. His voice had an unusual but unmistakable ring of authority (v. 29). And no wonder: they were listening to the King Himself! ◆

that they may see your good works and glorify your Father
in heaven.

The Morality of Christ

5:17–48
see pg. 24

17"Do not think that I came to destroy
the Law or the Prophets. I did not come
to destroy but to fulfill. 18For assuredly, I say to you, till
heaven and earth pass away, one jot or one tittle will by no

5:19

means pass from the law till all is fulfilled. 19Whoever therefore breaks one of
the least of these commandments, and teaches men so, shall
be called least in the kingdom of heaven; but whoever does
and teaches *them,* he shall be called great in the kingdom of
heaven. 20For I say to you, that unless your righteousness
exceeds *the righteousness* of the scribes and Pharisees, you
will by no means enter the kingdom of heaven.

21"You have heard that it was said to those of old, 'You
shall not murder,[a] and whoever murders will be in danger
of the judgment.' 22But I say to you that whoever is angry
with his brother without a cause[a] shall be in danger of the
judgment. And whoever says to his brother, 'Raca!' shall be
in danger of the council. But whoever says, 'You fool!' shall

5:21 [a]Exodus 20:13; Deuteronomy 5:17 *5:22* [a]NU-Text omits *without a cause.*

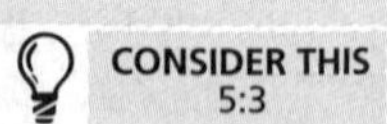

The Way Up Is Down

Of all the virtues Christ commended in the Beatitudes, it is significant that the first is humility, being "poor in spirit" (v. 3). That underlies all the others:

- *You cannot mourn (v. 4) without appreciating how insufficient you are to handle life in your own strength. That is humility.*
- *You cannot be meek (v. 5) unless you have needed gentleness yourself. Knowing that need is humility.*
- *You cannot hunger and thirst for righteousness (v. 6) if you proudly think of yourself as already righteous. Longing to fill that spiritual appetite demands humility. In a parable that Luke recorded, a humble tax collector prayed, "God, be merciful to me a sinner!" He went away justified, unlike a proud Pharisee who boasted of his righteousness (Luke 18:13).*
- *You cannot be merciful (Matt. 5:7) without recognizing your own need for mercy. Jesus said that it's the person who is forgiven much that loves much (Luke 7:47). To*

be in danger of hell fire. 23Therefore if you bring your gift to
the altar, and there remember that your brother has something against you, 24leave your gift there before the altar,
and go your way. First be reconciled to your brother, and
then come and offer your gift. 25Agree with your adversary
quickly, while you are on the way with him, lest your adversary deliver you to the judge, the judge hand you over to
the officer, and you be thrown into prison. 26Assuredly, I say
to you, you will by no means get out of there till you have
paid the last penny.
27"You have heard that it was said to those of old,[a] 'You
shall not commit adultery.'[b] 28But I say to you that whoever
looks at a woman to lust for her has already committed adultery with her in his heart. 29If your right eye causes
you to sin, pluck it out and cast *it* from you; for it is more
profitable for you that one of your members perish,
than for your whole body to be cast into hell. 30And if
your right hand causes you to sin, cut it off and cast *it*
from you; for it is more profitable for you that one of your
members perish, than for your whole body to be cast into
hell.

(Bible text continued on page 26)

5:27 [a]NU-Text and M-Text omit *to those of old.* [b]Exodus 20:14; Deuteronomy 5:18

confess your sin and ask God and others for forgiveness takes humility.

- *You cannot be pure in heart (Matt. 5:8) if your heart is filled with pride. God promises to exalt the humble, not the proud (James 4:10).*
- *You cannot be a peacemaker (Matt. 5:9) if you believe that you are always right. To admit your own fallibility takes humility. Peace results when both warring parties move toward each other.*
- *Finally, identifying with Christ no matter what the reaction of others (vv. 10–12) demands a certain death to yourself and a renunciation of your own rights. Standing up under persecution demands Christlike humility.* ◆

Humility is the scandalous virtue! See Phil. 2:3.

WHAT ABOUT THE OLD TESTAMENT LAW?

CONSIDER THIS 5:19

Jesus' critics claimed that His teaching encouraged people to violate the Mosaic Law, allowing them to get away with sin. Actually, He warned people to avoid the hypocrisies of the rabbis. While making an outward show of righteousness they took ethical shortcuts and carried out wicked schemes. In this portion of the the Sermon on the Mount (vv. 17–20), Jesus turned the tables on His opponents by appealing to the Law as the basis for His moral code—not the Law as they taught it, but as God intended it.

Jesus' words are crucial for Christians today. While God does not require us to live by the specific regulations of the Old Testament Law, He still expects us to honor Old Testament morality. What might that look like in today's ethically complicated marketplace? See "Ten Commandments for Practical Living," James 2:8–13.

The Old Testament Law was part of the covenant that set Israel apart as God's people. It governed their worship, their relationship to God, and their social relationships with one another. See "The Law," Rom. 2:12.

SULFA DRUGS AND STREET LIGHTS

Following Christ goes far beyond private spirituality. It also involves a believer's public life, particularly through work and participation in the community. Jesus used two metaphors to describe that dynamic: salt (v. 13) and light (vv. 14–16).

In Jesus' day, salt was used to preserve foods like fish from decay. In the same way, believers can help to preserve society from moral and spiritual decay. Of course, in our culture, salt has given way to chemical preservatives (many of which have come under attack in recent years for their alleged role in causing cancer). So Jesus might use a different metaphor were He speaking today.

Perhaps He would talk in terms of an infection-fighting drug, such as an antibiotic like penicillin, or the sulfa drugs developed in the '40s that have proved so valuable in fighting meningitis and pneumonia. Christians can help to ward off spiritual infections and diseases in the larger society. One of the most powerful arenas for influence is the workplace, particularly jobs that affect values, laws, and public opinion. That's why believers need to pursue careers in education, government, and journalism, among many others. They may not be able to transform the entire society, but they can use whatever influence they have to promote Christlike values and hinder evil.

THE MORALITY OF CHRIST

"Jesus was a great moral teacher. Mainly He taught that people should love each other." Have you ever heard someone summarize Christ's life and ministry that way?

It is true that Jesus was a great moral teacher. But of course, He was much more—He was also the Son of God (see "Ten Myths of Christianity, Myth #1: Jesus Christ Was Only a Great Moral Teacher," Matt. 13:34–35). Likewise, He certainly taught that people should love each other. But He taught a great deal more. In this section of the Sermon on the Mount (5:17–48), we discover much about Jesus' concept of morality.

Unfortunately, numerous misunderstandings have come from this passage. Jesus makes a number of statements that sound extreme to our ears (vv. 22, 30, 37, 39–42). How can we make sense out of them?

First, it's important to know that when Jesus referred to "the Law" and "the Prophets" (v. 17), He was referring to the express moral teaching of the Old Testament. His listeners were Jews, so their moral conduct and character were governed by those Scriptures. At least, they were supposed to be.

Jesus also called His followers "the light of the world" (v. 14), an image that fits perfectly into modern society. The Lord's first-century listeners would be astonished at the availability and importance of light in our culture. We use it not only to illuminate but also to communicate. Thus, Jesus wants us as His followers to shine, to be visible and attractive, not to bring attention to ourselves, but to bring people to God (v. 16). Again, our vocations are one of the primary means we have to reflect Christ to others.

Jesus' teaching here challenges us as His followers to ask: How are we engaging our society? What spiritual infections are we fighting to overcome? What positive changes are we trying to promote? What impact for God are we having through our work? Have we lost our saltiness (v. 13)? Are we standing like burned-out street lights, ineffective and waiting to be removed? Or are we shining brilliantly with the love and truth of Christ? ◆

Spreading Christ's message involves far more than just broadcasting a statement or a set of facts. See "Faith Impacts the World," Mark 16:15–16.

In reality, the people were taught a heavily doctored version of Old Testament truth by their rabbis. Sometimes these teachers stressed the letter of the Law, rather than its spirit, and sometimes they favored their own traditions over the actual teaching of God (12:9–12; 15:1–9). And sometimes they actually perverted the Law to suit their own ends (19:3–8). No wonder Jesus labeled them hypocrites and warned people not to follow their example (23:1–36).

That helps to explain the formula that Jesus uses here: "You have heard it said . . . but I say to you" (vv. 21–22, 27–28, 33–34, 38–39, 43–44). The people had heard the Law and the Prophets, but not in their purity. By contrast, Jesus spoke with integrity and authority to five areas of morality: murder (vv. 21–26), adultery (vv. 27–32), vows and oaths (vv. 33–37), vengeance (vv. 38–42), and love and hate (vv. 43–47).

Framing these remarks is an introduction in which the Lord appealed to His listeners to fulfill the Law (vv. 17–20) and a conclusion in which He challenged them to act as the Father would act (v. 48). ◆

"YOU HAVE HEARD THAT IT WAS SAID. . . . BUT I SAY TO YOU. . . ."
—Matthew 5:21–22

[31]"Furthermore it has been said, 'Whoever divorces his
5:32 wife, let him give her a certificate of divorce.' [32]But I say to you that whoever divorces his wife for any reason except sexual immorality[a]
causes her to commit adultery; and whoever marries a
woman who is divorced commits adultery.

[33]"Again you have heard that it was said to those of old,
'You shall not swear falsely, but shall perform your oaths to
the Lord.' [34]But I say to you, do not swear at all: neither by
heaven, for it is God's throne; [35]nor by the earth, for it is His
footstool; nor by Jerusalem, for it is the city of the great
King. [36]Nor shall you swear by your head, because you cannot make one hair white or black. [37]But let your 'Yes' be
'Yes,' and your 'No,' 'No.' For whatever is more than these is
from the evil one.

5:38–42 see pg. 28 [38]"You have heard that it was said, 'An
eye for an eye and a tooth for a tooth.'[a]
[39]But I tell you not to resist an evil person. But whoever
slaps you on your right cheek, turn the other to him also.
[40]If anyone wants to sue you and take away your tunic, let
him have *your* cloak also. [41]And whoever compels you to go
one mile, go with him two. [42]Give to him who asks you, and
from him who wants to borrow from you do not turn away.

5:43–48 [43]"You have heard that it was said, 'You
shall love your neighbor[a] and hate your
enemy.' [44]But I say to you, love your enemies, bless those
who curse you, do good to those who hate you, and pray
for those who spitefully use you and persecute you,[a] [45]that
you may be sons of your Father in heaven; for He makes
His sun rise on the evil and on the good, and sends rain on
the just and on the unjust. [46]For if you love those who love
you, what reward have you? Do not even the tax collectors
do the same? [47]And if you greet your brethren[a] only, what
do you do more *than others?* Do not even the tax collectors[b]
do so? [48]Therefore you shall be perfect, just as your Father
in heaven is perfect.

(Bible text continued on page 29)

5:32 [a]Or *fornication* *5:38* [a]Exodus 21:24; Leviticus 24:20; Deuteronomy 19:21
5:43 [a]Compare Leviticus 19:18 *5:44* [a]NU-Text omits three clauses from this verse, leaving, *"But I say to you, love your enemies and pray for those who persecute you."*
5:47 [a]M-Text reads *friends.* [b]NU-Text reads *Gentiles.*

A New Respect for Women

CONSIDER THIS 5:32 *Greek, Roman, and Jewish laws of Jesus' day afforded men many opportunities to divorce their wives. Perhaps the most painful for the women was infertility. But in vv. 31–32, Jesus insisted on a different understanding of women—and the relative importance of childbearing. Only the severing of the marriage bond through sexual immorality was to be grounds for divorce, not the lack of an heir.*

Living the Way God Wants Us To

A CLOSER LOOK 5:43–48 *Jesus' moral standard seems high. But it's not to be reached by just our own ability. When we are Christ's, we are made into new creatures. The Holy Spirit lives through us as we become more like Jesus. See "New Creatures with New Character," Gal. 5:22–23.*

There are two reasons not to feel frustrated by the expectations we see here: First, eternal life is not earned but is God's gift. Second, godly principles enable us to live stable, joyful lives. See "Rules That Lead to Joy," 1 John 2:3–6.

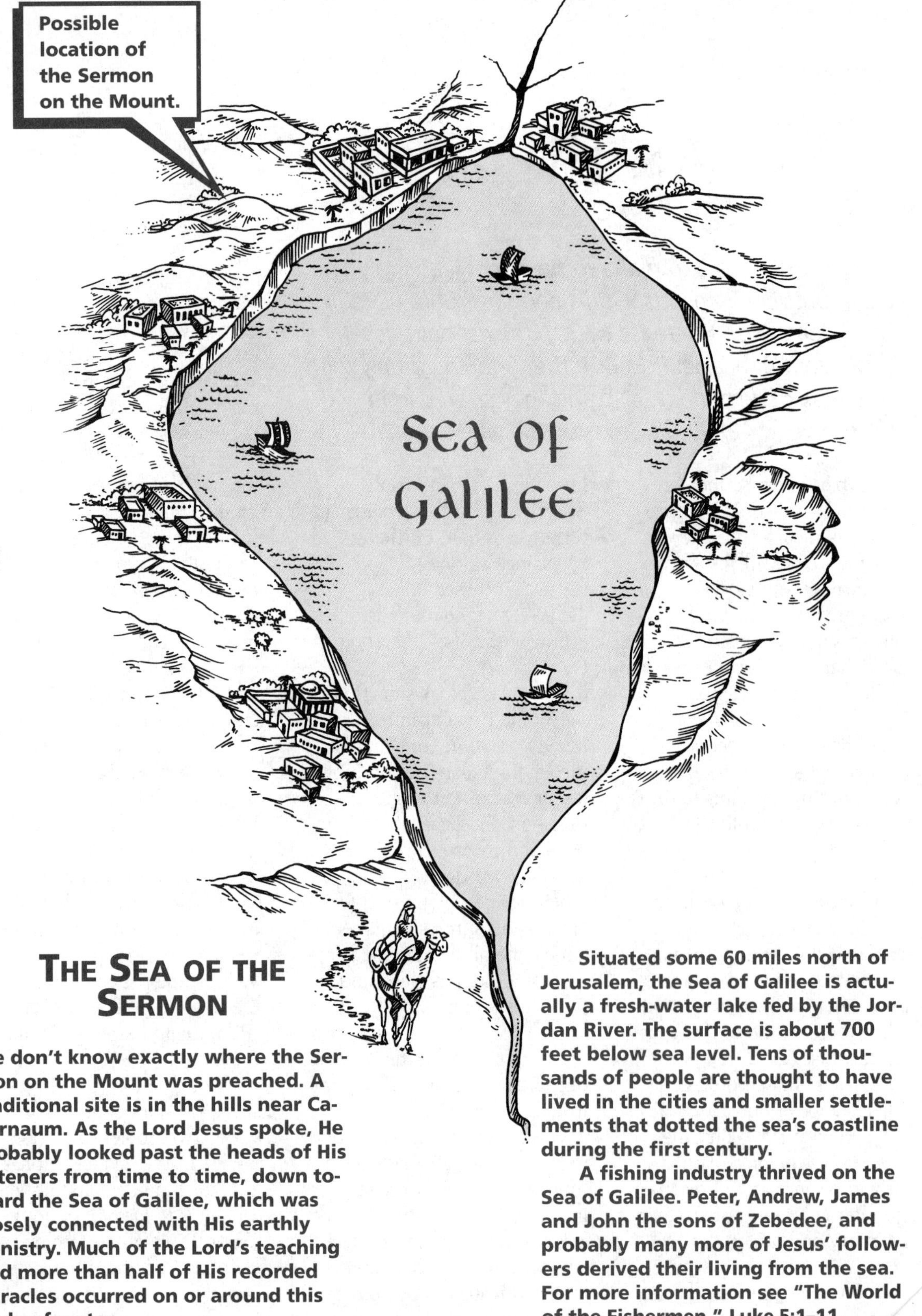

The Sea of the Sermon

We don't know exactly where the Sermon on the Mount was preached. A traditional site is in the hills near Capernaum. As the Lord Jesus spoke, He probably looked past the heads of His listeners from time to time, down toward the Sea of Galilee, which was closely connected with His earthly ministry. Much of the Lord's teaching and more than half of His recorded miracles occurred on or around this body of water.

Situated some 60 miles north of Jerusalem, the Sea of Galilee is actually a fresh-water lake fed by the Jordan River. The surface is about 700 feet below sea level. Tens of thousands of people are thought to have lived in the cities and smaller settlements that dotted the sea's coastline during the first century.

A fishing industry thrived on the Sea of Galilee. Peter, Andrew, James and John the sons of Zebedee, and probably many more of Jesus' followers derived their living from the sea. For more information see "The World of the Fishermen," Luke 5:1–11.

An Eye for an Eye

Jesus appears to make some stark, seemingly impossible demands: God's people should never use force in self-defense (v. 39); they should never contest a lawsuit (v. 40); they should comply with every type of demand (v. 41); and they should lend without reserve (v. 42). Could Jesus possibly be serious?

In this part of the Sermon on the Mount, the Lord is addressing the issue of justice. He was alluding to the Old Testament Law dealing with *public* vengeance. The Law limited damages in criminal cases to no more than the loss suffered—"an eye for an eye" (v. 38; Ex. 21:24–25). Nevertheless, as might be expected, people tended to justify *personal* vengeance by appealing to the same texts. We would call it "taking the law into your own hands."

But Jesus' morality challenged that. To be sure, some circumstances call for resistance and self-defense. The Law specifically sanctioned self-protection when there was no other apparent recourse (Ex. 22:2). Likewise, Jesus Himself protested when slapped (John 18:22–23).

But He warned against the needless use of force, particularly in revenge. In self-defense, the alternative to resistance may be injury or death. But in vengeance, one inflicts harm even though immediate danger [illegible]st. A slap on the cheek is little more than an insult. There's no place for violence in response to that. Furthermore, vengeance belongs to God (Deut. 32:35; see Rom. 12:19–21), who often uses governing authorities to carry it out (13:4).

In the case of lawsuits (Matt. 5:40), the Law permitted demanding a tunic (or shirt) in pledge for a loan, but prohibited taking a cloak (or coat) overnight, because it was needed for warmth (Ex. 22:26–27). However, Jesus' listeners commonly pressed for the cloak—for ruinous damages—almost literally "suing the pants off each other," as we would say. But Christ's point was that if lawsuits have to go to extremes, they ought to be in the extreme of charity. (Paul argued similarly in 1 Cor. 6:1–8.)

What about going the second mile (Matt. 5:41)? The word "compels" is a technical term meaning "to requisition or press into service." Ancient Persian law permitted postal carriers to *compel* private citizens to help carry their loads. The Romans were no different; for example, Roman soldiers compelled Simon of Cyrene to carry Jesus' cross (27:32). So Jesus was speaking of someone with legitimate authority who might compel one of His followers to go a "thousand paces," or one Roman mile, roughly nine-tenths of an English mile.

How should a believer respond to such requests? With resistance? Perhaps complying grudgingly, but only to a minimum degree? Again, Jesus challenged His followers to grace and integrity. Imagine the reputation that Christians would have if we always did twice what the law required! What would tax auditors think if we not only followed the rules, but paid more than the law required of us? What would our employers think if we consistently rendered double the expected service?

The same pattern holds in the case of lending (v. 42; see "Running to Extremes," Luke 6:29).

Throughout vv. 17–48, Jesus speaks in stark contrasts and strong hyperboles (overstatements for the sake of emphasis). The key to understanding this section is to keep in mind the major thrust of His teaching: good not evil, grace not vengeance, love not hatred. That is the morality of Christ. ◆

CHAPTER 6

Spiritual Disciplines

6:1–4

1"Take heed that you do not do your charitable deeds before men, to be seen by them. Otherwise you have no reward from your Father in heaven. 2Therefore, when you do a charitable deed, do not sound a trumpet before you as the hypocrites do in the synagogues and in the streets, that they may have glory from men. Assuredly, I say to you, they have their reward. 3But when you do a charitable deed, do not let your left hand know what your right hand is doing, 4that your charitable deed may be in secret; and your Father who sees in secret will Himself reward you openly.[a]

5"And when you pray, you shall not be like the hypocrites. For they love to pray standing in the synagogues and on the corners of the streets, that they may be seen by men. Assuredly, I say to you, they have their reward. 6But you, when you pray, go into your room, and when you have shut your door, pray to your Father who *is* in the secret *place;* and your Father who sees in secret will reward you openly.[a] 7And when you pray, do not use vain repetitions as the heathen *do.* For they think that they will be heard for their many words.

8"Therefore do not be like them. For your Father knows the things you have need of before you ask Him. 9In this manner, therefore, pray:

Our Father in heaven,
Hallowed be Your name.
10 Your kingdom come.
Your will be done
On earth as *it is* in heaven.

6:11

11 Give us this day our daily bread.
12 And forgive us our debts,
As we forgive our debtors.

6:4 [a]NU-Text omits *openly.* *6:6* [a]NU-Text omits *openly.*

Anonymous Donors

CONSIDER THIS 6:1–4 **Jesus' words in vv. 1–4 challenge a lot of what goes on today in fund-raising and charitable causes. As any fund-raiser knows, one of the biggest motivations for people who give large gifts is the prestige that results.**

Jesus questioned that spirit of giving, however. He detested people who made a great show of presenting their gifts in the temple and elsewhere (Mark 12:41–44) as if they were generous and upright, but behind the scenes practiced the worst sorts of greed and immorality (Matt. 23:23–24). He was not attacking giving but hypocrisy.

How can we be sure that we are giving with the right motives? One way is to give anonymously (6:3–4). That way, our gifts will affect no one's opinion of us one way or the other. The matter will stay between us and God—and He can evaluate our motives.

"YOU SHALL NOT BE LIKE THE HYPOCRITES." —Matthew 6:5

Our Daily Bread

A CLOSER LOOK 6:11

The request for daily bread (v. 11) acknowledges that God ultimately provides for our needs. He gives us skills and strength, jobs and income, and a world rich with resources to that end. For more on God's provision, see "God—The Original Worker," John 5:17.

6:13

[13] And do not lead us into temptation,
But deliver us from the evil one.
For Yours is the kingdom and the power and the glory
forever. Amen.[a]

[14]"For if you forgive men their trespasses, your heavenly
Father will also forgive you. [15]But if you do not forgive men
their trespasses, neither will your Father forgive your trespasses.
[16]"Moreover, when you fast, do not be like the hypocrites,
with a sad countenance. For they disfigure their faces that
they may appear to men to be fasting. Assuredly, I say to
you, they have their reward. [17]But you, when you fast,
anoint your head and wash your face, [18]so that you do not
appear to men to be fasting, but to your Father who *is* in

6:13 [a]NU-Text omits *For Yours* through *Amen.*

Do Not Lead Us into Temptation

A CLOSER LOOK 6:13

God has committed Himself to helping His children avoid, flee, confess, and resist temptation (v. 13). See "Pay Attention to Temptation!" at 1 Cor. 10:12–13.

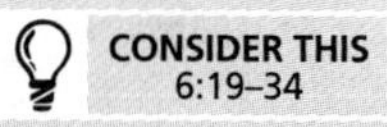

CONSIDER THIS 6:19–34

DON'T WORRY!

Of the texts in Scripture that discuss money and work, vv. 19–34 are among the most frequently cited. Unfortunately, they are often used to imply that Jesus was against money and considered everyday work a distraction to things that "really" matter.

However, a careful reader will notice that Jesus condemned worry, *not work (vv. 25, 27–28, 31, 34). He never told us to stop working. Rather, He called us to correctly focus our faith on God, the ultimate supplier of our needs (v. 32).*

God provides for people in many ways. The most common is through everyday work. He expects us to work diligently with whatever resources He gives us (2 Thess. 3:6–12). Of course, sometimes that normal means of provision fails for a variety of reasons: ill health, divorce from or death of a provider, loss of a job, natural disaster, changing markets, and other circumstances beyond our control.

It is precisely the fear of those possibilities that tempts us to worry so much and forget about trusting God. Why rely on Him, we figure, if He can't keep us from troubles like that? Why not just rely on ourselves and trust to our

the secret *place;* and your Father who sees in secret will reward you openly.[a]

Treasures on Earth

6:19–34

[19]"Do not lay up for yourselves treasures on earth, where moth and rust destroy and where thieves break in and steal; [20]but lay up for yourselves treasures in heaven, where neither moth nor rust destroys and where thieves do not break in and steal. [21]For where your treasure is, there your heart will be also.

[22]"The lamp of the body is the eye. If therefore your eye is good, your whole body will be full of light. [23]But if your eye is bad, your whole body will be full of darkness. If therefore the light that is in you is darkness, how great *is* that darkness!

[24]"No one can serve two masters; for either he will hate the one and love the other, or else he will be loyal to the one and despise the other. You cannot serve God and mammon.

[25]"Therefore I say to you, do not worry about your life,

6:18 [a]NU-Text and M-Text omit *openly.*

own devices? All the while we forget that God never promised that we wouldn't face hard times, and that He has many ways to help us through them when we do: family members, church communities, neighbors, charities, inheritances, even public agencies and non-profit groups.

Certainly we need to pay attention to our physical and material needs. But Jesus urged us to stop worrying about things so that they dominate our lives and values. We can't do that and serve God at the same time (v. 24). Instead, we need to redirect our focus onto God's kingdom and righteousness (v. 33). That means adopting the values of the King and bringing Him into our work and lives. Jesus said that's what "really" matters. ◆

God has given work as a gift to be used in service to others. See "People at Work," Heb. 2:7.

Contrary to what many people think, work is not a curse. See "Is Work a Curse?" Rom. 8:20–22.

Bringing Christ into our everyday work has a tangible effect on how we do our jobs. See "Your Workstyle," Titus 2:9–10.

"FOR WHERE YOUR TREASURE IS, THERE YOUR HEART WILL BE ALSO."
—Matthew 6:21

Judge Not!

CONSIDER THIS 7:1–5 What was Jesus calling for when He ordered His followers to "judge not" (v. 1)? Did He want us to close our eyes to error and evil? Did He intend that managers forgo critical performance reviews of their employees? Or that news editors and art critics pull their punches? Or that juries refrain from judgment? Should we decline any assessment of others, since none of us is perfect?

No, those would all be misapplications of Jesus' teaching. In the first place, He was not commanding blind acceptance, but grace toward others. Since all of us are sinners, we need to stop bothering with the failings of others and start attending to serious issues of our own (vv. 3–5). His words here extend His earlier exposé of hypocrisy (6:1–18). Don't blame or put down others while excusing or exalting yourself, Jesus was saying.

Is there room, then, to assess others, especially when we know we are not perfect? Yes, but only in Jesus' way: with empathy and fairness (7:12) and with a readiness to freely and fully forgive (Matt. 6:12, 14). When we are called upon to correct others, we should act like a good doctor whose purpose is to bring healing—not like an enemy who attacks.

Scripture gives clear guidelines to believers in cases where judgments need to be rendered. See Matt. 18:15–17; 1 Cor. 6:1–8; and Gal. 6:1–5.

what you will eat or what you will drink; nor about your
body, what you will put on. Is not life more than food and
the body more than clothing? 26Look at the birds of the air,
for they neither sow nor reap nor gather into barns; yet
your heavenly Father feeds them. Are you not of more value
than they? 27Which of you by worrying can add one cubit
to his stature?

28"So why do you worry about clothing? Consider the
lilies of the field, how they grow: they neither toil nor spin;
29and yet I say to you that even Solomon in all his glory was
not arrayed like one of these. 30Now if God so clothes the
grass of the field, which today is, and tomorrow is thrown
into the oven, *will He* not much more *clothe* you, O you of
little faith?

31"Therefore do not worry, saying, 'What shall we eat?' or
'What shall we drink?' or 'What shall we wear?' 32For after
all these things the Gentiles seek. For your heavenly Father
knows that you need all these things. 33But seek first the
kingdom of God and His righteousness, and all these things
shall be added to you. 34Therefore do not worry about tomorrow,
for tomorrow will worry about its own things. Sufficient
for the day *is* its own trouble.

CHAPTER 7

"Judge Not"

7:1–5

1"Judge not, that you be not judged.
2For with what judgment you judge, you
will be judged; and with the measure you use, it will be
measured back to you. 3And why do you look at the speck
in your brother's eye, but do not consider the plank in your
own eye? 4Or how can you say to your brother, 'Let me remove
the speck from your eye'; and look, a plank *is* in your
own eye? 5Hypocrite! First remove the plank from your
own eye, and then you will see clearly to remove the speck
from your brother's eye.

6"Do not give what is holy to the dogs; nor cast your
pearls before swine, lest they trample them under their feet,
and turn and tear you in pieces.

Asking and Receiving

7"Ask, and it will be given to you; seek, and you will find;
knock, and it will be opened to you. 8For everyone who
asks receives, and he who seeks finds, and to him who
knocks it will be opened. 9Or what man is there among you
who, if his son asks for bread, will give him a stone? 10Or if
he asks for a fish, will he give him a serpent? 11If you then,

being evil, know how to give good gifts to your children,
how much more will your Father who is in heaven give
good things to those who ask Him!

7:12

12Therefore, whatever you want men to
do to you, do also to them, for this is the Law and the
Prophets.

A Challenge to Obedience

13"Enter by the narrow gate; for wide *is* the gate and
broad *is* the way that leads to destruction, and there are
many who go in by it. 14Because[a] narrow *is* the gate and difficult *is* the way which leads to life, and there are few who
find it.
15"Beware of false prophets, who come to you in sheep's
clothing, but inwardly they are ravenous wolves. 16You will
know them by their fruits. Do men gather grapes from
thornbushes or figs from thistles? 17Even so, every good tree
bears good fruit, but a bad tree bears bad fruit. 18A good
tree cannot bear bad fruit, nor *can* a bad tree bear good
fruit. 19Every tree that does not bear good fruit is cut down
and thrown into the fire. 20Therefore by their fruits you will
know them.
21"Not everyone who says to Me, 'Lord, Lord,' shall enter
the kingdom of heaven, but he who does the will of My
Father in heaven. 22Many will say to Me in that day,
'Lord, Lord, have we not prophesied in Your name, cast
out demons in Your name, and done many wonders
in Your name?' 23And then I will declare to them, 'I
never knew you; depart from Me, you who practice lawlessness!'
24"Therefore whoever hears these sayings of Mine, and
does them, I will liken him to a wise man who built his
house on the rock: 25and the rain descended, the floods
came, and the winds blew and beat on that house; and it
did not fall, for it was founded on the rock.
26"But everyone who hears these sayings of Mine, and
does not do them, will be like a foolish man who built his
house on the sand: 27and the rain descended, the floods
came, and the winds blew and beat on that house; and it
fell. And great was its fall."

7:29 see pg. 34

28And so it was, when Jesus had ended
these sayings, that the people were astonished at His teaching, 29for He taught them as one having
authority, and not as the scribes.

7:14 [a]NU-Text and M-Text read *How . . . !*

QUOTE UNQUOTE

CONSIDER THIS 7:12 *The "golden rule" (v. 12) is one of the best known teachings of Scripture. The great Reformer, Martin Luther, applied it specifically to the workplace:*

If you are a manual laborer, you find that the Bible has been put in your workshop, into your hand, into your heart. It teaches and preaches how you should treat your neighbor. Just look at your tools—at your needle or thimble, . . . your goods, your scales or yardstick or measure—and you will read this statement inscribed on them. Everywhere you look it stares at you. Nothing you handle every day is so tiny that it does not continually tell you this, if only you will listen. Indeed, there is no shortage of preaching. You have as many preachers as you have transactions, goods, tools, and other equipment in your house and home. All this is continually crying out to you: "Friend use me in your relations with your neighbor just as you would want your neighbor to use his property in his relations with you."

Martin Luther

Jesus had much more to say about the Law and the Prophets (v. 12). See "The Morality of Christ," Matt. 5:17–48.

JESUS' AUTHORITY

CONSIDER THIS 7:29 *Scribes were members of a learned class in Israel who studied the Scriptures and tradition, and who served as copyists, editors, and teachers (see Luke 20:39). But while they held* positions *of authority, Jesus was a* person *of authority (v. 29). His authority was a function of who He was, not of what He had learned.*

CHAPTER 8

Jesus Heals a Leper

[1]When He had come down from the mountain,
8:2 great multitudes followed Him. [2]And
behold, a leper came and worshiped
Him, saying, "Lord, if You are willing, You can make me
clean."
[3]Then Jesus put out *His* hand and touched him, saying, "I
am willing; be cleansed." Immediately his leprosy was
cleansed.
[4]And Jesus said to him, "See that you tell no one; but go
your way, show yourself to the priest, and offer the gift that
Moses commanded, as a testimony to them."

CONSIDER THIS 8:5–13

UNDER AUTHORITY

The centurion pointed out that, like Jesus, he was also "a man under authority" (v. 9). The encounter between the two suggests several lessons of authority and leadership:

(1) Effective leaders willingly admit when they need help (v. 5). The centurion faced a problem that went beyond his own considerable power. But he was willing to go outside his resources to enlist Jesus to deal with the situation.

(2) Effective leaders respond to matters of the heart and spirit (vv. 6, 8). The centurion was moved by compassion for his suffering servant, and perceived that Jesus had insight and power that went beyond a physician's skill.

(3) Effective leaders are able to approach others on their terms (vv. 5, 8). The centurion came in faith, pleading with Jesus to help his servant. As a Roman officer, he could have ordered Jesus, or offered Him money. But instead, he approached the Lord in a manner consistent with His nature.

(4) Effective leaders understand and accept the nature of authority (v. 9). The centurion understood what submission is all about. When he issued a command, his soldiers simply obeyed. He recognized that Jesus had the same authority over illness.

(5) Effective leaders invest trust in those under their authority (vv. 9–10). Great leaders display great faith in their people. The centurion trusted that Jesus could do what He said He would do.

Jesus Heals a Centurion's Servant

8:5–13

5Now when Jesus had entered Capernaum, a centurion came to Him, plead-
ing with Him, 6saying, "Lord, my servant is lying at home
paralyzed, dreadfully tormented."
7And Jesus said to him, "I will come and heal him."
8The centurion answered and said, "Lord, I am not worthy that You should come under my roof. But only speak a
word, and my servant will be healed. 9For I also am a man
under authority, having soldiers under me. And I say to this
one, 'Go,' and he goes; and to another, 'Come,' and he
comes; and to my servant, 'Do this,' and he does *it.*"

8:10 see pg. 36

10When Jesus heard *it,* He marveled,
and said to those who followed, "As-
suredly, I say to you, I have not found such great faith, not

(Bible text continued on page 37)

◆ ◆ ◆ ◆ ◆ ◆ ◆ ◆ ◆ ◆ ◆ ◆ ◆ ◆ ◆ ◆

(6) Effective leaders know who to trust (v. 10). Trust is only as useful as the trustworthiness of the one in whom it is placed. The centurion's faith was marvelous because it was invested in the right person—Jesus. Leadership based on blind faith, either in others or in a system, is foolhardy.

In light of these observations:

- *Do you rely too much on your own competence, or do you honestly assess both your strengths and your weaknesses?*
- *Do you respond to people only in terms of "the facts," or are you sensitive to the feelings and unexpressed needs of others (as well as your own)?*
- *Are you willing to meet and work with people on their terms, in their arena? Or must everyone come to you and play by your rules?*
- *Are you willing to be in charge, but unwilling to submit?*
- *In whom and in what do you place your faith?* ◆

Centurions played a powerful role in Rome's occupation of Palestine. See Mark 15:39.

In praising the centurion, Jesus tweaked the ethnic attitudes of the Jews. A Gentile with greater faith than any of them? Scandalous! See "A Soldier's Surprising Faith," Luke 7:1–10.

LEPROSY

FOR YOUR INFO 8:2 **Lepers like the man mentioned in v. 2 were common in the ancient world. They suffered from a slowly progressing, ordinarily incurable skin disease that was believed to be highly contagious and therefore greatly feared. As a result, anyone who appeared to have leprosy, even if the symptoms were caused by some other condition, was banished from the community.**

True leprosy is caused by a bacterium that spreads across the skin, creating sores, scabs, and white shining spots. The most serious problem, however, is a loss of sensation. Without the ability to feel, lepers injure their tissue, leading to further infection, deformity, muscle loss, and eventual paralysis. Fortunately, modern medicine has all but eliminated the disease.

Old Testament Law was quite detailed in its instructions regarding recognition and quarantine of leprous persons. Priests became the central figures for diagnosis, care of patients, and taking sanitary precautions to protect the rest of the community. The Law required that a leper be isolated from the rest of society (Lev. 13:45–46). Infected persons were required to wear mourning clothes, leave their hair in disorder, keep their beards covered, and cry "Unclean! Unclean!" so that others could avoid them. Any contact would defile the person who touched a leper.

Sometimes lepers were miraculously cured, as in the case of Moses (Ex. 4:7), Miriam, his sister (Num. 12:10), and Naaman (2 Kin. 5:1,10).

In the New Testament, Jesus intentionally healed lepers as a sign to vindicate His ministry. On one occasion He healed ten, but only one returned to thank Him (Luke 17:11–15).

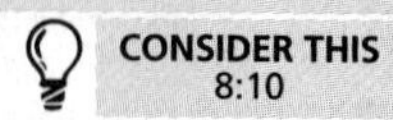

JESUS' GLOBAL CONNECTIONS

While Matthew's Gospel portrays Jesus in terms of His Jewish roots, it also shows that Jesus is an international Savior, a Messiah for the whole world. Notice some of Jesus' global connections:

Jesus' Roots (Matt. 1:1–16)

Jesus' genealogy includes at least two, and possibly three, Gentiles:

- David's great-great-grandmother, Rahab, a Canaanite prostitute of Jericho (Matt. 1:5; Josh. 2:1–24; 6:22–25).
- David's great-grandmother Ruth, a Moabite (Matt. 1:5; Ruth 1:1—4:22).
- Perhaps David's lover, Bathsheba, wife of Uriah the Hittite whom David murdered (Matt. 1:6; 2 Sam. 11:1—12:25). It is possible that Bathsheba was also a Hittite, though more likely she was a Hebrew who married a Hittite sojourner.

Wise Men from the East (Matt. 2:1–12)

In Matthew, the first worshipers of the baby Jesus were not Jews but Gentiles from the East. These wise men (*magi*) may have been astrologers from Persia (modern-day Iran). They came looking for the King of the Jews—their Messiah!

The Flight to Egypt (Matt. 2:13–14)

Egypt, a Gentile nation, provided a refuge for the infant Messiah from an outraged Herod the Great. In the same way, centuries before, Egypt had saved Jacob's family from starvation and had become a home where the family grew into a nation (Gen. 41:46—46:7).

Jesus' Childhood in Galilee (Matt. 2:22–23)

Jesus grew up in Nazareth, a small town of Galilee in the northern part of Palestine. The region was called Galilee of the Gentiles because of its mixed population (Matt. 4:15). Jesus began His ministry there, and many of His early followers were Gentiles from Syria and the Decapolis, a Gentile region (4:23–25).

"Undesirables" in Matthew

Jesus broke with many discriminatory traditions of His culture, reaching out to Samaritans, Gentiles, and other undesirables, as the following table of passages from Matthew shows:

A VARIETY OF PEOPLE AND RESPONSES

Text	People Involved	Jesus' Response
8:2–4	A leper, physically diseased and religiously unclean	Touched him when others would not
8:5–10	A Roman centurion	Healed his servant; praised his great faith
8:28–34	Two demon-possessed men from a Gentile region	Delivered them when the town rejected them
9:9–13	Matthew, a tax collector, and his disreputable friends	Called Matthew; dined with his friends
9:20–22	A hemorrhaging woman	Healed her; praised her faith
11:20–24	Tyre, Sidon, and Sodom (Gentile cities)	Said they will be better off than Jewish cities in the judgment, because of Jewish unbelief
12:39–42	Nineveh and the Queen of the South	Praised their repentance; said they would judge the generation of Jews that knew Jesus
14:34–36	People of Gennesaret, a Gentile region	Healed their sick
15:21–28	A Canaanite woman from the region of Tyre and Sidon	Healed her daughter; praised her great faith

◆

The roots of hostility between Jews and Gentiles stretched deep into Israel's history. See "Jews, Gentiles, and Jesus," Matt. 15:24.

even in Israel! [11]And I say to you that many will come from
east and west, and sit down with Abraham, Isaac, and Jacob
in the kingdom of heaven. [12]But the sons of the kingdom
will be cast out into outer darkness. There will be weeping
and gnashing of teeth." [13]Then Jesus said to the centurion,
"Go your way; and as you have believed, *so* let it be done
for you." And his servant was healed that same hour.

Peter's Mother-in-Law Healed

8:14–15

[14]Now when Jesus had come into Peter's house, He saw his wife's mother lying sick with a fever. [15]So He touched her hand, and the
fever left her. And she arose and served them.[a]

[16]When evening had come, they brought to Him many
who were demon-possessed. And He cast out the spirits
with a word, and healed all who were sick, [17]that it might
be fulfilled which was spoken by Isaiah the prophet, saying:

"He Himself took our infirmities
And bore *our* sicknesses."[a]

Following Jesus Has Its Costs

[18]And when Jesus saw great multitudes about Him, He
gave a command to depart to the other side. [19]Then a certain scribe came and said to Him, "Teacher, I will follow
You wherever You go."

8:20 see pg. 38

[20]And Jesus said to him, "Foxes have
holes and birds of the air *have* nests, but
the Son of Man has nowhere to lay *His* head."

[21]Then another of His disciples said to Him, "Lord, let me
first go and bury my father."

[22]But Jesus said to him, "Follow Me, and let the dead
bury their own dead."

Jesus Calms a Storm

8:23–27

[23]Now when He got into a boat, His
disciples followed Him. [24]And suddenly a
great tempest arose on the sea, so that the boat was covered
with the waves. But He was asleep. [25]Then His disciples
came to *Him* and awoke Him, saying, "Lord, save us! We are
perishing!"

[26]But He said to them, "Why are you fearful, O you of

8:15 [a]NU-Text and M-Text read *Him.* *8:17* [a]Isaiah 53:4

A Surprise in Peter's Household

CONSIDER THIS 8:14–15 *Households in Jesus' day tended to be much larger than those of today, with more children and more relatives from the extended family.*

But Peter's home (v. 14) was somewhat unusual in that his mother-in-law lived with the family. Peter was not required by law or custom to provide her with a home. A widow usually moved back to her father's home, if he were still alive, or else joined a son's household.

It was fortunate for Peter's mother-in-law that Peter befriended Jesus. The Lord's compassion extended to widowed mothers-in-law even when He was a house guest! He healed her from her fever and she began to serve Him—a response that indicated a changed life and a deeply grateful attitude.

Does your faith cause you to respond to the needs of others like Jesus did?

The Storms of Galilee

A CLOSER LOOK 8:23–27 *Galilee was and is the site of frequent violent storms such as the one described in vv. 23–27. For an explanation of this phenomenon, see the diagram, "What Kind of Storm Was This?" at Luke 8:22.*

Jesus—A Homeless Man?

CONSIDER THIS 8:20

Jesus was born poor and lived poor. His comment in v. 20 even suggests that He was homeless. He never celebrated poverty, but He did ask His followers to forsake the common belief that real security comes from having wealth (Matt. 6:19–34).

Does that seem too difficult for those of us living in a society that craves financial security and independence? If so, consider that Christ is not asking us to do anything that He did not do Himself. He wants us to learn to hold what we have very lightly.

little faith?" Then He arose and rebuked the winds and the
sea, and there was a great calm. 27So the men marveled, saying, "Who can this be, that even the winds and the sea obey
Him?"

Two Demon-possessed Men Healed

28When He had come to the other side, to the country of
the Gergesenes,[a] there met Him two demon-possessed *men*,
coming out of the tombs, exceedingly fierce, so that no one
8:29 could pass that way. 29And suddenly they
cried out, saying, "What have we to do
with You, Jesus, You Son of God? Have You come here to
torment us before the time?"

30Now a good way off from them there was a herd of
many swine feeding. 31So the demons begged Him, saying,
"If You cast us out, permit us to go away[a] into the herd of
swine."

32And He said to them, "Go." So when they had come
out, they went into the herd of swine. And suddenly the

8:28 [a]NU-Text reads *Gadarenes.* *8:31* [a]NU-Text reads *send us.*

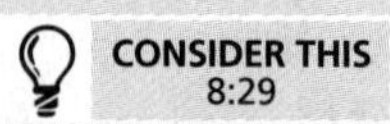

CONSIDER THIS 8:29

Spiritual Realities Beyond You

Jesus often encountered demons like those that possessed the men at Gadara (vv. 28–34). The mention of demons affirms the reality of powerful spiritual forces in the universe. Scripture has much to say about angels and demons.

***Angels** are members of an order of heavenly beings who are superior to humans in power and intelligence (Heb. 2:7; 2 Pet. 2:11). However, unlike God they are not all-powerful or all-knowing (Ps. 103:20; 2 Thess. 1:7). God often sends them to announce good news, such as the birth of Jesus (Luke 1:30–31), or to warn of coming dangers, such as the destruction of Sodom (Gen. 18:16—19:29).*

Angels played a particularly active role in the events surrounding Jesus' birth, resurrection, and ascension. They:

- *counseled Joseph to wed Mary (Matt. 1:20);*
- *warned Joseph to flee to Egypt with Mary and the Christ child (2:13);*
- *instructed Joseph to return the family to Palestine (2:19);*
- *foretold to Zacharias the birth of John the Baptist (Luke 1:11–38);*
- *announced to shepherds the birth of Christ (2:8–15);*
- *appeared to Jesus in the Garden of Gethsemane to strengthen Him (Luke 22:43);*

whole herd of swine ran violently down the steep place into the sea, and perished in the water.

[33]Then those who kept *them* fled; and they went away into the city and told everything, including what *had happened* to the demon-possessed *men.* [34]And behold, the whole city came out to meet Jesus. And when they saw Him, they begged *Him* to depart from their region.

CHAPTER 9

Jesus Heals a Paralytic

[1]So He got into a boat, crossed over, and came to His own
city. [2]Then behold, they brought to Him a paralytic lying on
a bed. When Jesus saw their faith, He said to the paralytic, "Son, be of good cheer; your sins are forgiven you."
[3]And at once some of the scribes said within themselves, "This Man blasphemes!"
9:4–8 [4]But Jesus, knowing their thoughts, said, "Why do you think evil in your
hearts? [5]For which is easier, to say, '*Your* sins are forgiven

(Bible text continued on page 41)

- *rolled back the stone from Jesus' empty tomb (Matt. 28:2);*
- *appeared to women at the empty tomb to announce Jesus' resurrection (Luke 24:4–7, 23; John 20:12);*
- *promised Jesus' return after His ascension (Acts 1:9–11).*

Since Pentecost, the frequency of angelic activity in human affairs appears to have diminished, perhaps because of the larger role played by the Holy Spirit in the lives of believers.

Demons *are fallen angels that have been cast out of heaven. They seek to undermine the cause of righteousness in the world (1 Pet. 3:19–20; 2 Pet. 2:4; Jude 6). Scripture describes them with various names: "unclean spirits" (Mark 6:7), "wicked or evil spirits" (Luke 7:21; Acts 19:12–13), "spirit of divination" (Acts 16:16), "deceiving spirits" (1 Tim. 4:1), and "spirit of error" (1 John 4:6).* ◆

Scripture presents demons not as mythological creatures, but as real beings involved in historical events. See "Demons," Luke 11:14.

The Power of Forgiveness

CONSIDER THIS 9:4–8 **The crowd that watched Jesus heal the paralytic responded enthusiastically to His dramatic display of power (v. 8). But they overlooked His more significant ability to forgive sins—a power that deeply troubled the scribes (vv. 2–3).**

The power of forgiveness is immeasurable. Jesus challenged us as His followers to forgive others who have wronged or hurt us (6:14–15; 18:21–35). That may seem like a simple act, but anyone who has struggled with pain and anger knows that it takes enormous power to authentically forgive—to lay aside one's hurt and reach out to an offender with the embrace of a pardon. On the other side, forgiveness can release the wrongdoer from paralyzing guilt and even turn around the course of that person's life (James 5:19–20).

Forgiveness is as powerful and liberating as the healing of a paralytic. And it's a power that Jesus has delegated to His followers (John 20:23).

We are called to forgive others as Christ has forgiven us. See Matt. 9:48 and Col. 3:13.

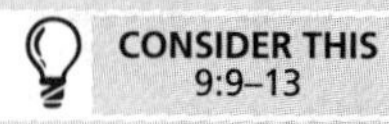

A Rich Man Enters the Kingdom

Jesus said it would be hard for the rich to enter the kingdom of heaven (Matt. 19:23). The remark has led some to believe that rich people can't enter the kingdom, and others to feel that Jesus was opposed to wealth and the wealthy. But Matthew's response to Jesus' call (9:9–13) contradicts both of those assumptions.

The incident recorded here contrasts sharply with Jesus' encounter with the rich young ruler (Matt. 19:16–30; Mark 10:17–31; Luke 18:18–30). In many ways, the ruler seemed to make a more likely prospect than Matthew for membership in Jesus' burgeoning movement. (See table below.)

Yet despite the young ruler's apparent edge, it was Matthew who ended up following Jesus. The other "went away sorrowful" (19:22). What accounts for the difference? For one thing, the wealthy young man clearly perceived himself as already righteous (19:17–20). He felt that he was able to meet God's requirements on his own merits (19:16). But no one had to convince Matthew that he needed the Great Physician (9:11–12). As a tax collector, he was among the most despised members of Jewish society.

Yet there was a more fundamental difference between these two men, a difference that depended on Jesus' attitude more than on theirs. His words to the Pharisees explained the matter clearly: "I desire mercy and not sacrifice. For I did not come to call the righteous, but sinners, to repentance" (v. 13). In calling Matthew but turning away the rich young ruler, Jesus demonstrated in real-life parables precisely this point: that salvation depends on the mercy of God, not on the merits or sacrifice of people.

In the end, the crucial difference between the rich man who followed and the rich man who rejected was the merciful choice of God. Of course, none of us knows that choice beforehand. Therefore, we as believers need to be equally eager to present the gospel of Christ to everyone, rich or poor, wise or foolish, mighty or weak. ◆

Two Different Rich Men

Rich Young Ruler	Matthew
Probably enjoyed inherited wealth	Rich most likely because of his work as a tax collector
Had lived a good life	Like most tax collectors, was probably dishonest and ruthless
Came to Jesus	Sat at his tax table; Jesus approached him
Displayed interest in spiritual things	Was collecting money when Jesus found him
Indicated a willingness to make sacrifices to gain eternal life	Gave no such indication

Scripture has much to say to believers about their wealth. See "Christians and Money," 1 Tim. 6:6–19, and "Getting Yours," James 5:1–6.

you,' or to say, 'Arise and walk'? 6But that you may know
that the Son of Man has power on earth to forgive sins"—
then He said to the paralytic, "Arise, take up your bed, and
go to your house." 7And he arose and departed to his house.
8Now when the multitudes saw *it,* they marveled[a] and
glorified God, who had given such power to men.

Matthew Follows Jesus

9As Jesus passed on from there, He saw a man named
Matthew sitting at the tax office. And He said to him, "Follow Me." So he arose and followed Him.

9:10

10Now it happened, as Jesus sat at the
table in the house, *that* behold, many tax
collectors and sinners came and sat down with Him and His
disciples. 11And when the Pharisees saw *it,* they said to His
disciples, "Why does your Teacher eat with tax collectors
and sinners?"

9:9–13

12When Jesus heard *that,* He said to
them, "Those who are well have no need
of a physician, but those who are sick. 13But go and learn
what *this* means: 'I desire mercy and not sacrifice.'[a] For I did
not come to call the righteous, but sinners, to repentance."[b]

The Old and the New

14Then the disciples of John came to Him, saying, "Why
do we and the Pharisees fast often,[a] but Your disciples do
not fast?"
15And Jesus said to them, "Can the friends of the bridegroom mourn as long as the bridegroom is with them? But
the days will come when the bridegroom will be taken away
from them, and then they will fast. 16No one puts a piece of
unshrunk cloth on an old garment; for the patch pulls away
from the garment, and the tear is made worse. 17Nor do
they put new wine into old wineskins, or else the wineskins
break, the wine is spilled, and the wineskins are ruined. But
they put new wine into new wineskins, and both are preserved."

Four Dramatic Healings

18While He spoke these things to them, behold, a ruler
came and worshiped Him, saying, "My daughter has just
died, but come and lay Your hand on her and she will live."
19So Jesus arose and followed him, and so *did* His disciples.

9:20–22
see pg. 43

20And suddenly, a woman who had a
flow of blood for twelve years came from
behind and touched the hem of His garment. 21For she said

(Bible text continued on page 43)

9:8 [a]NU-Text reads *were afraid.* *9:13* [a]Hosea 6:6 [b]NU-Text omits *to repentance.*
9:14 [a]NU-Text brackets *often* as disputed.

Who Were Those Tax Collectors?

CONSIDER THIS 9:10 **Tax collectors (v. 10) were agents or contract workers who collected taxes for the government during Bible times. Some translations incorrectly call them "publicans," but publicans were wealthy men, usually non-Jewish, who contracted with the Roman government to be responsible for the taxes of a particular district. They were often backed by military force. By contrast, tax collectors were employed by publicans to do the actual collecting of monies. They were Jews, usually not very wealthy.**

Tax collectors gathered several different types of taxes. Depending on the kind of rule in a given Jewish province, Rome levied a land tax, a poll tax, even a tax for the operation of the temple (Matt. 17:24–27). Some provinces, like Galilee, were not under an imperial governor, so their taxes remained in the province rather than going to the imperial treasury at Rome. Perhaps these inequities prompted the Pharisees in Judea (an imperial province) to ask Jesus, "Is it lawful to pay taxes to Caesar, or not?" (Matt. 22:17).

As a class, tax collectors were despised by their fellow Jews, and were generally associated with "sinners" (Matt. 9:10–11; Mark 2:15). They often gathered more than the government required and pocketed the excess amount—a practice that John the Baptist specifically preached against (Luke 3:12–13). But tax collectors were also hated because their fellow citizens viewed them as mercenaries working for the Roman oppressors.

In Jesus' day, Jews were probably paying no less than 30 or 40 percent of their income on taxes and religious dues. See "Taxes," Mark 12:14.

Zacchaeus was called the chief tax collector in Jericho, which may mean he was a publican. Nevertheless, he responded to Jesus' call. See Luke 19:1–10.

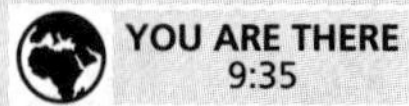

JESUS—A CITY PREACHER

Popular opinion frequently regards the Bible in general and the ministry of Jesus in particular in rural terms. Perhaps it's the Christmas story, with its quaint references to a donkey, a manger, and shepherds. Perhaps it's the memorable parables, such as the sower and the seed, the wheat and the weeds, and the prodigal son. Perhaps it's Jesus' origins in a small town. Whatever the cause, the popular image of Jesus and His world seems fixed on a rural environment. But that is somewhat misleading.

Palestine in Jesus' day was undergoing rapid urban development. Its population of around 2.5 to 3 million people lived in numerous preindustrial cities and towns that revolved around Jerusalem, the hub of the region. The Holy City had a population conservatively estimated by modern scholars at between 55,000 and 90,000. (Josephus, a first-century Jewish historian, placed the number at 3 million; the Talmud gives an incredible 12 million.)

So as Jesus carried out His ministry, He focused on the urban centers of Palestine (v. 35; 11:1; Luke 4:43; 13:22) and visited Jerusalem at least three times. This brought Him into contact with a greater number and wider variety of people than He would have encountered in a purely rural campaign—women, soldiers, religious leaders, the rich, merchants, tax collectors, Gentiles, prostitutes, beggars, and the poor. These He attracted in large crowds as He visited each city.

Jesus' urban strategy established a model for His disciples and the early church. When He sent the disciples on preaching tours, He directed them toward cities (Matt. 10:5, 11–14; Luke 10:1, 8–16). And later, the movement spread throughout the Roman empire by using an urban strategy that planted communities of believers in no less than 40 cities by the end of the first century (see "Churches—Keys to the Cities," Acts 11:22).

In light of the vital role that cities played in the ministry of Jesus, we who follow Him today need to ask: What are we doing to relate the message of Christ to our increasingly urban, multicultural, and pluralistic world? Our Lord's example in urban Palestine has much to teach us. ◆

Jerusalem dominated life in first-century Palestine. To find out why, see Matt. 23:37.

Don't miss the explosive start of the worldwide church! See "A Surprising First Fulfillment of Acts 1:8," Acts 2:8–11.

An urban strategy for ministry can be explosive—and unpredictable. See "The Ephesus Approach: How the Gospel Penetrates a City," Acts 19:8–41.

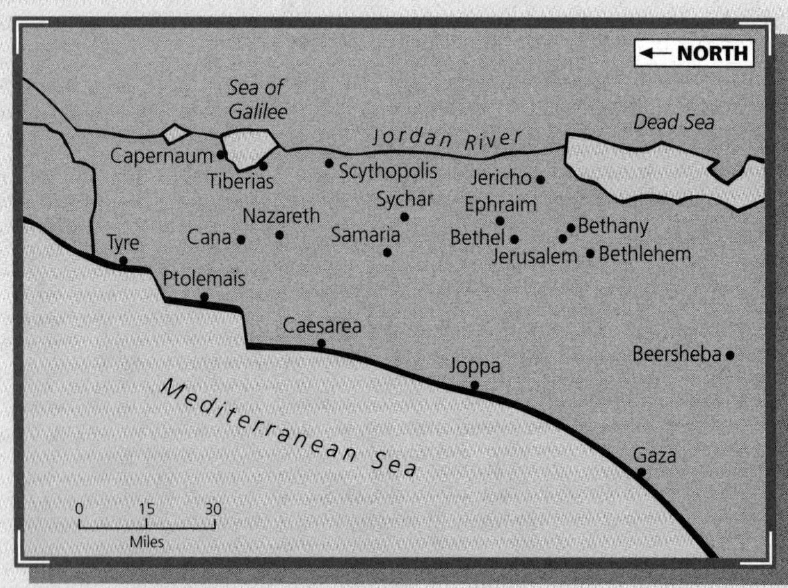

CITIES OF PALESTINE IN CHRIST'S TIME

to herself, "If only I may touch His garment, I shall be made
well." 22But Jesus turned around, and when He saw her He
said, "Be of good cheer, daughter; your faith has made you
well." And the woman was made well from that hour.

9:23 23When Jesus came into the ruler's
house, and saw the flute players and the
noisy crowd wailing, 24He said to them, "Make room, for
the girl is not dead, but sleeping." And they ridiculed Him.
25But when the crowd was put outside, He went in and
took her by the hand, and the girl arose. 26And the report of
this went out into all that land.

27When Jesus departed from there, two blind men followed Him, crying out and saying, "Son of David, have
mercy on us!"

28And when He had come into the house, the blind men
came to Him. And Jesus said to them, "Do you believe that I
am able to do this?"

They said to Him, "Yes, Lord."

29Then He touched their eyes, saying, "According to your
faith let it be to you." 30And their eyes were opened. And Jesus sternly warned them, saying, "See *that* no one knows *it*."
31But when they had departed, they spread the news about
Him in all that country.

32As they went out, behold, they brought to Him a man,
mute and demon-possessed. 33And when the demon was

The Mourners

CONSIDER THIS 9:23 *In the ancient world, paid professional mourners (v. 23), most often women, aided families in their public expression of grief upon the death of a loved one. They composed poems or dirges praising the deceased, which they chanted to the accompaniment of a flute or other musical instrument in an attempt to stir the audience emotionally. They usually wore sackcloth and scattered dust in the air and on their heads. Weeping, wailing, and beating their breasts, they created an unmistakable tone of grief. There was no denial of death or distancing themselves from loss.*

Perhaps Jesus was making use of the image of professional mourners when He spoke of those who mourn in the Sermon on the Mount (Matt. 5:2).

The Hemorrhaging Woman

CONSIDER THIS 9:20–22 For twelve years the woman in vv. 20–22 had sought a cure for her condition. Perhaps worse than the drain on her physical strength and finances was the stigma of uncleanness. Jews considered women ritually unclean during menstruation, and whoever touched a menstruating woman was made unclean until evening. If a woman experienced bleeding other than at her normal menses, she was considered unclean until the bleeding stopped (Lev. 15:19–27). That meant exclusion from participating in the life and worship of the community.

Scripture is silent on the source of this woman's livelihood. Perhaps she lived off an inheritance, or perhaps she was divorced and her dowry had been returned to her. Whatever her means of support, it was gone. Jesus was her last hope.

So she approached Him, breaking a rule that made it an unclean person's responsibility to keep away from others. In desperation, she reached out and touched Jesus.

Perceiving that power had gone out from Him, Jesus sought her out. Perhaps as she explained her disease the crowd backed away, not wanting to contaminate themselves. But Jesus didn't withdraw. Rather He drew her to Him with the affectionate term "daughter" and sent her away in peace, healed at last.

Who are the "untouchables" in your world? Who is desperately trying to reach out for help? How can you respond to their needs with Christlikeness?

WHAT IT MEANS TO BE LIKE JESUS

CONSIDER THIS
8:1—9:38

Jesus indicated that those who follow Him will become like Him (10:25). What does it mean to **"be like Jesus"** *in today's complex world? Matthew paints eight portraits of what Christlikeness looks like, including:*

#7: To Be Like Jesus Means TO SERVE OTHERS

The Sermon on the Mount (Matt. 5–7) was immediately followed by "deeds in the valley" (Matt. 8–9). Christlike values lead to servant actions—and it was obedient action that Jesus cared about, not just sermonizing (7:21–29). Jesus modeled how to *do* the will of God by actively serving more than 25 different people (chs. 8–9). These included such undesirables as lepers, an officer of the Roman occupation troops, the sick, the demon-possessed, cave dwellers, tax collectors, and a diseased, outcast woman. If we want to be like Jesus, we need to befriend those who are weak, under oppression, or without Christ. Like Him, we need to become "a friend of sinners" (11:19). He offered much more than religious information—He served them.

For a summary of all eight portraits of Christlikeness, see "What It Means to Be Like Jesus" at 10:25. The next item in the series can be found at 10:1–42.

cast out, the mute spoke. And the multitudes marveled,
saying, "It was never seen like this in Israel!"
34But the Pharisees said, "He casts out demons by the
ruler of the demons."

Jesus Feels Compassion for the Crowds

9:35 see pg. 42

35Then Jesus went about all the cities
and villages, teaching in their syna-
gogues, preaching the gospel of the kingdom, and healing
every sickness and every disease among the people.[a] 36But
when He saw the multitudes, He was moved with compassion for them, because they were weary[a] and scattered, like
sheep having no shepherd. 37Then He said to His disciples,
"The harvest truly *is* plentiful, but the laborers *are* few.
38Therefore pray the Lord of the harvest
to send out laborers into His harvest."

8:1—9:38

CHAPTER 10

The Twelve

10:1–42

1And when He had called His twelve
disciples to *Him,* He gave them power
over unclean spirits, to cast them out, and to heal all kinds
of sickness and all kinds of disease. 2Now
the names of the twelve apostles are
these: first, Simon, who is called Peter, and Andrew his
brother; James the *son* of Zebedee, and John his brother;
3Philip and Bartholomew; Thomas and Matthew the tax collector; James the *son* of Alphaeus, and Lebbaeus, whose surname was[a] Thaddaeus; 4Simon the Cananite,[a] and Judas Iscariot, who also betrayed Him.

10:2

Jesus Sends and Warns the Twelve

5These twelve Jesus sent out and commanded them, saying: "Do not go into the way of the Gentiles, and do not enter a city of the Samaritans. 6But go rather to the lost sheep
of the house of Israel. 7And as you go,
preach, saying, 'The kingdom of heaven
is at hand.' 8Heal the sick, cleanse the lepers, raise the
dead,[a] cast out demons. Freely you have received, freely
give. 9Provide neither gold nor silver nor copper in your
money belts, 10nor bag for *your* journey, nor two tunics, nor
sandals, nor staffs; for a worker is worthy of his food.
11"Now whatever city or town you enter, inquire who in it
is worthy, and stay there till you go out. 12And when you go
into a household, greet it. 13If the household is worthy, let
your peace come upon it. But if it is not worthy, let your

10:7–10 see pg. 46

9:35 [a]NU-Text omits *among the people.* *9:36* [a]NU-Text and M-Text read *harassed.*
10:3 [a]NU-Text omits *Lebbaeus, whose surname was.* *10:4* [a]NU-Text reads *Cananaean.*
10:8 [a]NU-Text reads *raise the dead, cleanse the lepers;* M-Text omits *raise the dead.*

peace return to you. 14And whoever will not receive you
nor hear your words, when you depart from that house or
city, shake off the dust from your feet. 15Assuredly, I say to
you, it will be more tolerable for the land of Sodom and
Gomorrah in the day of judgment than for that city!
16"Behold, I send you out as sheep in the midst of wolves.
Therefore be wise as serpents and harmless as doves. 17But
beware of men, for they will deliver you up to councils and
scourge you in their synagogues. 18You will be brought before governors and kings for My sake, as a testimony to
them and to the Gentiles. 19But when they deliver you up,
do not worry about how or what you should speak. For it
will be given to you in that hour what you should speak;
20for it is not you who speak, but the Spirit of your Father
who speaks in you.

(Bible text continued on page 47)

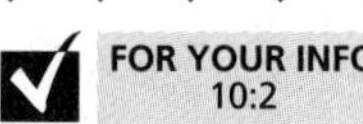

THE TWELVE

Apostle	Description
Simon (Peter) (Mark 1:16)	Fisherman from Galilee, Andrew's brother
Andrew (John 1:40)	Fisherman from Galilee, Peter's brother
James	Son of Zebedee, brother to John; from Capernaum
John (Introduction to John)	Son of Zebedee, brother to James; from Capernaum
Philip	From Bethsaida
Bartholomew (Nathanael)	From Cana in Galilee
Thomas (Didymus)	Possibly also a fisherman
Matthew (Levi) (Matt. 9:9)	Tax collector in Capernaum; son of Alphaeus, possibly James' brother
James	Son of Alphaeus, possibly Matthew's brother
Lebbaeus Thaddeus (Judas)	May have taken the name Thaddeus ("warm-hearted") because of the infamy that came to be attached to the name Judas
Simon (the Cananite)	From Cana; one of the Zealots, Jewish revolutionaries who opposed Rome
Judas Iscariot (Matt. 26:14)	From Kerioth, and possibly the only Judean among the Twelve

(Biblical references are to Personality Profiles.)

Matthew called these twelve "apostles." What did that term mean? See 2 Cor. 11:5.

What It Means To Be Like Jesus

Jesus indicated that those who follow Him will become like Him (10:25). What does it mean to **"be like Jesus"** *in today's complex world? Matthew paints eight portraits of what Christlikeness looks like, including:*

#8: To Be Like Jesus Means TO AFFIRM OTHER LEADERS

Jesus invested Himself in the development of other people, particularly the Twelve. He gave them responsibility and authority, resisting the temptation to get the job done "right" by doing it Himself. In doing so, He accepted the risk that they might fail. Of course, He gave them adequate preparation before sending them out, and on their return He affirmed them on their successful completion of the mission. Jesus calls us to help others grow. If we want to be like Him, we will share the joys and risks of working together with our brothers and sisters.

For a summary of all eight portraits of Christlikeness, see "What It Means to Be Like Jesus" at 10:25. This is the last item in the series.

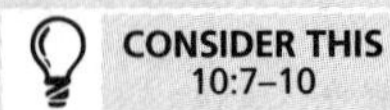

A Prayer of the Laity

He was born into a noble family in Assisi, Italy in 1182. Although christened Giovanni Bernadone, he went by the nickname Francis—a reminder that his merchant father had been away in France when he was born. The privileges of his childhood fostered a pursuit of wealth, education, and fun, and when he came of age he joined the army as the simplest avenue to achieving those goals.

But young Francis' life took a dramatic turn when serious illness interrupted his plans. While convalescing, he took a new and profound interest in religion. Once on his feet, he made a pilgrimage to Rome, a common discipline for the spiritually devoted.

But he was shocked at what he found there. Lepers and beggars languished in cathedrals fallen into disrepair. Moved to compassion and inspired by his newfound faith, he exercised one of the few options available to concerned laity at the time: he sold his horse and some of his father's cloth supplies and gave the money to a local priest, assuming that the cleric would restore the buildings. But to his surprise, the priest rejected the gift when he learned that it had come from the Bernadone family's commercial ventures. To make matters worse, Francis' father disowned him upon learning of his actions.

Penniless, he managed to find refuge with a bishop. But he continued his mission to the poor, begging enough money over a two-year span to repair four church buildings. It was during that period that he heard a sermon on Matthew 10:7–10. The text galvanized his thinking, and he made a decision to live the rest of his life as a beggar, serving the poor through preaching and healing.

His example motivated others to follow. A wealthy woman from Assisi began a sister movement, as well as one for married laity. Those who joined were reacting against widespread corruption in the church and a general confusion about the meaning and practice of spirituality for laypeople. Not all of the newcomers were sincere. Some tried to introduce changes away from a singleminded focus on the poor and unbelievers. And, as the movement became fashionable, Francis had to constantly resist the clergy's attempts to bring the work under their auspices and "upgrade" the status of the lay workers to agents of the church.

The spirit of Francis' vision was captured in a prayer that he penned, "Make me an instrument of Thy peace." Today, it has become quite well known. Perhaps its popularity springs from its simple yet eloquent statement of the aspirations of a very concerned and committed layperson who determined to make a difference for God in the world as he found it. ◆

The Prayer of St. Francis

Lord,
Make me an instrument of Thy peace;
Where there is hatred, let me sow love;
Where there is injury, pardon;
Where there is doubt, faith;
Where there is despair, hope;
Where there is darkness, light; and
Where there is sadness, joy.
Divine Master,
Grant that I may not so much
seek to be consoled as to console;
To be understood as to understand;
To be loved as to love;
For it is in giving that we receive;
It is in pardoning that we are pardoned;
And it is in dying
that we are born to eternal life.

21"Now brother will deliver up brother to death, and a father *his* child; and children will rise up against parents and cause them to be put to death. 22And you will be hated by all for My name's sake. But he who endures to the end will be saved. 23When they persecute you in this city, flee to another. For assuredly, I say to you, you will not have gone through the cities of Israel before the Son of Man comes.

24"A disciple is not above *his* teacher, nor a servant above his master. 25It is enough for a disciple that he be like his teacher, and a servant like his master. If they have called the master of the house Beelzebub,[a] how much more *will they call* those of his household! 26Therefore do not fear them. For there is nothing covered that will not be revealed, and hidden that will not be known.

10:25

27"Whatever I tell you in the dark, speak in the light; and what you hear in the ear, preach on the housetops. 28And do not fear those who kill the body but cannot kill the soul. But rather fear Him who is able to destroy both soul and body in hell. 29Are not two sparrows sold for a copper coin? And not one of them falls to the ground apart from your Father's will. 30But the very hairs of your head are all numbered. 31Do not fear therefore; you are of more value than many sparrows.

32"Therefore whoever confesses Me before men, him I will also confess before My Father who is in heaven. 33But whoever denies Me before men, him I will also deny before My Father who is in heaven.

34"Do not think that I came to bring peace on earth. I did not come to bring peace but a sword. 35For I have come to 'set a man against his father, a daughter against her mother, and a daughter-in-law against her mother-in-law'; 36and 'a man's enemies will be those of his *own* household.'[a] 37He who loves father or mother more than Me is not worthy of Me. And he who loves son or daughter more than Me is not worthy of Me. 38And he who does not take his cross and follow after Me is not worthy of Me. 39He who finds his life will lose it, and he who loses his life for My sake will find it.

40"He who receives you receives Me, and he who receives Me receives Him who sent Me. 41He who receives a prophet in the name of a prophet shall receive a prophet's reward. And he who receives a righteous man in the name of a righteous man shall receive a righteous man's reward. 42And whoever gives one of these little ones only a cup of cold *water* in the name of a disciple, assuredly, I say to you, he shall by no means lose his reward."

10:25 [a]NU-Text and M-Text read *Beelzebul.* *10:36* [a]Micah 7:6

WHAT IT MEANS TO BE LIKE JESUS

CONSIDER THIS 10:25 **Jesus' statement in v. 25 implies that His disciples will be like Him. To His first-century followers, that included the prospect of persecution and martyrdom. But what else does it mean to "be like Jesus," especially for Christians in today's marketplace? Eight portraits in Matthew's eye-witness account give us some clues:**

#1: To be like Jesus means to accept our roots (1:1–17).

#2: To be like Jesus means to engage the world's pain and struggle (1:18—2:23).

#3: To be like Jesus means to commit ourselves to other believers, no matter how "weird" they appear to be (3:1–17).

#4: To be like Jesus means to admit our vulnerability to temptation (4:1–11).

#5: To be like Jesus means to openly proclaim the message of Christ (4:12–25).

#6: To be like Jesus means to commit ourselves to changed thinking and behavior (5:1—7:27).

#7: To be like Jesus means to serve others, especially those who are oppressed or without Christ (8:1—9:38).

#8: To be like Jesus means to affirm others in leadership (10:1–42).

For more on each of these points, see the articles at the texts indicated.

CHAPTER 11

Jesus Speaks about John the Baptist

1Now it came to pass, when Jesus finished commanding
His twelve disciples, that He departed from there to teach
and to preach in their cities.

11:2–6

2And when John had heard in prison
about the works of Christ, he sent two of[a]
his disciples 3and said to Him, "Are You the Coming One,
or do we look for another?"

4Jesus answered and said to them, "Go and tell John the
things which you hear and see: 5*The* blind see and *the* lame
walk; *the* lepers are cleansed and *the* deaf hear; *the* dead are
raised up and *the* poor have the gospel preached to them.
6And blessed is he who is not offended because of Me."

7As they departed, Jesus began to say to the multitudes
concerning John: "What did you go out into the wilderness
to see? A reed shaken by the wind? 8But what did you go
out to see? A man clothed in soft garments? Indeed, those
who wear soft *clothing* are in kings' houses. 9But what did
you go out to see? A prophet? Yes, I say to you, and more
than a prophet. 10For this is *he* of whom it is written:

'Behold, I send My messenger before Your face,
Who will prepare Your way before You.'[a]

11"Assuredly, I say to you, among those born of women
there has not risen one greater than John the Baptist; but he
who is least in the kingdom of heaven is greater than he.
12And from the days of John the Baptist until now the kingdom of heaven suffers violence, and the violent take it by
force. 13For all the prophets and the law prophesied until
John. 14And if you are willing to receive *it,* he is Elijah who
is to come. 15He who has ears to hear, let him hear!

16"But to what shall I liken this generation? It is like children sitting in the marketplaces and calling to their companions, 17and saying:

'We played the flute for you,
And you did not dance;
We mourned to you,
And you did not lament.'

18For John came neither eating nor drinking, and they say,
'He has a demon.' 19The Son of Man came eating and drinking, and they say, 'Look, a glutton and a winebibber, a
friend of tax collectors and sinners!' But wisdom is justified
by her children."[a]

11:2 [a]NU-Text reads *by* for *two of.* *11:10* [a]Malachi 3:1 *11:19* [a]NU-Text reads *works.*

Some Surprising Evidence

CONSIDER THIS 11:2–6 **John the Baptist wanted reassurance about who Jesus was and what He was doing (vv. 2–3). Jesus replied with a list of things He had done that revealed God's presence, power, and love (vv. 4–5). The most telling evidence was His work among the poor, the downtrodden, and the needy.**

Our culture today wants to know whether Christ is still alive among His people. Like John, observers are asking whether those of us who claim to be Christ's followers are truly of God, or whether they should look elsewhere. They especially pay attention to our posture toward the poor. So it's worth asking: Are we as involved and concerned with the material needs of our neighbors as we are with their spiritual needs? Do we respond to physical needs as intentionally as Christ did, even if we have only material help to offer rather than miracles of healing? Is there unmistakable evidence of Christ working within us?

Scripture has a great deal to say about Christians' responsibilities to the poor and needy. See "I Have Not Coveted," Acts 20:33–38; "Giving It All Away," 1 Cor. 13:3; "Christ Became Poor," 2 Cor. 8:9; and "Take a Cardiogram," 1 John 3:16–21.

Unbelieving Cities Condemned

[20]Then He began to rebuke the cities in which most of His mighty works had been done, because they did not repent: 11:21 [21]"Woe to you, Chorazin! Woe to you, Bethsaida! For if the mighty works which were done in you had been done in Tyre and Sidon, they would have repented long ago in sackcloth and ashes. [22]But I say to you, it will be more tolerable for Tyre and Sidon in the day of judgment than for you. [23]And you, Capernaum, who are exalted to heaven, will be[a] brought down to Hades; for if the mighty works which were done in you had been done in Sodom, it would have remained until this day. [24]But I say to you that it shall be more tolerable for the land of Sodom in the day of judgment than for you."

An Invitation

[25]At that time Jesus answered and said, "I thank You, Father, Lord of heaven and earth, that You have hidden these things from *the* wise and prudent and have revealed them to babes. [26]Even so, Father, for so it seemed good in Your sight. [27]All things have been delivered to Me by My Father, and no one knows the Son except the Father. Nor does anyone know the Father except the Son, and *the one* to whom the Son wills to reveal *Him.* [28]Come to Me, all *you* who labor and are heavy laden, and I will give you rest. [29]Take My yoke upon you and learn from Me, for I am gentle and lowly in heart, and you will find rest for your souls. [30]For My yoke *is* easy and My burden is light."

CHAPTER 12

Sabbath Controversies

12:1–13 [1]At that time Jesus went through the grainfields on the Sabbath. And His disciples were hungry, and began to pluck heads of grain and to eat. [2]And when the Pharisees saw *it,* they said to Him, "Look, Your disciples are doing what is not lawful to do on the Sabbath!"

[3]But He said to them, "Have you not read what David did when he was hungry, he and those who were with him:

11:23 [a]NU-Text reads *will you be exalted to heaven? No, you will be.*

Why This Anger?

What was it that so enraged the Pharisees when they saw the disciples picking grain and Jesus healing a man's withered hand? And why did Jesus refuse to allow their grumbling to go unchallenged? See "Jesus Confronts the Legalists," Luke 6:1–11.

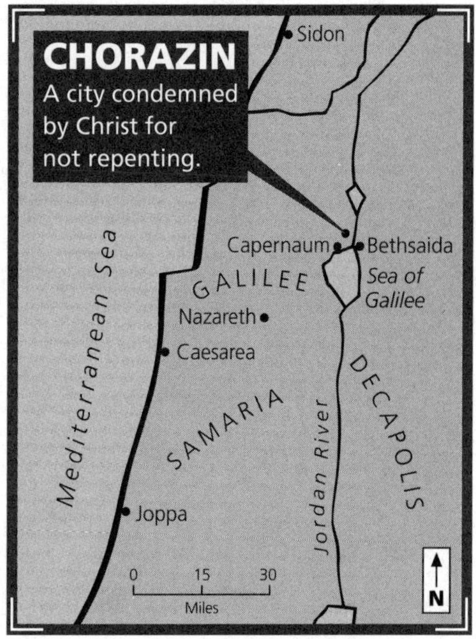

CHORAZIN

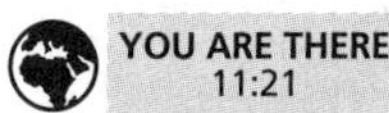

- **A town north of the Sea of Galilee, built on the basalt hills two and one-half miles north of Capernaum.**
- **Name means "secret."**
- **Mentioned in the Talmud as a distribution point for wheat.**
- **Known for the black, volcanic rock ruins of its synagogue. The famed *cathedra Mosis,* a carved judgment seat of Moses (compare Matt. 23:2), has been found there (in modern-day Khirbet Kerazeh).**

4how he entered the house of God and ate the showbread
which was not lawful for him to eat, nor for those who were
with him, but only for the priests? 5Or have you not read in
the law that on the Sabbath the priests in the temple profane the Sabbath, and are blameless? 6Yet I say to you that
in this place there is *One* greater than the temple. 7But if
you had known what *this* means, 'I desire mercy and not
sacrifice,'[a] you would not have condemned the guiltless.
8For the Son of Man is Lord even[a] of the Sabbath."

9Now when He had departed from there, He went into
their synagogue. 10And behold, there was a man who had a
withered hand. And they asked Him, saying, "Is it lawful to
heal on the Sabbath?"—that they might accuse Him.

11Then He said to them, "What man is there among you
who has one sheep, and if it falls into a pit on the Sabbath,
will not lay hold of it and lift *it* out? 12Of how much more
value then is a man than a sheep? Therefore it is lawful to
do good on the Sabbath." 13Then He said to the man,
"Stretch out your hand." And he stretched *it* out, and it was

12:7 [a]Hosea 6:6 *12:8* [a]NU-Text and M-Text omit *even*.

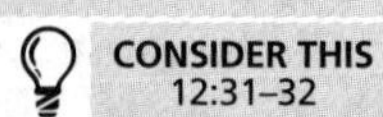

CONSIDER THIS
12:31–32

No Forgiveness!

People speak of committing the "unpardonable sin," but in His severe comments to the Pharisees (vv. 31–32), Jesus indicated that it is more than just a figure of speech—it is a matter with eternal consequences!

Can people ever sin so badly that God cannot forgive them? The answer is yes and no. It's important to realize that the blood of Jesus Christ on the cross paid for all of the sin of the world (John 1:29; Rom. 5:12–21; 8:3). There is no sin that God has not overcome through Christ. That means that no one ever has to fear going beyond the scope of God's grace or power. Sometimes people despair because they have committed certain sins that to them seem unforgivable. But no matter what their failure has been, God can and will forgive their sin if they come to Him in repentance (Acts 2:38; 1 John 1:9).

At the same time, it is possible to willfully place oneself beyond the grace of God—to persist in rebellion and sin and resist His call to repentance. This, essentially, is what the Pharisees and other Jewish leaders did (compare Acts 7:51–52). Jesus had healed a demon-possessed man by the power of the Holy Spirit (v. 28). His enemies claimed that He cast them out by the power of Satan ("Beelze-

12:14

restored as whole as the other. [14]Then the
Pharisees went out and plotted against
Him, how they might destroy Him.

Jesus Seeks a Low Profile

[15]But when Jesus knew *it,* He withdrew from there. And
great multitudes[a] followed Him, and He healed them all.
[16]Yet He warned them not to make Him known, [17]that it
might be fulfilled which was spoken by Isaiah the prophet,
saying:

18 "Behold! My Servant whom I have chosen,
My Beloved in whom My soul is well pleased!

12:15 [a]NU-Text brackets *multitudes* as disputed.

Political Intrigue

A CLOSER LOOK 12:14

The Pharisees feared Jesus as much as they hated Him. They were concerned that His popularity might have political repercussions, drawing Roman troops to the area and causing the loss of what little independence the nation had. So they plotted to destroy Him. The mastermind behind their plans was Caiaphas the high priest, a Sadducee rather than a Pharisee, but equally opposed to Jesus. Find out more about this man at Matt. 26:3.

bub," v. 24). The accusation was evidence that they had rejected Him.

It also slandered the Holy Spirit, revealing their spiritual blindness, a warping and perversion of their moral nature that put them beyond hope of repentance and faith—and therefore beyond forgiveness.

Is there an "unpardonable sin?" Not for those who cry out like the tax collector in a parable of Jesus, "God, be merciful to me a sinner!" (Luke 18:13). But those who, like the Pharisee in the same parable (as well the Pharisees in this incident), trust to their own self-righteousness, reject Christ, and slander His Holy Spirit—they reveal a spiritual cancer so advanced that they are beyond any hope of healing and forgiveness. ◆

Our culture tends to dismiss demon possession as a quaint, archaic way of trying to explain physical and psychological conditions. But the Bible presents demons and demon possession not as myth, but as reality. See "Demons," Luke 11:14.

"OF HOW MUCH MORE VALUE THEN IS A MAN THAN A SHEEP?"
—Matthew 12:12

I will put My Spirit upon Him,
And He will declare justice to the Gentiles.
19 He will not quarrel nor cry out,
Nor will anyone hear His voice in the streets.
20 A bruised reed He will not break,
And smoking flax He will not quench,
Till He sends forth justice to victory;
21 And in His name Gentiles will trust."[a]

Allegations of Satanism

22Then one was brought to Him who was demon-
possessed, blind and mute; and He healed him, so that the
blind and[a] mute man both spoke and saw. 23And all the
multitudes were amazed and said, "Could this be the Son of
David?"

24Now when the Pharisees heard *it* they said, "This *fellow*
does not cast out demons except by Beelzebub,[a] the ruler of
the demons."

12:21 [a]Isaiah 42:1–4 *12:22* [a]NU-Text omits *blind and.* *12:24* [a]NU-Text and M-Text read *Beelzebul.*

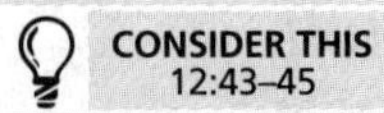
CONSIDER THIS
12:43–45

Turning Back Is Awful

Do you intend to overcome evil? If so, make sure to replace it with good or else, as Jesus warns, the evil may return with its friends, producing more evil than ever (vv. 43–45).

This teaching warns us to persevere in the journey of faith. That can be hard to do when everything in us wants to quit, the way an exhausted long-distance runner wants to drop out of a marathon. Besides (we reason), look how far we've already come!

Yes, but God's goal is not just to make us nicer people or better people, but to make us Christlike *people. That won't happen completely until we're with Him. For now, He wants us to keep growing in that direction. Stopping short can bring disaster. In a warning similar to Jesus' words here, the writer of Hebrews urges us to "go on to perfection" and describes in sobering words the fate of those who "fall away" (Heb. 6:1–12).*

Fortunately, God lends us help to prevent us from falling back. As Hebrews also says, He disciplines us for our good. His stern efforts can feel harsh, but they are the loving protection of a caring Father (12:3–11). ◆

It is dangerous to compare ourselves with others when evaluating our worth. God has a better way of self-assessment. See "Do You Suffer from 'Comparisonitis'?" Rom. 12:3.

25But Jesus knew their thoughts, and said to them: "Every kingdom divided against itself is brought to desolation, and every city or house divided against itself will not stand. 26If Satan casts out Satan, he is divided against himself. How then will his kingdom stand? 27And if I cast out demons by Beelzebub, by whom do your sons cast *them* out? Therefore they shall be your judges. 28But if I cast out demons by the Spirit of God, surely the kingdom of God has come upon you. 29Or how can one enter a strong man's house and plunder his goods, unless he first binds the strong man? And then he will plunder his house. 30He who is not with Me is against Me, and he who does not gather with Me scatters abroad.

12:31–32
see pg. 50

31"Therefore I say to you, every sin and blasphemy will be forgiven men, but the blasphemy *against* the Spirit will not be forgiven men. 32Anyone who speaks a word against the Son of Man, it will be forgiven him; but whoever speaks against the Holy Spirit, it will not be forgiven him, either in this age or in the *age* to come.

33"Either make the tree good and its fruit good, or else make the tree bad and its fruit bad; for a tree is known by *its* fruit. 34Brood of vipers! How can you, being evil, speak good things? For out of the abundance of the heart the mouth speaks. 35A good man out of the good treasure of his heart[a] brings forth good things, and an evil man out of the evil treasure brings forth evil things. 36But I say to you that for every idle word men may speak, they will give account of it in the day of judgment. 37For by your words you will be justified, and by your words you will be condemned."

38Then some of the scribes and Pharisees answered, saying, "Teacher, we want to see a sign from You."

39But He answered and said to them, "An evil and adulterous generation seeks after a sign, and no sign will be given to it except the sign of the prophet Jonah. 40For as Jonah was three days and three nights in the belly of the great fish, so will the Son of Man be three days and three nights in the heart of the earth. 41The men of Nineveh will rise up in the judgment with this generation and condemn it, because they repented at the preaching of Jonah; and indeed a greater than Jonah *is* here. 42The queen of the South will rise up in the judgment with this generation and condemn it, for she came from the ends of the earth to hear the wisdom of Solomon; and indeed a greater than Solomon *is* here.

12:43–45

43"When an unclean spirit goes out of a man, he goes through dry places, seeking

(Bible text continued on page 55)

12:35 [a]NU-Text and M-Text omit *of his heart.*

Family Loyalty

CONSIDER THIS
12:46–50

Ancient society placed great emphasis on faithfulness to blood relatives. So Jesus' words in vv. 48–50 must have sounded quite foreign to the crowd. He seemed to be breaking with tradition and disowning His family. But notice: Jesus didn't deny that the woman and the men at the door were His family. He merely pushed beyond the normal understanding of family to a larger reality—the claims of spiritual kinship. This new "family" included anyone who does the will of the Father in heaven.

In no way was Jesus denying the value or benefits of solid family relationships. See "The Family: A Call to Long-Term Work," Eph. 5:21.

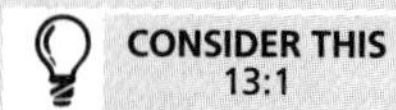

WORK-WORLD STORIES DESCRIBE THE KINGDOM

Jesus captivated His listeners by presenting truth in terms that they could understand. Here in chapter 13 we find no less than eight different images from the work world. Clearly, Jesus knew how to relate to the world in which everyday people lived and worked.

No wonder: Jesus probably spent most of His life working in His family's carpentry business. We know almost nothing of His youth from adolescence until He began His public ministry at about age 30. But we know that His father was a carpenter (Matt. 13:55) and that Jesus also practiced the trade (Mark 6:3). Carpenters worked with wood, metal, and stone to produce furniture and farm implements, and constructed houses and public buildings.

Jesus may have continued His occupation even after He began to teach and travel. Rabbis (or teachers) of the day commonly spent anywhere from one-third to one-half of their time working (most likely with their hands) to provide for themselves. And while Jesus' opponents, many of them rabbis, attacked Him on numerous grounds, they never accused Him of laziness or free-loading. Indeed, He was known to them as a carpenter.

That reputation passed on to the early church. One writer described Jesus as "working as a carpenter when among men, making ploughs and yokes, by which He taught the symbols of righteousness and an active life."

Little wonder, then, that Jesus' teaching was filled with workplace images and analogies such as those recorded here. Using parables—brief tales illustrating moral principles—He frequently spoke about the nature of His kingdom. Matthew 13 collects eight of these as listed below (with possible interpretations):

(1) *The parable of the soils* (vv. 1–23) addresses the receptivity of those who hear about the kingdom.

(2) *The parable of the wheat and the weeds* (vv. 24–30) warns that people who pretend to be part of the kingdom may be able to fool others, but they can't fool God.

(3) *The parable of the mustard seed* (vv. 31–32) is a promise that the kingdom would become a force to be reckoned with. Do not despise small beginnings!

(4) *The parable of the leaven* (v. 33) describes the influence of the kingdom: it quietly but effectively spreads among people and accomplishes significant results.

(5) *The parable of the hidden treasure* (v. 44) puts a value on the kingdom: it's the most important thing one can possess.

(6) *The parable of the pearl of great price* (vv. 45–46) also describes the kingdom's value: it's worth sacrificing everything in order to possess it.

(continued on next page)

rest, and finds none. [44]Then he says, 'I will return to my house from which I came.' And when he comes, he finds *it* empty, swept, and put in order. [45]Then he goes and takes with him seven other spirits more wicked than himself, and they enter and dwell there; and the last *state* of that man is worse than the first. So shall it also be with this wicked generation."

Family Loyalty

12:46–50 see pg. 53

[46]While He was still talking to the multitudes, behold, His mother and brothers stood outside, seeking to speak with Him. [47]Then one said to Him, "Look, Your mother and Your brothers are standing outside, seeking to speak with You."

[48]But He answered and said to the one who told Him, "Who is My mother and who are My brothers?" [49]And He stretched out His hand toward His disciples and said, "Here are My mother and My brothers! [50]For whoever does the will of My Father in heaven is My brother and sister and mother."

CHAPTER 13

Parables by the Sea

13:1

[1]On the same day Jesus went out of the house and sat by the sea. [2]And great multitudes were gathered together to Him, so that He got into a boat and sat; and the whole multitude stood on the shore.

Soils

[3]Then He spoke many things to them in parables, saying: "Behold, a sower went out to sow. [4]And as he sowed, some *seed* fell by the wayside; and the birds came and devoured them. [5]Some fell on stony places, where they did not have much earth; and they immediately sprang up because they had no depth of earth. [6]But when the sun was up they were scorched, and because they had no root they withered away. [7]And some fell among thorns, and the thorns sprang up and choked them. [8]But others fell on good ground and yielded a crop: some a hundredfold, some sixty, some thirty. [9]He who has ears to hear, let him hear!"

[10]And the disciples came and said to Him, "Why do You speak to them in parables?"

[11]He answered and said to them, "Because it has been given to you to know the mysteries of the kingdom of heaven, but to them it has not been given. [12]For whoever has, to him more will be given, and he will have abundance; but whoever does not have, even what he has will be taken away from him. [13]Therefore I speak to them in parables,

(continued from previous page)

(7) The parable of the dragnet (vv. 47–50) warns that a day of reckoning is coming, when those who accept the kingdom will be separated from those who reject it.

(8) The parable of the householder (vv. 51–52) places a responsibility on those who understand about the kingdom to share their insight with others.

Jesus' stories connected with the real world of agriculture (sowing, harvesting, growing), the food industry (baking, fishing), real estate (land purchasing, home ownership), and retailing (the sale of pearls). His images and language helped bring His message alive to common people. It showed clearly that God takes an interest in the workplace, and desires people to serve Him in the "secular" arena.

Work is one of the most important means that believers today have to accomplish God's purposes. See "Faith Impacts the World," Mark 16:15–16.

Like Jesus, Paul was able to support himself through a "secular" occupation. See "Paul's 'Real' Job," Acts 18:1–3.

If Jesus might have supported Himself while carrying out His ministry, is there any reason why modern Christian leaders shouldn't at least consider that as an option today? See "Paying Vocational Christian Workers," 1 Cor. 9:1–23.

because seeing they do not see, and hearing they do not hear, nor do they understand. 14And in them the prophecy of Isaiah is fulfilled, which says:

> 'Hearing you will hear and shall not
> understand,
> And seeing you will see and not perceive;
> 15 For the hearts of this people have grown dull.
> *Their* ears are hard of hearing,
> And their eyes they have closed,
> Lest they should see with *their* eyes and hear
> with *their* ears,
> Lest they should understand with *their* hearts
> and turn,
> So that I should[a] heal them.'[b]

16But blessed *are* your eyes for they see, and your ears for they hear; 17for assuredly, I say to you that many prophets and righteous *men* desired to see what you see, and did not see *it,* and to hear what you hear, and did not hear *it.*

18"Therefore hear the parable of the sower: 19When anyone hears the word of the kingdom, and does not understand *it,* then the wicked *one* comes and snatches away what was sown in his heart. This is he who received seed by the wayside. 20But he who received the seed on stony places, this is he who hears the word and immediately receives it with joy; 21yet he has no root in himself, but endures only for a while. For when tribulation or persecution arises because of the word, immediately he stumbles. 22Now he who received seed among the thorns is he who hears the word, and the cares of this world and the deceitfulness of riches choke the word, and he becomes unfruitful. 23But he who received seed on the good ground is he who hears the word and understands *it,* who indeed bears fruit and produces: some a hundredfold, some sixty, some thirty."

Wheat and Tares

24Another parable He put forth to them, saying: "The kingdom of heaven is like a man who sowed good seed in his field; 25but while men slept, his enemy came and sowed tares among the wheat and went his way. 26But when the grain had sprouted and produced a crop, then the tares also appeared. 27So the servants of the owner came and said to him, 'Sir, did you not sow good seed in your field? How then does it have tares?' 28He said to them, 'An enemy has done this.' The servants said to him, 'Do you want us then to go and gather them up?' 29But he said, 'No, lest while you gather up the tares you also uproot the wheat with them. 30Let both grow together until the harvest, and at the time of harvest I will say to the reapers, "First gather together the tares and bind them in bundles to burn them, but gather the wheat into my barn." ' "

A Mustard Seed

31Another parable He put forth to them, saying: "The kingdom of heaven is like a mustard seed, which a man took and sowed in his field, 32which indeed is the least of all the seeds; but when it is grown it is greater than the herbs and becomes a tree, so that the birds of the air come and nest in its branches."

Leaven

13:33
see pg. 58

33Another parable He spoke to them: "The kingdom of heaven is like leaven, which a woman took and hid in three measures[a] of meal till it was all leavened."

The Use of Parables

13:34–35

34All these things Jesus spoke to the multitude in parables; and without a parable He did not speak to them, 35that it might be fulfilled which was spoken by the prophet, saying:

> "I will open My mouth in parables;
> I will utter things kept secret from the
> foundation of the world."[a]

Wheat and Tares Explained

36Then Jesus sent the multitude away and went into the house. And His disciples came to Him, saying, "Explain to us the parable of the tares of the field."

(Bible text continued on page 58)

13:15 [a]NU-Text and M-Text read *would.* [b]Isaiah 6:9, 10 *13:33* [a]Greek *sata,* approximately two pecks in all *13:35* [a]Psalm 78:2

CONSIDER THIS
13:34–35

MYTH #1

10 MYTHS ABOUT CHRISTIANITY

MYTH: JESUS CHRIST WAS ONLY A GREAT MORAL TEACHER

Many people today accept a number of myths about Christianity, with the result that they never respond to Jesus as He really is. This is one of ten articles that speak to some of those misconceptions. For a list of all ten, see 1 Tim. 1:3–4.

People marveled at the teaching of Jesus. Whether He spoke in interesting parables (v. 34) or gave more straightforward, extended discourses (for instance, Matt. 5–7), people followed Him everywhere, hanging on His every word (Matt. 7:28). "No man ever spoke like this Man!" His listeners remarked (John 7:46). And they were right. Jesus was a master teacher and communicator.

Moreover, beyond simply teaching the highest moral and spiritual principles ever known, Jesus actually *lived* them. He told people to love their enemies; He forgave those who crucified Him. He told people to lay down their lives for others; He laid down His own life for the world. He told people not to worry about material possessions; He owned no more than the clothes on His back. Jesus' example makes Him the most remarkable of all teachers.

And yet that legacy almost makes it too easy for people to dismiss Him, ignoring both His message and His person: "Jesus? Yes, He was a great moral teacher." What they really mean is that, for them, Jesus was *only* a teacher—a great teacher, perhaps the greatest the world has ever seen, but a teacher and nothing more.

Neither He nor His followers would allow for that. Jesus was either very much more than a great teacher or else very much less than one. For in addition to His great moral precepts, He made astonishing claims that no other sane person has ever made, and behaved in ways that no other decent human has. For instance:

- He claimed to forgive people's sins (Matt. 9:2; Luke 7:47–48).
- He accepted people's worship (Matt. 8:2–3; 9:18–19; 14:33).
- He said that He alone was the way to God, the truth of God, and the life of God (John 5:40; 6:44; 7:16–17; 14:6).
- He said that He had come to seek and to save the lost (Luke 19:10).
- He promised that He would rise from the dead (Matt. 20:19; 27:63).
- He claimed that humanity would ultimately be accountable to Him (Matt. 7:21–23; 25:31–46).
- He claimed to be God and allowed others to call Him God (Matt. 16:15–16; 26:63–64; John 8:58).

These are astonishing claims. Any teacher who would make them had better be telling the truth or else He would be the worst of all liars and neither great nor moral.

The evidence suggests that Jesus was telling the truth. For in addition to His explicit claims are the implicit claims of fulfilled Old Testament prophecies and the performance of supernatural miracles. And there is also the fact that countless others who have examined His words and actions have come away convinced that He was not merely a great moral teacher, but the very Son of God. Among them have been determined and supposedly unshakable skeptics like Thomas and adamant opponents like the brilliant Saul of Tarsus who ended up becoming His most ardent follower.

(continued on next page)

(continued from previous page)

To believe that Jesus was simply a great moral teacher is untenable. As C. S. Lewis put it,

A man who was merely a man and said the sort of things Jesus said would not be a great moral teacher. He would either be a lunatic—on a level with the man who says he is a poached egg—or else He would be the Devil of Hell. You must make your choice. Either this man was, and is, the Son of God: or else a madman or something worse. You can shut Him up for a fool, you can spit at Him and kill Him as a demon; or you can fall at His feet and call Him Lord and God. But let us not come with any patronizing nonsense about His being a great human teacher. He has not left that open to us. He did not intend to.

(C. S. Lewis, *Mere Christianity,* p. 56) ◆

37He answered and said to them: "He who sows the good
seed is the Son of Man. 38The field is the world, the good
seeds are the sons of the kingdom, but the tares are the sons
of the wicked *one.* 39The enemy who sowed them is the
devil, the harvest is the end of the age, and the reapers are
the angels. 40Therefore as the tares are gathered and burned
in the fire, so it will be at the end of this age. 41The Son of
Man will send out His angels, and they will gather out of
His kingdom all things that offend, and those who practice
lawlessness, 42and will cast them into the furnace of fire.
There will be wailing and gnashing of teeth. 43Then the
righteous will shine forth as the sun in the kingdom of their
Father. He who has ears to hear, let him hear!

◆ ◆ ◆ ◆ ◆ ◆ ◆ ◆ ◆ ◆ ◆ ◆ ◆ ◆

FIFTY POUNDS OF FLOUR

Perhaps when Jesus told the parable of the leaven (v. 33), laughter rippled through the crowd from the women who were listening. "Doesn't He know anything about baking?" *they might have chuckled—or maybe Jesus was humoring them with an inside joke.*

Jewish women did not use fresh yeast each day to leaven their barley or wheat bread, but a small piece of fermented dough from the previous day's batch. However, three measures was an enormous amount of flour—close to fifty pounds! How could that much flour be leavened by the usual amount of previously leavened dough?

Jesus' parable—and its point—must have come to mind every day afterwards as the women kneaded their dough. Fifty pounds of flour leavened by such a small amount of dough . . . the kingdom of God brought about by way of such a small number of faithful people.

Two other images that Jesus used to describe the influence His followers can have on society were salt and light. See "Sulfa Drugs and Street Lights," Matt. 5:13–16.

On another occasion, Jesus talked about leaven in a much more negative connection. See "Danger Ahead," Mark 8:14–21.

Hidden Treasure

13:44–46

44"Again, the kingdom of heaven is like
treasure hidden in a field, which a man
found and hid; and for joy over it he goes and sells all that
he has and buys that field.

A Pearl of Great Price

45"Again, the kingdom of heaven is like a merchant seeking beautiful pearls, 46who, when he had found one pearl of
great price, went and sold all that he had and bought it.

A Dragnet

47"Again, the kingdom of heaven is like a dragnet that was
cast into the sea and gathered some of every kind, 48which,
when it was full, they drew to shore; and they sat down and
gathered the good into vessels, but threw the bad away. 49So
it will be at the end of the age. The angels will come forth,
separate the wicked from among the just, 50and cast them
into the furnace of fire. There will be wailing and gnashing
of teeth."

A Householder

51Jesus said to them,[a] "Have you understood all these
things?"

They said to Him, "Yes, Lord."[b]

13:52 see pg. 60

52Then He said to them, "Therefore
every scribe instructed concerning[a] the
kingdom of heaven is like a householder who brings out of
his treasure *things* new and old."

Jesus Dishonored in His Own Country

53Now it came to pass, when Jesus had finished these
parables, that He departed from there. 54When He had
come to His own country, He taught them in their synagogue, so that they were astonished and said, "Where did
this *Man* get this wisdom and *these* mighty works? 55Is this
not the carpenter's son? Is not His mother called Mary? And
His brothers James, Joses,[a] Simon, and Judas? 56And His sisters, are they not all with us? Where then did this *Man* get
all these things?" 57So they were offended at Him.

But Jesus said to them, "A prophet is not without honor
except in his own country and in his own house." 58Now
He did not do many mighty works there because of their
unbelief.

(Bible text continued on page 61)

13:51 [a]NU-Text omits *Jesus said to them.* [b]NU-Text omits *Lord.* *13:52* [a]Or *for*
13:55 [a]NU-Text reads *Joseph.*

The Incomparable Value of the Kingdom

CONSIDER THIS 13:44–46 **The two parables in vv. 44–46 describe the incomparable value of the kingdom. Nothing was worth more, Jesus told His followers. Nothing is too great to sacrifice for it—certainly not material wealth (Matt. 6:33; 19:16–30).**

In light of Jesus' words here, maybe it's worth pausing to reflect on your own life and choices. What has your commitment to Christ cost you? Or has it cost you anything? Has it made any difference in decisions about your career, lifestyle, investments, or purchases? What would you sell in order to gain the King and His kingdom (v. 46)?

CONSIDER THIS
13:52

TREASURES NEW AND OLD

One of the most exciting aspects of Christian truth is that it is inexhaustible. One can never come to the end of it. No matter how long we may have been in the faith, no matter how much theology we may master, we can never come to the end of what God has revealed in Christ and in the Bible. Jesus spoke to this fact in His parable of the householder (v. 52).

The key to understanding this parable is the question Jesus asked His followers: "Have you understood all these things?" (v. 51). "These things" refers to the series of parables on the kingdom that He had just told (vv. 1–50). Amazingly, the disciples answered yes. Apparently they thought they had absorbed everything Jesus had to say.

But how could they? They could not possibly perceive the vast implications of these stories for day-to-day life, let alone the theological issues involved in a doctrine as complex as the kingdom. Theologians still debate these matters (see "The King Declares His Kingdom," Matt. 4:17).

Jesus recognized that the disciples were claiming more insight than they actually possessed. So He gave them the parable of the householder to characterize the situation. Householders were what we would call heads of households, persons with authority over what went on in a given home.

If one were to visit the home, the master of the house might bring out some of the treasures of the home to delight and impress his guest. He might bring out something old—perhaps one of the family heirlooms—or something new—maybe a recent purchase.

Jesus likened His disciples to heads of the family in possession of His truth. Over the years they would tell people about the "old treasures"—the basics of the gospel—and about "new treasures"—the way in which His teaching applied to new situations.

In effect, they would be like "scribe[s] instructed concerning the kingdom of heaven" (v. 52). Scribes were a learned class of scholars who studied the Scriptures and served as copyists, editors, and teachers. They occupied a prestigious position, as only ordained teachers could transmit and create religious tradition. Just as the Jewish scribes studied the Law, recalling old truths recognized for centuries as well as "new" truths that applied Scripture to the demands of new situations, so the disciples were storing up Jesus' teaching and—someday—would repeat it to others, write it down, and teach from it, passing on "things new and old."

Today we possess the written record of these treasures. But like Jesus' first disciples, we can find both old and new. As we confront situations, we can look back to the "old" truths, the fundamental things that never change, and we can also discern how to apply biblical truth to new issues in ways that are fresh and alive. ◆

To become a scribe required constant study, often beginning at age 14 and continuing to the age of 40. Learn more about these elite scholars of Jewish society at Luke 20:39.

CHAPTER 14

Herod Executes John the Baptist

14:1

1At that time Herod the tetrarch heard the report about Jesus 2and said to his servants, "This is John the Baptist; he is risen from the dead,

14:3

and therefore these powers are at work in him." 3For Herod had laid hold of John and bound him, and put *him* in prison for the sake of Herodias, his brother Philip's wife. 4Because John had said to him, "It is not lawful for you to have her." 5And although he wanted to put him to death, he feared the multitude, because they counted him as a prophet.

14:6–10

6But when Herod's birthday was celebrated, the daughter of Herodias danced before them and pleased Herod. 7Therefore he promised with an oath to give her whatever she might ask.

8So she, having been prompted by her mother, said, "Give me John the Baptist's head here on a platter."

9And the king was sorry; nevertheless, because of the oaths and because of those who sat with him, he commanded *it* to be given to *her.* 10So he sent and had John beheaded in prison. 11And his head was brought on a platter and given to the girl, and she brought *it* to her mother. 12Then his disciples came and took away the body and buried it, and went and told Jesus.

Jesus Feeds 5,000

14:13–14 see pg. 62

13When Jesus heard *it,* He departed from there by boat to a deserted place by Himself. But when the multitudes heard it, they followed Him on foot from the cities. 14And when Jesus went out He saw a great multitude; and He was moved with compassion for them, and healed their sick. 15When it was evening, His disciples came to Him, saying, "This is a deserted place, and the hour is already late. Send the multitudes away, that they may go into the villages and buy themselves food."

Herod the Tetrarch

The son of King Herod, Herod Antipas inherited the title of "tetrarch" (ruler of a fourth part; see Luke 9:7). Read about his infamous family in "The Herods," Acts 12:1–2.

Herod's Rash Promise

Charmed by his stepdaughter and no doubt intoxicated, Herod rashly made a promise that cost John the Baptist his life (vv. 6–10). "A Reckless Choice" at Mark 6:23, discusses how decisions with far-reaching consequences are often made in haste, in a flush of wild excitement.

HATEFUL HERODIAS

CONSIDER THIS 14:3

Herodias (v. 3) was a powerful woman. The wife of Palestine's appointed ruler, she enjoyed privilege and position. But one thing she had no control over was the outspoken tongue of John the Baptist.

John had publicly condemned Herodias' marriage to Herod Antipas. A granddaughter of Herod the Great, Herodias had first married her father's brother, Herod Philip I. But she left Philip to marry his half-brother, Herod Antipas, who divorced his wife to marry Herodias.

John denounced their immorality, and Herodias was determined to silence the troublesome prophet. So she persuaded Herod to have John arrested and imprisoned. However, she could not convince her husband to execute the man.

Eventually, however, an opportunity presented itself when Herod's lust led him to foolishly promise Herodias' daughter Salome anything (v. 7). The extent of Herodias' evil and cunning is evident from her daughter's unusual request. Imagine the control she must have had over the girl's mind!

The Bible records terrible stories truthfully. This woman's choice, to use her daughter to work her vengeance on an innocent man, ranks among the worst.

16But Jesus said to them, "They do not need to go away.
You give them something to eat."
17And they said to Him, "We have here only five loaves
and two fish."
18He said, "Bring them here to Me." 19Then He commanded the multitudes to sit down on the grass. And He
took the five loaves and the two fish, and looking up to
heaven, He blessed and broke and gave the loaves to the
disciples; and the disciples gave to the multitudes. 20So they
all ate and were filled, and they took up twelve baskets full
of the fragments that remained. 21Now those who had eaten
were about five thousand men, besides women and children.

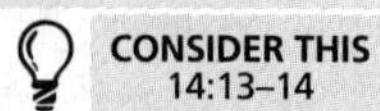

THE PUBLIC SIDE OF OUR FAITH

Much of the Christianity that has come down to us today dwells on private spirituality—prayers, private devotions and Bible reading, self-examination and confession, personal holiness, individual acts of charity, and so on. This is all to the good, inasmuch as Christ is a Person who seeks a relationship with individuals.

But what about the public *side of our faith? For example:*

- *How do we as believers live as Christians in the public arenas—work, community, relationships, civic responsibilities, and so on?*
- *What about our communities of faith, such as our churches? How vibrant and strategic is our collective witness as God's people to a watching world?*

Jesus Walks on Water

[22]Immediately Jesus made His disciples get into the boat
and go before Him to the other side, while He sent the multitudes away. [23]And when He had sent the multitudes away,
He went up on the mountain by Himself to pray. Now
when evening came, He was alone there. [24]But the boat was
now in the middle of the sea,[a] tossed by the waves, for the
wind was contrary.

14:25 see pg. 64

[25]Now in the fourth watch of the night
Jesus went to them, walking on the sea.
[26]And when the disciples saw Him walking on the sea, they

14:24 [a]NU-Text reads *many furlongs away from the land.*

- *In what ways do we as believers influence our society as a whole—its institutions, its needs, and its values?*

These are broad, complex questions that have no easy answers. But we cannot afford to ignore them—not when we consider the public side of Jesus' ministry. Unlike others of His day who withdrew from society to practice and perfect their own, private spirituality (such as the Essenes, Matt. 16:1), Jesus actively engaged His culture. He participated in its rituals. He focused His work on its cities (see "Jesus—A City Preacher," Matt. 9:35). He interacted with its leaders. He welcomed its crowds (as seen here in vv. 13–14). He particularly reached out to its poor—not only the financially poor but the "poor in spirit," those left behind, those left without hope.

In short, Jesus not only affects our private lives, but our public lives as well. We need to recover that dimension of the gospel today. As believers we are no longer simply individuals, but have been made part of a "royal priesthood" and a "holy nation." Out of those who were once "no people," we are now "the people of God" (1 Pet. 2:9–10). We need to discover how to live out our faith in visible, public ways, as the collective people of God, in order to powerfully impact our world. ◆

Jesus used two metaphors to describe a believer's public life, particularly work and participation in the community. See "Sulfa Drugs and Street Lights," Matt. 5:13–16.

HE SAW A GREAT MULTITUDE; AND HE WAS MOVED WITH COMPASSION FOR THEM. . . .
—Matthew 14:14

were troubled, saying, "It is a ghost!" And they cried out for
fear.

27But immediately Jesus spoke to them, saying, "Be of
good cheer! It is I; do not be afraid."

28And Peter answered Him and said, "Lord, if it is You,
command me to come to You on the water."

29So He said, "Come." And when Peter had come down
out of the boat, he walked on the water to go to Jesus. 30But
when he saw that the wind *was* boisterous,[a] he was afraid;
and beginning to sink he cried out, saying, "Lord, save me!"

31And immediately Jesus stretched out *His* hand and
caught him, and said to him, "O you of little faith, why did
you doubt?" 32And when they got into the boat, the wind
ceased.

33Then those who were in the boat came and[a] worshiped
Him, saying, "Truly You are the Son of God."

14:30 [a]NU-Text brackets *that* and *boisterous* as disputed. *14:33* [a]NU-Text omits *came and.*

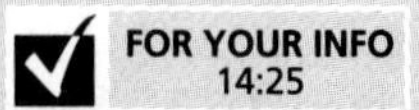

TELLING TIME

Matthew records that Jesus came walking on the sea "in the fourth watch of the night" (v. 25). That would make it near sunrise, indicating that the disciples had spent virtually the entire night struggling with the stormy conditions!

In those days, time was not reckoned as precisely as it is today. In cultures that lacked electricity and were far more agriculturally based than our own, time was an approximation. Thus when the men of Jabesh Gilead came to Saul for help, he promised them, "Tomorrow, by the time the sun is hot, you shall have help" (1 Sam. 11:9), indicating that reinforcements would arrive sometime in midmorning. Likewise, God is said to have walked in the garden of Eden "in the cool of the day" (Gen. 3:8), suggesting evening.

However, the Hebrews did divide the period of daylight (yom) *into 12 hours, as follows:*

Sunrise	*6:00 a.m.*
1st hour	*7:00 a.m.*
2nd hour	*8:00 a.m.*
3rd hour	*9:00 a.m.*
4th hour	*10:00 a.m.*
5th hour	*11:00 a.m.*
6th hour	*12:00 noon*
7th hour	*1:00 p.m.*

Many Healed in Gennesaret

34When they had crossed over, they came to the land of[a]
Gennesaret. 35And when the men of that place recognized
Him, they sent out into all that surrounding region, brought
to Him all who were sick, 36and begged Him that they
might only touch the hem of His garment. And as many as
touched *it* were made perfectly well.

CHAPTER 15

Debates over Tradition

15:1–3

1Then the scribes and Pharisees who
were from Jerusalem came to Jesus, saying,
2"Why do Your disciples transgress the tradition of the
elders? For they do not wash their hands when they eat
bread."

14:34 [a]NU-Text reads *came to land at.*

8th hour .... 2:00 p.m.
9th hour .... 3:00 p.m.
10th hour .... 4:00 p.m.
11th hour .... 5:00 p.m.
12th hour .... 6:00 p.m.

Obviously these times could vary substantially, depending on the season. To complicate matters, the Romans reckoned the day (as we do) in two twelve-hour periods beginning at midnight and noon.

Nighttime was divided into "watches," so called because of the changing shifts of watchmen who stood guard on city walls and at the gates. In the New Testament, the influence of the Romans created four watches estimated as follows (again depending on the season):

Beginning around . . .
1st watch .... 6:00 p.m.
2nd watch .... 9:00 p.m.
3rd watch .... midnight
4th watch .... 3:00 a.m. ◆

TRADITION

CONSIDER THIS 15:1–3 **Tradition. Is it the bedrock of intelligent change or the stumbling block to any change? Should leaders embrace and personify traditional values, or should they be mavericks, breaking with tradition and striking out in new directions?**

Jesus rebuked the scribes and Pharisees for allowing their rabbinic traditions to actually supersede the express commands of God (v. 3). The specific issue here was a tradition about ritual washings connected with the preparation and serving of food. Not only must one's hands be washed, but also the bowls, cups, pitchers, and other utensils.

In modern American culture we do not follow the rigid pronouncements of a priestly class. Yet there are numerous traditions and expectations—most of which are unspoken—that govern our behavior in powerful ways. This creates tension for believers in the workplace, particularly managers. They are called upon to be both sustainers and breakers of tradition. There are no simple formulas to help one decide how to respond to tradition, but it might help to reflect on questions such as:

- **What values and principles does the tradition seek to embody? How do those square with the values of Christ?**
- **Why does the tradition exist? Why is it maintained? Are there any major objections to it?**
- **In maintaining a tradition, who benefits and who suffers? If it changes, who might be helped or hurt? How would the organization be affected?**

Tradition is an important area in which faith impacts the world. See Mark 16:15–16.

3He answered and said to them, "Why do you also transgress the commandment of God because of your tradition?
4For God commanded, saying, 'Honor your father and your
mother';[a] and, 'He who curses father or mother, let him be
put to death.'[b] 5But you say, 'Whoever says to his father or
mother, "Whatever profit you might have received from me
is a gift *to God*"— 6then he need not honor his father or
mother.'[a] Thus you have made the commandment[b] of God
of no effect by your tradition. 7Hypocrites! Well did Isaiah
prophesy about you, saying:

8 'These people draw near to Me with their mouth,
And[a] honor Me with *their* lips,
But their heart is far from Me.
9 And in vain they worship Me,
Teaching *as* doctrines the commandments of men.' "[a]

Jesus Denounces the Pharisees

10When He had called the multitude to *Himself*, He said
to them, "Hear and understand: 11Not what goes into the
mouth defiles a man; but what comes out of the mouth, this
defiles a man."
12Then His disciples came and said to Him, "Do You
know that the Pharisees were offended when they heard
this saying?"
13But He answered and said, "Every plant which My heavenly Father has not planted will be uprooted. 14Let them
alone. They are blind leaders of the blind. And if the blind
leads the blind, both will fall into a ditch."
15Then Peter answered and said to Him, "Explain this
parable to us."
16So Jesus said, "Are you also still without understanding?
17Do you not yet understand that whatever enters the
mouth goes into the stomach and is eliminated? 18But those
things which proceed out of the mouth come from the
heart, and they defile a man. 19For out of the heart proceed
evil thoughts, murders, adulteries, fornications, thefts, false
witness, blasphemies. 20These are *the things* which defile a
man, but to eat with unwashed hands does not defile a
man."

A Canaanite Woman's Plea

15:21–28

21Then Jesus went out from there and
departed to the region of Tyre and Sidon.
22And behold, a woman of Canaan came from that region

(*Bible text continued on page 68*)

15:4 [a]Exodus 20:12; Deuteronomy 5:16 [b]Exodus 21:17 *15:6* [a]NU-Text omits *or mother.* [b]NU-Text reads *word.* *15:8* [a]NU-Text omits *draw near to Me with their mouth, And.* *15:9* [a]Isaiah 29:13

Persistence Pays Off

CONSIDER THIS 15:21–28 **Jesus took His disciples to the seacoast towns of Tyre and Sidon (v. 21), probably to rest (Mark 7:24). As far as we can tell, He had no intention of preaching or healing in that area.**

But as so often happens when one has no intention of being available, someone interrupted His vacation. Today, phone calls prove to be the major source of interruptions. But in ancient times it was worse: interruptions arrived at one's doorstep and stayed until someone answered.

In this instance, a woman who supposedly had no claim on Jesus' attention begged Him to deliver her daughter from demons. She had probably already tried to heal the girl and failed. In ancient societies, women usually tended the sick and nursed the dying.

Jesus hardly encouraged this woman. As He pointed out, she had no ethnic or religious claim on Him. But somehow she recognized that He was capable of doing what she could not—heal her daughter. In the end, her courage, faith, and sheer persistence won out.

How persistent are you in crying out to God for people who matter a lot to you? Like the woman, will you keep coming back to God in faith?

Jesus' treatment of the woman seems a contradiction to His image. She came in utter sincerity and with great respect, yet He put her off with severe words. Why would He do that? See "Jesus and Ethnicity," Mark 7:24–30.

On another occasion, Jesus told His followers an interesting story about the need for persistence in prayer. See Luke 18:1–8.

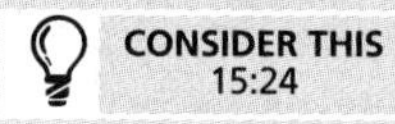

Jews, Gentiles, and Jesus

At the time Jesus was born, Hebrews saw the world divided into two types of people—Jews and everyone else. Jews regarded foreigners (known as Gentiles*, or "nations") as morally unclean and spiritually lost. Jews were God's people; Gentiles were not. The attitude was well expressed by Peter upon meeting Cornelius, a Roman centurion: "You know how unlawful it is for a Jewish man to keep company with or go to one of another nation" (Acts 10:28).*

The roots of this separation stretched deep into Israel's history. One important development occurred in about 450 B.C. when a remnant of Jews returned from captivity in Babylon to rebuild Jerusalem. Their leader, Ezra the priest, called for purification from all pagan influences, such as foreign-born wives (Ezra 10:2–4).

Later, after centuries of domination by the Greeks and Romans, Jews developed a hatred for all Gentiles and tried to avoid contact with foreigners. According to Tacitus, a Roman historian, "they regard the rest of mankind with all the hatred of enemies" (*Histories,* v. 5).

In Matthew's Gospel we see a recognition of the tension between the two groups. He presents Jesus as the long-awaited Christ of the Jews (Matt. 15:24). Jesus fulfilled numerous Old Testament messianic prophecies (for example, Matt. 1:23; 2:6, 14, 18, 23). But Matthew also shows Jesus breaking through the Jew/Gentile wall of hatred and separation. Jesus dealt with Jews and Gentiles alike, shattering the caste system of His day—and shocking His Jewish brothers.

What ethnic or racial walls would Jesus tear down in the modern era? Perhaps He would have joined black slaves in the United States and lived among them as an equal. Perhaps He would have violated the customs of segregation and eaten with blacks in white restaurants earlier in this century. Perhaps He would open His door to Haitians in Miami, Chinese in Vancouver, or Vietnamese in Houston. Perhaps He would make friends with Palestinians in Israel, or reach out to Moslems in Iraq and Iran. Perhaps He would heal both Roman Catholics and Protestants in Northern Ireland.

Racism and ethnic hatred have never been God's desire. They come from the sin of men and women. Jesus repudiated such sin wherever He found it. As Matthew shows, His heart is for all the nations. ◆

While Matthew's Gospel portrays Jesus in terms of His Jewish roots, it also shows that Jesus is an international Savior, a Messiah for the whole world. See "Jesus' Global Connections," Matt. 8:10.

Part-Jew, part-Gentile, Samaritans were treated with unusual scorn by their Hebrew cousins. See John 4:4.

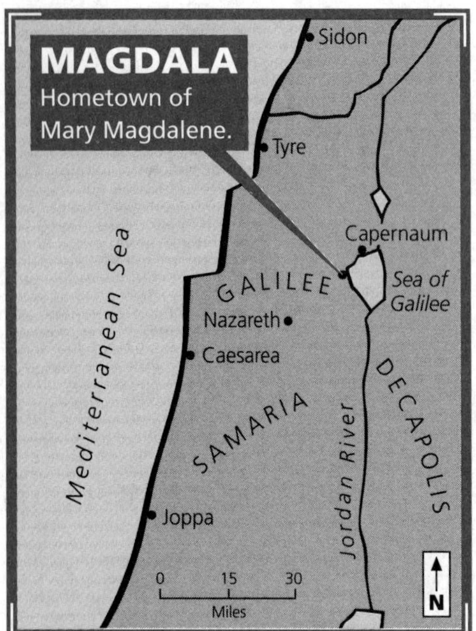

Magdala

YOU ARE THERE 15:39

- A city on the west shore of the Sea of Galilee, a short distance from Tiberias.
- Also known as Taricheae and called *Migdal* ("tower"), suggesting its significance militarily.
- A flourishing center of the region's fishing industry, shipping salted and pickled fish to Jerusalem, Damascus, and even as far away as Spain.
- Also known for agriculture, shipbuilding, and trade.
- Mostly Gentile in population and very wealthy.
- Boasted a hippodrome (stadium for chariot racing).
- Modern-day Mejdel the likely site of the ancient city.

and cried out to Him, saying, "Have mercy on me, O Lord, Son of David! My daughter is severely demon-possessed."
23But He answered her not a word.
And His disciples came and urged Him, saying, "Send her away, for she cries out after us."

15:24 see pg. 67

24But He answered and said, "I was not sent except to the lost sheep of the house of Israel."
25Then she came and worshiped Him, saying, "Lord, help me!"
26But He answered and said, "It is not good to take the children's bread and throw *it* to the little dogs."
27And she said, "Yes, Lord, yet even the little dogs eat the crumbs which fall from their masters' table."
28Then Jesus answered and said to her, "O woman, great *is* your faith! Let it be to you as you desire." And her daughter was healed from that very hour.

Jesus Heals on a Mountain

29Jesus departed from there, skirted the Sea of Galilee,
and went up on the mountain and sat down there. 30Then
great multitudes came to Him, having with them *the* lame, blind, mute, maimed, and many others; and they laid them
down at Jesus' feet, and He healed them. 31So the multitude
marveled when they saw *the* mute speaking, *the* maimed made whole, *the* lame walking, and *the* blind seeing; and they glorified the God of Israel.

Jesus Feeds 4,000

32Now Jesus called His disciples to *Himself* and said, "I have compassion on the multitude, because they have now continued with Me three days and have nothing to eat. And I do not want to send them away hungry, lest they faint on the way."
33Then His disciples said to Him, "Where could we get enough bread in the wilderness to fill such a great multitude?"
34Jesus said to them, "How many loaves do you have?"
And they said, "Seven, and a few little fish."
35So He commanded the multitude to sit down on the
ground. 36And He took the seven loaves and the fish and gave thanks, broke *them* and gave *them* to His disciples;
and the disciples *gave* to the multitude. 37So they all ate and
were filled, and they took up seven large baskets full of the
fragments that were left. 38Now those who ate were four thousand men, besides women and chil-

15:39

dren. 39And He sent away the multitude,
got into the boat, and came to the region of Magdala.[a]

15:39 [a]NU-Text reads *Magadan*.

CHAPTER 16

Leaders Ask for a Sign

16:1
see pg. 70

1Then the Pharisees and Sadducees came, and testing Him asked that He would show them a sign from heaven. 2He answered and said to them, "When it is evening you say, '*It will be* fair weather, for the sky is red'; 3and in the morning, '*It will be* foul weather today, for the sky is red and threatening.' Hypocrites![a] You know how to discern the face of the sky, but you cannot *discern* the signs of the times. 4A wicked and adulterous generation seeks after a sign, and no sign shall be given to it except the sign of the prophet[a] Jonah." And He left them and departed.

"Beware of the Leaven of the Pharisees"

5Now when His disciples had come to the other side, they had forgotten to take bread. 6Then Jesus said to them, "Take heed and beware of the leaven of the Pharisees and the Sadducees."

7And they reasoned among themselves, saying, "*It is* because we have taken no bread."

8But Jesus, being aware of *it,* said to them, "O you of little faith, why do you reason among yourselves because you have brought no bread?[a] 9Do you not yet understand, or remember the five loaves of the five thousand and how many baskets you took up? 10Nor the seven loaves of the four thousand and how many large baskets you took up? 11How is it you do not understand that I did not speak to you concerning bread?—*but* to beware of the leaven of the Pharisees and Sadducees." 12Then they understood that He did not tell *them* to beware of the leaven of bread, but of the doctrine of the Pharisees and Sadducees.

"You Are the Christ"

16:13–20

13When Jesus came into the region of Caesarea Philippi, He asked His disciples, saying, "Who do men say that I, the Son of Man, am?"

(Bible text continued on page 72)

16:3 [a]NU-Text omits *Hypocrites.* *16:4* [a]NU-Text omits *the prophet.* *16:8* [a]NU-Text reads *you have no bread.*

"YOU CANNOT DISCERN THE SIGNS OF THE TIMES."
—Matthew 16:3

Standing at the Gates of Hell

A CLOSER LOOK
16:13–20

When Jesus queried His disciples as to His identity (vv. 13, 15), they were standing in the shadow of a city named in honor of Rome's emperor. See "You Are the Christ," Mark 8:27–33, and "Caesarea," Acts 10:24.

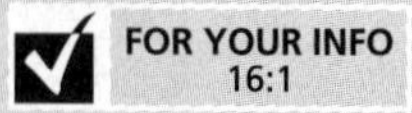

Party Politics of Jesus' Day

What were the politics of Jesus? We may speculate on what His preferences might be today. But what political ideals did He favor during His earthly life? What leaders did He endorse, if any? What causes did He support? For that matter, was political choice even an issue for Him? Did politics even matter?

In the end, it would be difficult if not impossible to determine any satisfactory answers. Jesus seemed acutely aware of the power brokers in His society. He also showed remarkable skill at political gamesmanship. But He never addressed or practiced politics in any formal sense. And He lived in a system completely different from our own.

However, even if we cannot know precisely what Jesus' affiliations were, we can at least understand some of the political dynamics at work in Palestine in the first half of the first century. For example, we know that there were at least five major political parties among the Hebrews of that day.

The Herodians—Loyal Defenders of the Status Quo

- Took their name from Herod the Great (37–4 B.C.) and his supporters. (See "The Herods," Acts 12:1–2.)
- Supported the adoption of Graeco-Roman culture and policies in Palestine.
- Like the Pharisees, favored local political autonomy. Fearing military intervention by Rome, they stridently resisted challengers to the status quo, such as the Zealots, John the Baptist, Jesus, and the apostles.
- Joined forces with other parties in the plot to eliminate Jesus (Matt. 22:16; Mark 3:6; 12:13).

The Pharisees—Religious Legalists

- Probably derived from a group of the faithful called the *Hasidim*.
- Name means "to separate."
- Shared similar views with the Essenes, but chose to stay within the

larger society. Nevertheless, many chose to study the Law on their own, having lost respect for the priesthood as a result of its corruption.

- Many served on the council (see Acts 6:12).
- Considered the doctors of the Law; scribes were considered laymen.
- Collected and preserved the Talmud and the Mishnah, voluminous products of oral tradition and Old Testament commentary.
- By reputation, legalistic and fanatically devoted to rabbinic tradition. Some even refused to eat with non-Pharisees for fear of being contaminated by food not rendered ritually clean.
- Like the Herodians, favored local political autonomy.
- Differed with the Sadducees over the doctrine of the resurrection.
- Understood the coming kingdom as a literal fulfillment of the promise to David for a King to reign over Israel forever.
- Maintained an elaborate theology of angels, believing them to intervene in human affairs.

The Sadducees—The Urban Elite

- May have derived from Zadok, high priest under King David.
- Tended to represent the aristocrats, priests, merchants, and urban elite in Jerusalem and other cities in Judea.
- Hostile to Jesus and His followers.
- Many served on the council. Most of the high priests in the days of Jesus and the apostles were Sadducees.
- Denied the resurrection or life after death, along with the doctrines of everlasting punishment and a literal kingdom.
- Denied that God controls history, insisting on free will and the responsibility of humans to make wise choices according to the Law.
- Held only to the Law of Moses (the first five books of the Old Testament) as supremely authoritative.
- Denied the existence of angels.

The Zealots—Firebrands of Revolution

- Ardent nationalists who awaited an opportunity to revolt against Rome.
- Resisted paying taxes to Rome or to the temple.
- One particular tax revolt against Rome, led by Judas the Galilean (6 B.C.), secured Galilee's reputation as a seedbed of revolutionaries.
- Blamed by some for the collapse of Judea to Rome in the war of A.D. 66–70. Josephus, a Jewish historian, claimed that they degenerated into mere assassins or *sicarii* ("dagger-men").
- Sided with the Pharisees in supporting Jewish Law.
- Opposed the Herodians and Sadducees, who tried to maintain the political status quo.
- Intolerant of the Essenes and later the Christians for their tendencies toward nonviolence.
- Two recruited by Jesus were Judas Iscariot and Simon the Cananite.

The Essenes—Detached Purists

- A sect of ascetics that thrived between the middle of the second century B.C. until the Jewish-Roman war in A.D. 66–70.
- Once members of the *Hasidim,* but unlike the Pharisees separated from society, withdrawing into monastic communities like Qumran where the Dead Sea scrolls were found.
- Known today mostly through secondary sources.
- Lived in societies that held property in common.
- Believed in the immortality of the soul, angels, and an elaborate scheme of end-times prophecies. Some were looking for as many as three different Messiahs.
- Known for celibacy, pacifism, opposition to slavery, caring for their own sick and elderly, trading only within their own sect, simplicity in meals and dress, and the rejection of all ostentatious display.
- Paid more attention to ceremonial purity than did even the Pharisees, and carefully guarded the Sabbath.
- Practiced ritual baptism and a communal dinner called the messianic banquet.
- May have influenced some early Christian practices and rituals. ◆

In addition to the regional and local politics of Palestine, Jesus and His followers lived under the enormous influence of Rome. See "Roman Politics in the First Century A.D.," Luke 22:25.

[14]So they said, "Some *say* John the Baptist, some Elijah, and others Jeremiah or one of the prophets."

[15]He said to them, "But who do you say that I am?"

[16]Simon Peter answered and said, "You are the Christ, the Son of the living God."

[17]Jesus answered and said to him, "Blessed are you, Simon Bar-Jonah, for flesh and blood has not revealed *this* to

16:18

you, but My Father who is in heaven. [18]And I also say to you that you are Peter, and on this rock I will build My church, and the gates of Hades shall not prevail against it. [19]And I will give you the keys of the kingdom of heaven, and whatever you bind on earth will be bound in heaven, and whatever you loose on earth will be loosed[a] in heaven."

[20]Then He commanded His disciples that they should tell no one that He was Jesus the Christ.

Following Christ Means Sacrifice

[21]From that time Jesus began to show to His disciples that He must go to Jerusalem, and suffer many things from the elders and chief priests and scribes, and be killed, and be raised the third day.

16:22–23 see pg. 74

[22]Then Peter took Him aside and began to rebuke Him, saying, "Far be it from You, Lord; this shall not happen to You!"

[23]But He turned and said to Peter, "Get behind Me, Satan! You are an offense to Me, for you are not mindful of the things of God, but the things of men."

[24]Then Jesus said to His disciples, "If anyone desires to come after Me, let him deny himself, and take up his cross, and follow Me. [25]For whoever desires to save his life will lose it, but whoever loses his life for My sake will find it. [26]For what profit is it to a man if he gains the whole world, and loses his own soul? Or what will a man give in exchange for his soul? [27]For the Son of Man will come in the glory of His Father with His angels, and then He will reward each according to his works. [28]Assuredly, I say to you, there are some standing here who shall not taste death till they see the Son of Man coming in His kingdom."

"FOR WHAT PROFIT IS IT TO A MAN IF HE GAINS THE WHOLE WORLD, AND LOSES HIS OWN SOUL?" —Matthew 16:26

CHAPTER 17

The Transfiguration

[1]Now after six days Jesus took Peter, James, and John his brother, led them up on a high mountain by themselves; [2]and He was transfigured before them. His face shone like

(Bible text continued on page 74)

16:19 [a]Or *will have been bound . . . will have been loosed*

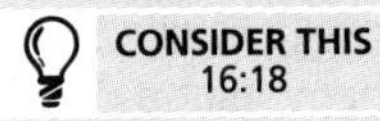

"The Gates of Hell"

Jesus referred to "the gates of Hades" (hell) in His bold statement to Peter (v. 18). For Matthew's original readers, the word "gates" held special significance.

Ancient cities erected walls to protect themselves from invaders. Here and there along the walls they inserted massive gates to allow traffic in and out. In times of trouble, they could close the gates against attacking armies or bandits.

City gates, then, tended to be thoroughfares through which communications and commerce passed with frequency. Not surprisingly, bazaars and forums tended to congregate around a city's gates, so that they became an important arena in a town's public life. Goods were traded there and decision-makers gathered to hear news and deliberate on events of the day. Such gates exist to this day in some cities of the world.

Given this phenomenon, "gates" became a metaphor signifying the economic and political life of a walled city. The influential and powerful did their business "in the gates." For example, the husband of the virtuous women of Proverbs 31 is "known in the gates, when he sits among the elders of the land" (Prov. 31:23). Boaz, the intended husband of Ruth, went to the gate to buy a marriage license (Ruth 4:1–12; also Deut. 25:7). War plans were devised and military treaties signed in the gates (Judg. 5:8, 11). Kings sat in the gates to address their people (2 Sam. 19:8). Even conspirators against kings hatched their plots and were exposed in the gates (Esth. 2:19–23).

So when Jesus spoke of the gates of Hades, He was drawing on a powerful image. Matthew's original readers would have seen it as a political metaphor, the way we use the terms *City Hall, the White House,* or *the Capitol* today. For them, the gates of Hades were not just a spiritual abstraction but actual forces of evil at work among human systems—the Roman government, for instance. While not evil in and of itself, first-century government was quickly becoming corrupted and also anti-Christian.

Jesus was alluding to a spiritual warfare of cosmic proportions. His followers are pitted against the powers of hell itself, which not only attack individual believers but seek to corrupt institutions, enlisting them in their campaign against Christ. Satan's guises can take many forms, as a look at any day's news will attest. (See "Spiritual Realities Beyond You," Matt. 8:29.)

Fortunately, Jesus also promised that in the end the gates of Hades would not succeed. That offers great hope to believers who live in difficult places and contend for good against powerful entities that, in ways known and unknown, are backed by spiritual forces of wickedness. In the midst of the fight Jesus has declared: "I will build My church!" ◆

the sun, and His clothes became as white as the light. 3And
behold, Moses and Elijah appeared to them, talking with
Him. 4Then Peter answered and said to Jesus, “Lord, it is
good for us to be here; if You wish, let us[a] make here three
tabernacles: one for You, one for Moses, and one for Elijah.”

17:5 see pg. 76

5While he was still speaking, behold, a
bright cloud overshadowed them; and
suddenly a voice came out of the cloud, saying, “This is My
beloved Son, in whom I am well pleased. Hear Him!” 6And
when the disciples heard *it,* they fell on their faces and were
greatly afraid. 7But Jesus came and touched them and said,
“Arise, and do not be afraid.” 8When they had lifted up
their eyes, they saw no one but Jesus only.

9Now as they came down from the mountain, Jesus commanded them, saying, “Tell the vision to no one until the
Son of Man is risen from the dead.”

10And His disciples asked Him, saying, “Why then do the
scribes say that Elijah must come first?”

11Jesus answered and said to them, “Indeed, Elijah is
coming first[a] and will restore all things. 12But I say to you
that Elijah has come already, and they did not know him
but did to him whatever they wished. Likewise the Son of
Man is also about to suffer at their hands.” 13Then the disciples understood that He spoke to them of John the Baptist.

17:4 [a]NU-Text reads *I will.* *17:11* [a]NU-Text omits *first.*

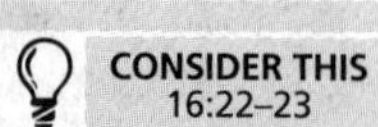

Living Within Your Limits

Are you impulsive? Are you quick to step forward with a plan of action? As the exchange between Peter and the Lord in vv. 22–23 shows there were times when Peter liked to take charge quickly and set the agenda for himself and others. But just as often he found himself in over his head:

- *When Jesus came walking on water to a storm-tossed boat that held His terrified disciples, Peter demanded that He show that it was He by bidding Peter also to walk on water. After a few steps, Peter noticed the wind and the waves and promptly sank, requiring Jesus to rescue him again (Matt. 14:22–32).*
- *He overstated his commitment to Christ, claiming that "even if I have to die with You, I will not deny You!" (26:35). Yet only a few hours later he denied having any association with the Lord (26:69–75).*
- *He took charge of defending Jesus against Roman soldiers when they came to arrest Him—even though he*

Jesus Heals an Epileptic Boy

14And when they had come to the multitude, a man came
to Him, kneeling down to Him and saying, 15"Lord, have
mercy on my son, for he is an epileptic[a] and suffers severely; for he often falls into the fire and often into the water. 16So I brought him to Your disciples, but they could not
cure him."

17Then Jesus answered and said, "O faithless and perverse
generation, how long shall I be with you? How long shall I
bear with you? Bring him here to Me." 18And Jesus rebuked
the demon, and it came out of him; and the child was cured
from that very hour.

19Then the disciples came to Jesus privately and said,
"Why could we not cast it out?"

20So Jesus said to them, "Because of your unbelief;[a] for assuredly, I say to you, if you have faith as a mustard seed,
you will say to this mountain, 'Move from here to there,'
and it will move; and nothing will be impossible for you.
21However, this kind does not go out except by prayer and
fasting."[a]

Jesus Predicts His Betrayal

22Now while they were staying[a] in Galilee, Jesus said to
them, "The Son of Man is about to be betrayed into the

(Bible text continued on page 77)

17:15 [a]Literally *moonstruck* *17:20* [a]NU-Text reads *little faith.* *17:21* [a]NU-Text omits this verse. *17:22* [a]NU-Text reads *gathering together.*

had failed to "watch and pray" with Christ as had been requested (26:36–46; John 18:1–11).

- *He refused to allow Jesus to wash his feet at the Last Supper, then called on Him to wash his hands and his head as well (John 13:5–11).*

Eventually Peter's leadership skills were captured in a more controlled spirit and he became a significant figure in the early church. Despite many false starts as a result of Peter's impetuous nature, Jesus enlisted this impulsive but loyal follower to "feed My sheep" (John 21:17).

Have your personality and skills become more mature and thoughtful? Or are you still in the raw stage, ready to jump at the first idea that occurs to you? ◆

Peter was not the only man who made an unlikely candidate for Jesus' "leadership training program." See "Would You Choose These for Leaders?" Matt. 26:35–74.

"O FAITHLESS AND PERVERSE GENERATION, HOW LONG SHALL I BE WITH YOU?"
—Matthew 17:17

FOR YOUR INFO
17:5

THE NAMES OF JESUS

The voice that the disciples heard during the Transfiguration said that Jesus was "My beloved Son" (v. 5). This term indicates a unique relationship that Jesus has with God the Father. Elsewhere Scripture calls Jesus by other names and titles to indicate other aspects of His nature, character, and roles:

Name or Title	Description
Adam (1 Cor. 15:45)	The first Adam brought death through sin; Jesus, "the last Adam," brought life through His righteousness.
The Alpha and the Omega (Rev. 21:6)	Jesus is eternal, "the Beginning and the End." Alpha is the first letter in the Greek alphabet, omega is the last.
Apostle (Heb. 3:1)	"Messenger." Jesus came to bring the good news of salvation to humanity.
The bread of life (John 6:35, 48)	Jesus is the heavenly manna, the spiritual food, given by the Father to those who ask for it.
The chief cornerstone (Eph. 2:20)	Jesus is the foundation of the church.
The Chief Shepherd (1 Pet. 5:4)	The title that Peter called Jesus, indicating His oversight of His "flock," the church.
The Christ (Matt. 1:1, 17; 16:16; Luke 2:11; John 1:40)	From the Greek word *Christos*, "Messiah" or "Anointed One." Jesus fulfills the Old Testament promise of a Messiah.
The Consolation of Israel (Luke 2:25)	Jesus came to bring comfort to the nation (Is. 40:1–2).
The firstborn from the dead (Col. 1:18)	Jesus overcame death in order to give life to believers.
The firstborn over all creation (Col. 1:15)	As God's Son, Jesus rules over everything that exists.
The good shepherd (John 10:11, 14; compare Heb. 13:20)	An image that Jesus used to describe His relationship to His people.
The head of the body, the church (Eph. 1:22–23; 4:15–16; Col. 1:18)	Jesus is the leader of His people and the source of their life.
High Priest (Heb. 3:1)	Like the Old Testament high priest, Jesus stands between God and people to offer an acceptable sacrifice for sin.
The Holy One of God (Mark 1:24; John 6:69)	Jesus is the sinless Messiah promised by God.
I AM (John 8:58)	A name by which God made Himself known to Moses (Ex. 3:14), related to the verb "to be."
The image of the invisible God (Col. 1:15)	Jesus expresses God in bodily form.
Immanuel (Matt. 1:23)	"God with us" (Is. 7:14).
Jesus (Matt. 1:21; Luke 1:30; Acts 9:5)	The name that God instructed Joseph and Mary to call their Son.
King of Kings and Lord of Lords (Rev. 19:16)	The formal title that Jesus has received, indicating His supremacy as the one to whom "every knee should bow" (Phil. 2:9–11).
King of the Jews (Matt. 2:2; 27:11–12; John 19:19)	As Messiah, Jesus is Israel's king, fulfilling God's promises to David (2 Sam. 7:12–16).
The Lamb of God (John 1:29, 35)	Jesus became the atoning sacrifice for sin.
The light of the world (John 9:5)	Jesus brings truth and hope to light in the midst of spiritual darkness.
Lord (Luke 2:11; 1 Cor. 2:8; Phil. 2:11)	A title indicating ultimate sovereignty.
Mediator between God and men (1 Tim. 2:5)	Jesus reestablishes the relationship between God and people.

Continued

hands of men, [23]and they will kill Him, and the third day
He will be raised up." And they were exceedingly sorrowful.

Jesus and Taxation

17:24–27
see pg. 78

[24]When they had come to Capernaum,[a]
those who received the *temple* tax came
to Peter and said, "Does your Teacher not pay the *temple*
tax?"
[25]He said, "Yes."
And when he had come into the house, Jesus anticipated
him, saying, "What do you think, Simon? From whom do
the kings of the earth take customs or taxes, from their sons
or from strangers?"
[26]Peter said to Him, "From strangers."
Jesus said to him, "Then the sons are free. [27]Nevertheless,
lest we offend them, go to the sea, cast in a hook, and take
the fish that comes up first. And when you have opened its
mouth, you will find a piece of money;[a] take that and give it
to them for Me and you."

CHAPTER 18

"Who Is Greatest in the Kingdom?"

[1]At that time the disciples came to Jesus, saying, "Who
then is greatest in the kingdom of heaven?"
[2]Then Jesus called a little child to Him, set him in the

17:24 [a]NU-Text reads *Capharnaum* (here and elsewhere). *17:27* [a]Greek *stater,* the exact amount to pay the temple tax (didrachma) for two

Continued

Name or Title	Description
The only Begotten of the Father (John 1:14)	Jesus is God's only Son.
The Prophet (Mark 6:15; John 7:40; Acts 3:22)	Jesus is the leader that God promised to "raise up" like Moses (Deut. 18:15, 18–19).
Rabbi (John 1:38; 3:2)	Friends and enemies alike recognized Jesus as Teacher.
Savior (Luke 1:47; 2:11)	Jesus came to save people from their sins.
Seed (of Abraham; Gal. 3:16)	God made promises to Abraham and his "Seed," whom Paul identified as Christ (Gen. 13:15; 17:8).
The Son of Abraham (Matt. 1:1)	Jesus descended from Abraham and fulfills the promises of God to Abraham (Gen. 22:18).
The Son of David (Matt. 1:1)	Jesus descended from David and fulfills the promises of God to David (2 Sam. 7:12–16).
The Son of God (John 1:24; 9:35–37)	Jesus is one of three Persons of the Trinity (Father, Son, and Holy Spirit).
The Son of Man (Matt. 18:11; John 1:51)	Though fully God, Jesus took on a human body (compare Phil. 2:5–8).
The Word (John 1:1; Rev. 19:13)	Jesus is fully God and therefore is the full expression of God.

midst of them, 3and said, "Assuredly, I say to you, unless
you are converted and become as little children, you will by
no means enter the kingdom of heaven. 4Therefore whoever
humbles himself as this little child is the greatest in the
kingdom of heaven. 5Whoever receives one little child like
this in My name receives Me.

6"But whoever causes one of these little ones who believe
in Me to sin, it would be better for him if a millstone were
hung around his neck, and he were drowned in the depth
of the sea. 7Woe to the world because of offenses! For offenses must come, but woe to that man by whom the offense comes!

18:8–9

8"If your hand or foot causes you to sin,
cut it off and cast *it* from you. It is better
for you to enter into life lame or maimed, rather than having two hands or two feet, to be cast into the everlasting

Jesus and Taxation

The odd episode in vv. 24–27 turns out to be a subtle and winsome reminder that Jesus claimed to be God. It's also a lesson in the proper exercise of moral liberty.

The temple tax of half a shekel was assessed annually on all Jews 20 years old and above. It paid for the support of the temple system (Ex. 30:13–15). Apparently Jesus and Peter had not yet paid their taxes, though Peter's response to the tax collectors indicated that they soon would (Matt. 17:24–25).

The irony, however, is that the temple tax collectors were demanding taxes from the Messiah Himself! How ludicrous—as Jesus pointed out in His question to Peter about who is taxed by a ruler (v. 25). As God's Son, Jesus was the Lord of the temple; technically, He was exempt from taxation.

God put His stamp of approval on Jesus' reasoning with the miracle of the coin (v. 27). Peter found "a piece of

fire. [9]And if your eye causes you to sin, pluck it out and cast
it from you. It is better for you to enter into life with one
eye, rather than having two eyes, to be cast into hell fire.
[10]"Take heed that you do not despise one of these little
ones, for I say to you that in heaven their angels always see
the face of My Father who is in heaven. [11]For the Son of
Man has come to save that which was lost.[a]
[12]"What do you think? If a man has a hundred sheep, and
one of them goes astray, does he not leave the ninety-nine
and go to the mountains to seek the one that is straying?
[13]And if he should find it, assuredly, I say to you, he rejoices
more over that *sheep* than over the ninety-nine that did not
go astray. [14]Even so it is not the will of your Father who is
in heaven that one of these little ones should perish.
[15]"Moreover if your brother sins against you, go and tell

18:11 [a]NU-Text omits this verse.

money" (a stater, a four-drachma coin) in the fish's mouth—the exact amount needed for the two of them. The collectors were satisfied, and the transaction cost Peter and Jesus nothing.

But consider: Jesus voluntarily paid the tax to avoid offending the religious leaders that the collectors represented (v. 27). In doing so, He demonstrated something about how His followers should live.

We as Christians are properly free in many areas because of our relationship with God. We are not bound by legalistic rules about eating, drinking, or special observances. Nonetheless, we must be careful not to use our liberty in a manner that offends other people. If the Son of God paid a voluntary tax in order to avoid offending those who did not understand who He was, how much more should we, as God's children, bend over backwards at times to avoid offending those who do not understand our liberty? ◆

Scripture offers help for believers in handling the "gray" areas of life in which God has prescribed no specific behavior. See "Matters of Conscience," Rom. 14:1–23; and "Gray Areas," 1 Cor. 8:1–13.

There were so many taxes during Jesus' time that the Jews were probably paying between 30 and 40 percent of their income on taxes and religious dues. See "Taxes," Mark 12:14.

Exaggerating to Make a Point

CONSIDER THIS 18:8–9 **Was Jesus speaking literally when He told His followers to cut off their hand or foot if it caused them to sin (v. 8)? Did He intend for them actually to rip out their eye if it caused them to sin (v. 9)? No, Jesus was using a customary teaching method called *hyperbole*—exaggerating to make a point. He frequently spoke in that manner, perhaps to hold His listeners' attention, to touch their imagination, or to show a bit of humor.**

After all, it's a bit silly to imagine what would happen if people actually followed these instructions literally. It's hard to sin without using a hand, a foot, or an eye, so it wouldn't be long before we all would be paralyzed and blind. Without our faculties, we simply couldn't function. And that's precisely Jesus' point. Sin makes it difficult if not impossible to function spiritually in the way God created us. Moreover, sin can do what no amputation can—keep us from God. That's why, to catch Jesus' serious point, it *would* be better to do without an arm or a leg than to live forever apart from God.

Seventy Times Seven—Still Not Enough!

CONSIDER THIS 18:21–35 **If Peter gasped when Jesus told him to forgive his brother up to seventy times seven times (v. 22), he must have gagged when he heard the parable that followed.**

The first servant owed 10,000 talents to the king (v. 24). The second servant owed 100 denarii to the first servant (v. 28). This was an extraordinary difference in indebtedness. A talent was a lot of money, perhaps $1,000 in today's currency. But in that culture, it probably represented far more. A talent equalled 6,000 denarii, and one denarius was what a common laborer could earn in one day, about 16¢ to 18¢.

So the first servant owed at least $10 million, but from the standpoint of common wages, *he would have had to work 60 million days to pay off his debt!* By contrast, the second servant owed $16 to $18, which he could earn in 100 days. In other words, the first servant owed the king more than the second servant owed the first servant by a ratio of at least 600,000-to-1!

Somehow, after Jesus finished that parable, seventy times seven probably didn't look so bad to Peter!

The power of forgiveness is immeasurable. It is a power that Jesus used often and even delegated to His followers. See "The Power of Forgiveness," Matt. 9:4–8.

The talent was one of several units of money in the ancient world. See the table, "Money in the New Testament," Rev. 16:21.

him his fault between you and him alone. If he hears you, you have gained your brother. 16But if he will not hear, take with you one or two more, that 'by the mouth of two or three witnesses every word may be established.'[a] 17And if he refuses to hear them, tell *it* to the church. But if he refuses even to hear the church, let him be to you like a heathen and a tax collector.

18"Assuredly, I say to you, whatever you bind on earth will be bound in heaven, and whatever you loose on earth will be loosed in heaven.

19"Again I say[a] to you that if two of you agree on earth concerning anything that they ask, it will be done for them by My Father in heaven. 20For where two or three are gathered together in My name, I am there in the midst of them."

About Forgiveness

18:21–35 21Then Peter came to Him and said, "Lord, how often shall my brother sin against me, and I forgive him? Up to seven times?"

22Jesus said to him, "I do not say to you, up to seven times, but up to seventy times seven. 23Therefore the kingdom of heaven is like a certain king who wanted to settle accounts with his servants. 24And when he had begun to settle accounts, one was brought to him who owed him ten thousand talents. 25But as he was not able to pay, his master commanded that he be sold, with his wife and children and all that he had, and that payment be made. 26The servant therefore fell down before him, saying, 'Master, have patience with me, and I will pay you all.' 27Then the master of that servant was moved with compassion, released him, and forgave him the debt.

28"But that servant went out and found one of his fellow servants who owed him a hundred denarii; and he laid hands on him and took *him* by the throat, saying, 'Pay me what you owe!' 29So his fellow servant fell down at his feet[a] and begged him, saying, 'Have patience with me, and I will pay you all.'[b] 30And he would not, but went and threw him into prison till he should pay the debt. 31So when his fellow servants saw what had been done, they were very grieved, and came and told their master all that had been done. 32Then his master, after he had called him, said to him, 'You wicked servant! I forgave you all that debt because you begged me. 33Should you not also have had compassion on your fellow servant, just as I had pity on you?' 34And his master was angry, and delivered him to the torturers until he should pay all that was due to him.

35"So My heavenly Father also will do to you if each of

18:16 [a]Deuteronomy 19:15 *18:19* [a]NU-Text and M-Text read *Again, assuredly, I say.* *18:29* [a]NU-Text omits *at his feet.* [b]NU-Text and M-Text omit *all.*

you, from his heart, does not forgive his brother his trespasses."[a]

CHAPTER 19

Marriage and Divorce

19:1–15
see pg. 82

1Now it came to pass, when Jesus had
finished these sayings, *that* He departed
from Galilee and came to the region of Judea beyond the
Jordan. 2And great multitudes followed Him, and He healed
them there.

3The Pharisees also came to Him, testing Him, and saying
to Him, "Is it lawful for a man to divorce his wife for *just*
any reason?"

4And He answered and said to them, "Have you not read
that He who made[a] *them* at the beginning 'made them male
and female,'[b] 5and said, 'For this reason a man shall leave
his father and mother and be joined to his wife, and the two
shall become one flesh' ?[a] 6So then, they are no longer two
but one flesh. Therefore what God has joined together, let
not man separate."

7They said to Him, "Why then did Moses command to
give a certificate of divorce, and to put her away?"

8He said to them, "Moses, because of the hardness of your
hearts, permitted you to divorce your wives, but from the
beginning it was not so. 9And I say to you, whoever divorces his wife, except for sexual immorality,[a] and marries
another, commits adultery; and whoever marries her who is
divorced commits adultery."

10His disciples said to Him, "If such is the case of the man
with *his* wife, it is better not to marry."

11But He said to them, "All cannot accept this saying, but
only *those* to whom it has been given: 12For there are eunuchs who were born thus from *their* mother's womb, and
there are eunuchs who were made eunuchs by men, and
there are eunuchs who have made themselves eunuchs for
the kingdom of heaven's sake. He who is able to accept *it*,
let him accept *it*."

Jesus Blesses Children

19:13–15

13Then little children were brought to
Him that He might put *His* hands on

(Bible text continued on page 84)

18:35 [a]NU-Text omits *his trespasses.* *19:4* [a]NU-Text reads *created.* [b]Genesis 1:27; 5:2
19:5 [a]Genesis 2:24 *19:9* [a]Or *fornication*

"WHAT GOD HAS JOINED TOGETHER, LET NOT MAN SEPARATE."
—Matthew 19:6

Please Bless Our Children

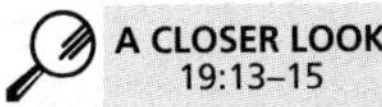
A CLOSER LOOK
19:13–15

In Jesus' day it was customary to ask famous rabbis to bless one's children. See "The Friend of Children" at Mark 10:13–16.

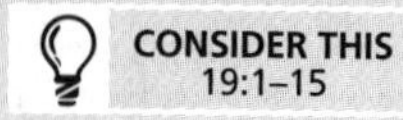

The Challenge of Commitment

Commitment is in jeopardy these days. Some even call it the "C" word, as if to shame it as something we won't even acknowledge. After all, the demands and costs are too great. Today, convenience usually wins out over the sacrifice involved in being committed to someone or something.

The situation was no less confused in Jesus' day. As He began to unveil a new way of life for His followers, critics appeared and challenged Him on the difficulties of keeping the marriage commitment (vv. 3, 7). Even His disciples quivered as they perceived the costs of maintaining one's marriage vows (v. 10). Later, they wanted to send away some bothersome children in order to deal with more "important" things (v. 13). It seems that Jesus was surrounded by men who were a little unsure about domestic matters.

The discussion of divorce followed appropriately on the heels of Jesus' remarks about the merits of boundless forgiveness (18:21–35). What better way to lead into the topic of commitment? Jesus didn't ignore the problems and failures of human relationships. Those very shortcomings are what make forgiveness—and commitment—crucial.

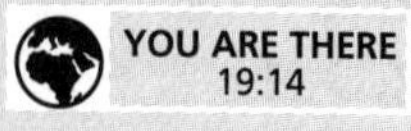

Children and Childcare

When Jesus welcomed the little children (v. 14), He was making a major statement to everyone standing by about the value and significance of children.

Perhaps the disciples, who rebuked the mothers who brought their babies to Jesus (v. 13), had adopted the prevailing Graeco-Roman view of childhood as an insignificant phase of life. To be sure, children were necessary for a family's survival, but they were not valued for their own sake.

Indeed, unwanted infants in pagan cultures were routinely abandoned on roadsides and at garbage dumps. Tragically, gender and economics often determined an infant's fate: more girls than boys were exposed since girls represented a future financial burden while boys could eventually contribute to the family's income.

Most exposed infants died but a few were rescued and raised to become slaves, gladiators, or prostitutes. Children were held in such low esteem in Jesus' time that some professional beggars collected exposed children, mutilated them, and then used their misery to gain sympathy and thus increase profits from their begging.

However, among the Jews children were traditionally

Those lessons were reinforced in Jesus' next encounter, with a rich man who wanted to ensure his possession of eternal life (19:16–30). The man proposed rule-keeping as the standard by which he should be judged, but Jesus countered with an appeal for service (v. 21). True wealth involved a higher commitment—serving the Lord and others rather than the idol of material gain (vv. 23, 29).

Followers of Christ need to be known for their commitment—to marriage, to family, to community, to work, above all to Christ. Such loyalty often means messy obedience, but it is the way of Christ. How desperately that is needed in a day when people make vows of convenience rather than commitment. ◆

Commitment makes all the difference when it comes to family relationships. See "Family: A Call to Long-term Work," Eph. 5:21—6:4.

Commitment is one of the hallmarks of a godly "workstyle." See Titus 2:9–10.

Peter echoed Jesus' words on marital faithfulness in his instructions to husbands, 1 Pet. 2:11–17.

considered a blessing from God, and childlessness a curse. In fact, children were so desired that barrenness was grounds for divorce.

Jewish fathers had ultimate authority over all aspects of their children's lives, but both fathers and mothers were instructed by the Law to nurture and care for their children. Fathers were particularly obligated to teach their children God's commands and to raise them as members of God's chosen people (Deut. 6:6–8). In return, children were obliged to honor both mother and father (5:16).

Mothers usually took care of infants who typically nursed until the age of two or three. In some wealthy Greek and Roman homes, women employed wet nurses and, as the children grew, slaves who were assigned to their total care. Poor women, however, worked while their babies hung from slings on their backs. But as soon as the children were old enough, they were taught to help.

First-century women did not have to confront the childcare dilemma faced by many women today. Their work and their homes were tightly linked, so they did not have to surmount the challenges of specialization and separation. ◆

"LET THE LITTLE CHILDREN COME TO ME. . . ."
—Matthew 19:14

19:14
see pg. 82

them and pray, but the disciples rebuked them. 14But Jesus said, "Let the little children come to Me, and do not forbid them; for of such is the kingdom of heaven." 15And He laid *His* hands on them and departed from there.

A Rich Young Man's Question

19:16–26

16Now behold, one came and said to Him, "Good[a] Teacher, what good thing shall I do that I may have eternal life?"

17So He said to him, "Why do you call Me good?[a] No one *is* good but One, *that is,* God.[b] But if you want to enter into life, keep the commandments."

18He said to Him, "Which ones?"

Jesus said, "'You shall not murder,' 'You shall not commit adultery,' 'You shall not steal,' 'You shall not bear false witness,' 19'Honor your father and *your* mother,'[a] and, 'You shall love your neighbor as yourself.' "[b]

20The young man said to Him, "All these things I have kept from my youth.[a] What do I still lack?"

21Jesus said to him, "If you want to be perfect, go, sell what you have and give to the poor, and you will have treasure in heaven; and come, follow Me."

22But when the young man heard that saying, he went away sorrowful, for he had great possessions.

23Then Jesus said to His disciples, "Assuredly, I say to you that it is hard for a rich man to enter the kingdom of heaven. 24And again I say to you, it is easier for a camel to go through the eye of a needle than for a rich man to enter the kingdom of God."

25When His disciples heard *it,* they were greatly astonished, saying, "Who then can be saved?"

26But Jesus looked at *them* and said to them, "With men this is impossible, but with God all things are possible."

"IT IS EASIER FOR A CAMEL TO GO THROUGH THE EYE OF A NEEDLE THAN FOR A RICH MAN TO ENTER THE KINGDOM OF GOD."
—Matthew 19:24

Rewards for the Twelve

27Then Peter answered and said to Him, "See, we have left all and followed You. Therefore what shall we have?"

19:16 [a]NU-Text omits *Good.* *19:17* [a]NU-Text reads *Why do you ask Me about what is good?* [b]NU-Text reads *There is One who is good.* *19:19* [a]Exodus 20:12–16; Deuteronomy 5:16–20 [b]Leviticus 19:18 *19:20* [a]NU-Text omits *from my youth.*

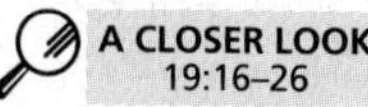

A CLOSER LOOK 19:16–26

"What Do I Still Lack?"

The rich young ruler asked the classic question of many who appear to have it all: "What do I still lack?" (v. 20). "The Man Who Had It All—Almost" (Mark 10:17–27) discusses the Lord's mysterious response and challenging perspective on wealth. In a similar situation (Luke 10:25–37), Jesus urged people to put feet on their good intentions.

28So Jesus said to them, "Assuredly I say to you, that in
the regeneration, when the Son of Man sits on the throne of
His glory, you who have followed Me will also sit on twelve
19:29
thrones, judging the twelve tribes of Israel. 29And everyone who has left houses
or brothers or sisters or father or mother or wife[a] or children or lands, for My name's sake, shall receive a hundredfold, and inherit eternal life. 30But many *who are* first will be
last, and the last first.

CHAPTER 20

A Parable about Wages

20:1–16 see pg. 86

1"For the kingdom of heaven is like a
landowner who went out early in the
morning to hire laborers for his vineyard. 2Now when he
had agreed with the laborers for a denarius a day, he sent
them into his vineyard. 3And he went out about the third
hour and saw others standing idle in the marketplace, 4and
said to them, 'You also go into the vineyard, and whatever is
right I will give you.' So they went. 5Again he went out
about the sixth and the ninth hour, and did likewise. 6And
about the eleventh hour he went out and found others
standing idle,[a] and said to them, 'Why have you been
standing here idle all day?' 7They said to him, 'Because no
one hired us.' He said to them, 'You also go into the vineyard, and whatever is right you will receive.'[a]
8"So when evening had come, the owner of the vineyard
said to his steward, 'Call the laborers and give them *their*
wages, beginning with the last to the first.' 9And when those
came who *were hired* about the eleventh hour, they each received a denarius. 10But when the first came, they supposed
that they would receive more; and they likewise received
each a denarius. 11And when they had received *it*, they
complained against the landowner, 12saying, 'These last *men*
have worked *only* one hour, and you made them equal to us
who have borne the burden and the heat of the day.' 13But
he answered one of them and said, 'Friend, I am doing you
no wrong. Did you not agree with me for a denarius? 14Take
what is yours and go your way. I wish to give to this last
man *the same* as to you. 15Is it not lawful for me to do what

19:29 [a]NU-Text omits *or wife*. *20:6* [a]NU-Text omits *idle*. *20:7* [a]NU-Text omits the last clause of this verse.

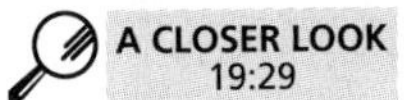

A CLOSER LOOK 19:29

An Eternal Inheritance

To have Christ is to have everything (v. 29). "What's in It for Me?" (Eph. 1:11) describes the inheritance we will enjoy as God's children.

A Pushy Mother

CONSIDER THIS 20:20–23

Overzealous mothers are not exclusive to the twentieth century, as the incident in vv. 20–23 makes clear. The woman's name remains unknown; she is remembered only as the mother of Zebedee's sons (James and John). Perhaps she was so caught up in managing her sons' lives that she had no other life, and therefore required no other designation than "mother." Naturally, she would have claimed that she only wanted what was best for her sons.

But when Jesus found out what she was seeking, He gave her and her sons a warning. He knew that suffering had to come before glory. Could James and John endure that suffering? The two men were quick to promise that they would. (Perhaps their mother prompted them to say so by giving them a stern look.) Jesus assured them that they would have the chance to back up their words.

Perhaps later James and John regretted making such bold promises. But how often are we like them—eager to promise whatever we have to in order to get what we want? Perhaps worse, how often do we push our children into things based on our own needs for pride and significance?

I wish with my own things? Or is your eye evil because I am good?' [16]So the last will be first, and the first last. For many are called, but few chosen."[a]

Jesus Predicts His Death

[17]Now Jesus, going up to Jerusalem, took the twelve disciples aside on the road and said to them, [18]"Behold, we are going up to Jerusalem, and the Son of Man will be betrayed to the chief priests and to the scribes; and they will condemn Him to death, [19]and deliver Him to the Gentiles to mock and to scourge and to crucify. And the third day He will rise again."

20:16 [a]NU-Text omits the last sentence of this verse.

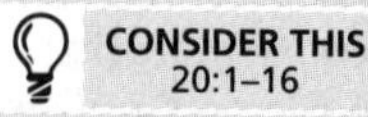

Jesus and Unjust Pay

Anyone who feels that they are not paid what they are worth can appreciate the reaction of the workers in the parable Jesus told (vv. 1–16). He spoke of an employer who hired workers for a full day, others for two-thirds of a day, others for half a day, and others for even less. Yet he paid them all the same (v. 9–11)! Naturally those who had worked longer demanded, "What's going on here?" (vv. 11–12). Good question!

The first thing to notice is that none of the workers was employed before the landowner hired them (vv. 3, 6, 7). The fact that they got a job was due to the employer's goodwill, not to anything they brought to the situation. Furthermore, the landowner promised the first group fair wages of a day's pay (a denarius, *v. 2; see "Money in the New Testament," Rev. 16:21) and the rest an undetermined amount ("whatever is right"). As it turned out, he paid everyone an entire day's wage.*

Jesus was trying to help His followers grasp something important about grace in the kingdom of God. They had been asking about the kingdom's makeup and benefits earlier (Matt. 19:16, 25, 27). Jesus was not encouraging unjust pay scales and discrimination. He was merely illustrating the nature of God's grace in terms that His followers could understand.

In the kingdom of God, grace is given because of the nature of the Giver, not the worthiness of the recipient. Receiving God's grace is a privilege for sinners—who, after all, really deserve nothing but condemnation. ◆

A Mother's Big Request

20:20–23 see pg. 85

[20]Then the mother of Zebedee's sons
came to Him with her sons, kneeling
down and asking something from Him.
[21]And He said to her, "What do you wish?"
She said to Him, "Grant that these two sons of mine may
sit, one on Your right hand and the other on the left, in
Your kingdom."
[22]But Jesus answered and said, "You do not know what
you ask. Are you able to drink the cup that I am about to
drink, and be baptized with the baptism that I am baptized
with?"[a]
They said to Him, "We are able."
[23]So He said to them, "You will indeed drink My cup, and
be baptized with the baptism that I am baptized with;[a] but
to sit on My right hand and on My left is not Mine to give,
but *it is for those* for whom it is prepared by My Father."
[24]And when the ten heard *it,* they were greatly displeased

20:25–28

with the two brothers. [25]But Jesus called
them to *Himself* and said, "You know that
the rulers of the Gentiles lord it over them, and those who
are great exercise authority over them. [26]Yet it shall not be
so among you; but whoever desires to become great among
you, let him be your servant. [27]And whoever desires to be

20:28 see pg. 88

first among you, let him be your slave—
[28]just as the Son of Man did not come to
be served, but to serve, and to give His life a ransom for
many."

Two Blind Men Healed at Jericho

20:29

[29]Now as they went out of Jericho, a
great multitude followed Him. [30]And be-
hold, two blind men sitting by the road, when they heard
that Jesus was passing by, cried out, saying, "Have mercy on
us, O Lord, Son of David!"
[31]Then the multitude warned them that they should be
quiet; but they cried out all the more, saying, "Have mercy
on us, O Lord, Son of David!"
[32]So Jesus stood still and called them, and said, "What do
you want Me to do for you?"

20:22 [a]NU-Text omits *and be baptized with the baptism that I am baptized with.*
20:23 [a]NU-Text omits *and be baptized with the baptism that I am baptized with.*

Servant-Leaders

CONSIDER THIS 20:25–28 **Responding to a controversy among the disciples (vv. 25–28), Jesus revealed a unique style of authority—servant leadership. What does it mean to be a "slave" in order to become great (v. 27)? What does it mean to define leadership in terms of servanthood? Jesus suggested that both involve seeking the highest good for others—good as evaluated from God's perspective.**

In light of Jesus' own example—particularly in giving up His own life as a "ransom for many" (v. 28)—we can observe that servant leadership means:

- **seeing ourselves as called by God to serve/lead others.**
- **knowing intimately the people we serve/lead.**
- **caring deeply about the people we serve/lead.**
- **being willing to sacrifice our own convenience to meet the needs of the people we serve/lead.**

The Dangerous Road to Jericho

A CLOSER LOOK 20:29

Jericho was notorious for the beggars and thieves who camped nearby, plundering travelers along the narrow, winding mountain road up to Jerusalem. See Luke 10:30.

QUOTE UNQUOTE

CONSIDER THIS 20:28 *Just as Jesus came to serve, He calls His followers to a life of service:*

That Christianity should be equated in the public mind, inside as well as outside the Church, with "organized religion" merely shows how far we have departed from the New Testament. For the last thing the Church exists to be is an organization for the religious. Its charter is to be the servant of the world.

John A.T. Robinson, *Honest To God*

Jesus used a powerful image when He compared true leadership to slavery. See "Slaves," Rom. 6:16.

33They said to Him, "Lord, that our eyes may be opened."
34So Jesus had compassion and touched their eyes. And immediately their eyes received sight, and they followed Him.

CHAPTER 21

Jesus Enters Jerusalem

21:1 1Now when they drew near Jerusalem,
and came to Bethphage,[a] at the Mount of
Olives, then Jesus sent two disciples, 2saying to them, "Go
into the village opposite you, and immediately you will find
a donkey tied, and a colt with her. Loose *them* and bring
them to Me. 3And if anyone says anything to you, you shall
say, 'The Lord has need of them,' and immediately he will
send them."
4All[a] this was done that it might be fulfilled which was
spoken by the prophet, saying:

5 "Tell the daughter of Zion,
'Behold, your King is coming to you,
Lowly, and sitting on a donkey,
A colt, the foal of a donkey.' "[a]

6So the disciples went and did as Jesus commanded them.
7They brought the donkey and the colt, laid their clothes on

21:1 [a]M-Text reads *Bethsphage.* *21:4* [a]NU-Text omits *All.* *21:5* [a]Zechariah 9:9

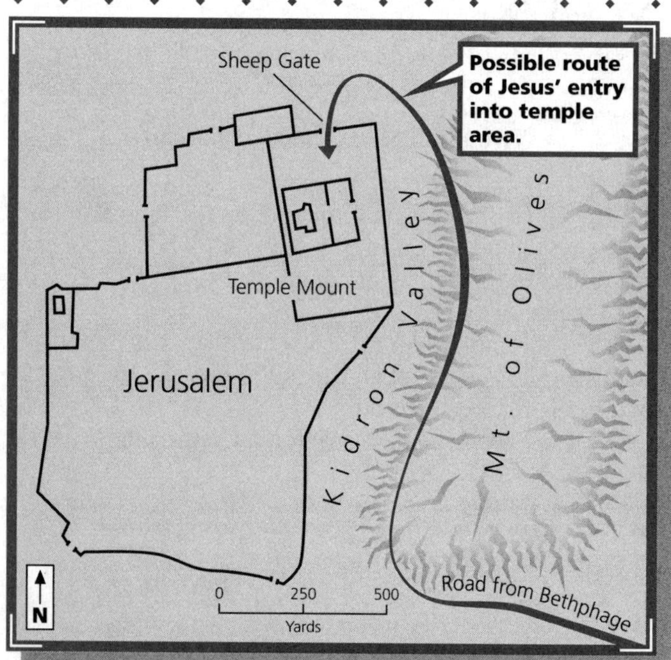

YOU ARE THERE 21:1 **JESUS' ENTRY**

21:8–11
see pg. 90

them, and set Him[a] on them. 8And a very
great multitude spread their clothes on
the road; others cut down branches from the trees and
spread *them* on the road. 9Then the multitudes who went
before and those who followed cried out, saying:

"Hosanna to the Son of David!
'Blessed *is* He who comes in the name of the Lord!'[a]
Hosanna in the highest!"

10And when He had come into Jerusalem, all the city was
moved, saying, "Who is this?"
11So the multitudes said, "This is Jesus, the prophet from
Nazareth of Galilee."

Jesus Purges the Temple

12Then Jesus went into the temple of God[a] and drove out
all those who bought and sold in the temple, and over-
turned the tables of the money changers and the seats of
those who sold doves. 13And He said to them, "It is written,
'My house shall be called a house of prayer,'[a] but you have
made it a 'den of thieves.' "[b]
14Then *the* blind and *the* lame came to Him in the temple,
and He healed them. 15But when the chief priests and
scribes saw the wonderful things that He did, and the children crying out in the temple and saying, "Hosanna to the
Son of David!" they were indignant 16and said to Him, "Do
You hear what these are saying?"
And Jesus said to them, "Yes. Have you never read,

'Out of the mouth of babes and nursing infants
You have perfected praise'? "[a]

17Then He left them and went out of the city to Bethany,
and He lodged there.

Jesus Curses a Fig Tree

18Now in the morning, as He returned to the city, He was
hungry. 19And seeing a fig tree by the road, He came to it
and found nothing on it but leaves, and said to it, "Let no
fruit grow on you ever again." Immediately the fig tree withered away.
20And when the disciples saw *it,* they marveled, saying,
"How did the fig tree wither away so soon?"
21So Jesus answered and said to them, "Assuredly, I say to
you, if you have faith and do not doubt, you will not only
do what was done to the fig tree, but also if you say to this

(Bible text continued on page 92)

" 'MY HOUSE SHALL BE CALLED A HOUSE OF PRAYER,' BUT YOU HAVE MADE IT A 'DEN OF THIEVES.' "
—Matthew 21:13

21:7 [a]NU-Text reads *and He sat.* *21:9* [a]Psalm 118:26 *21:12* [a]NU-Text omits *of God.*
21:13 [a]Isaiah 56:7 [b]Jeremiah 7:11 *21:16* [a]Psalm 8:2

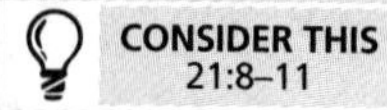

CONSIDER THIS
21:8–11

A New Style of Fame

If you've ever encountered a famous person, you may have felt somewhat intimidated, especially if that person seemed arrogant. People of status and image can easily make us feel inferior, as if we have nothing to offer by comparison. No wonder we long for the traits of compassion and humility in society's leaders.

Jesus became famous among His own people. But as He entered Jerusalem, the capital of Palestine, He modeled a new style for handling acclaim from the crowd. The city was wild with excitement during its peak season of tourists and celebration. What a moment for Jesus to bring His campaign to a climax! He even had the prophecies of Zechariah 9:9 and Isaiah 62:11 to bolster His confidence.

But instead of a parade of chariots and trumpets and a well-orchestrated ceremony, Jesus chose to ride into town on a donkey, a common beast of burden; no prancing warhorse for Him! And instead of walking arm-in-arm with powerful city officials and other celebrities, He was accompanied only by a small band of common fishermen, rural Galileans, and even a former tax collector. For once, the common folks had a parade (Matt. 21:8, 10).

Once arrived at the end of the parade route, Jesus did

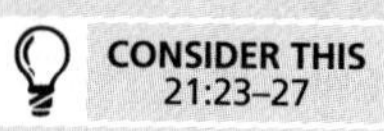

CONSIDER THIS
21:23–27

A Challenge to Authority

Sooner or later, almost all leaders have their authority questioned. Sometimes they are challenged directly, but more often indirectly by rumor and innuendo.

Jesus faced a direct challenge to His authority from the chief priests and elders, the top leadership in Israel (vv. 23–27). In this instance He didn't argue with them, but simply tossed the ball back into their court. He showed that one very effective way of responding to threatening questions is to ask questions in return.

But observe two aspects of the interaction between Jesus and the Jewish leaders:

(1) The motives of the challengers. *The scribes and Pharisees had no interest in an honest understanding of the nature or source of Jesus' authority. They were only concerned with protecting their own interests and power. In light of their behavior, you might ask yourself whether you ever question or resist people in authority over you because you are afraid or jealous of them.*

not go to the halls of the powerful. Instead He marched into the place of worship, a national center for the Jews. There He overthrew the tables of unjust businesses that manipulated the poor and made the temple a place of moneymaking (vv. 12–13). He focused on the blind, the lame, and children (vv. 14–16). And when He completed the day's tasks, He spent the night not in the fashionable home of a city leader but in a humble house in a nearby suburb, Bethany (v. 17).

Jesus' final activities before His death focused on those most ready to hear of His love, forgiveness, and hope—the little people in (or even outside) the system of privilege and power (Luke 4:18).

Do you know people who need to be invited to join the humble King's procession? Are there coworkers, neighbors, or family members who need to receive good news through you? How are you dealing with the temptation to rub shoulders only with the powerful and elite? ◆

Jesus liked to surround Himself with relatively average people of little social standing or influence. See "The Little People at Jesus' Death," Matt. 27:32.

(2) The security of Jesus. *Jesus was neither upset nor caught off guard by His attackers. For one thing, He had endured their criticism before, and no doubt expected it to increase. But He also knew with absolute certainty about the very thing that His challengers were attacking: He knew who He was and whose authority He wielded (28:18). His response is a reminder that intimidation is something we allow to occur. People may threaten and confront us, but only we allow ourselves to feel fear. The real question is, are we certain who we are as followers of the King?* ◆

To understand more about Jesus' sense of identity, see "Being Like Jesus," Matt. 10:25.

" 'Blessed is He who comes in the name of the Lord!' "
—Matthew 21:9

mountain, 'Be removed and be cast into the sea,' it will be
done. [22]And whatever things you ask in prayer, believing,
you will receive."

Pharisees Challenge Jesus' Authority

21:23–27 see pg. 90
[23]Now when He came into the temple,
the chief priests and the elders of the
people confronted Him as He was teaching, and said, "By
what authority are You doing these things? And who gave
You this authority?"

21:24–27
[24]But Jesus answered and said to them,
"I also will ask you one thing, which if
you tell Me, I likewise will tell you by what authority I do
these things: [25]The baptism of John—where was it from?
From heaven or from men?"
And they reasoned among themselves, saying, "If we say,

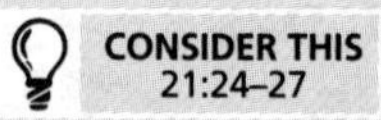
CONSIDER THIS 21:24–27

Is Evasion Ethical?

As you deal with people at work and in your family, you no doubt encounter situations where it might seem better not to reveal the whole truth. What should you do? Is anything less than the actual, complete truth ever ethical or biblical? Can believers practice cunning when Scripture calls us to be honest (for example, Eph. 4:15, 25, 29)?

Christ faced this dilemma when certain leaders challenged His authority (Matt. 21:23). He replied by asking them a question that was almost impossible for them to answer (vv. 24–27). Was He being fair?

Observe the context. Jesus' inquisitors were powerful religious leaders who felt threatened by His assault on their hypocrisies and His impact on the people. He had just challenged one of their sources of revenue by throwing the money changers out of the temple (vv. 12–17). Now they were launching a counterassault by challenging His authority.

Rather than being unethically evasive, Jesus was merely diverting an evil plot in a discrete manner by posing a difficult question. A simple yes or no answer would have played right into their hands. It probably would have touched off a confrontation prematurely. Jesus was more interested in accomplishing His long-range purposes than in exposing these hateful leaders on the spot.

Have you developed the ability to discern the gray areas of conflict and competition? Do you take a long-term view when you face confrontation? ◆

'From heaven,' He will say to us, 'Why then did you not believe him?' 26But if we say, 'From men,' we fear the multitude, for all count John as a prophet." 27So they answered
Jesus and said, "We do not know."

And He said to them, "Neither will I tell you by what authority I do these things.

A Parable about Two Sons

28"But what do you think? A man had two sons, and he
came to the first and said, 'Son, go, work today in my vineyard.' 29He answered and said, 'I will not,' but afterward he
regretted it and went. 30Then he came to the second and
said likewise. And he answered and said, 'I *go,* sir,' but he
did not go. 31Which of the two did the
will of *his* father?"

21:31–32 see pg. 94

They said to Him, "The first."

Jesus said to them, "Assuredly, I say to you that tax collectors and harlots enter the kingdom of God before you.
32For John came to you in the way of righteousness, and
you did not believe him; but tax collectors and harlots believed him; and when you saw *it,* you did not afterward re-
lent and believe him.

A Parable about a Vineyard Owner

33"Hear another parable: There was a certain landowner
who planted a vineyard and set a hedge around it, dug a
winepress in it and built a tower. And he leased it to vinedressers and went into a far country. 34Now when vintage-
time drew near, he sent his servants to the vinedressers, that
they might receive its fruit. 35And the vinedressers took his
servants, beat one, killed one, and stoned another. 36Again
he sent other servants, more than the first, and they did
likewise to them. 37Then last of all he sent his son to them,
saying, 'They will respect my son.' 38But when the vinedressers saw the son, they said among themselves, 'This is
the heir. Come, let us kill him and seize his inheritance.'
39So they took him and cast *him* out of the vineyard and
killed *him.*

40"Therefore, when the owner of the vineyard comes,
what will he do to those vinedressers?"

41They said to Him, "He will destroy those wicked men
miserably, and lease *his* vineyard to other vinedressers who
will render to him the fruits in their seasons."

42Jesus said to them, "Have you never read in the Scriptures:

'The stone which the builders rejected
Has become the chief cornerstone.

" 'THE STONE WHICH THE BUILDERS REJECTED HAS BECOME THE CHIEF CORNERSTONE.' "
—Matthew 21:42

This was the LORD's doing,
And it is marvelous in our eyes' ?[a]

43"Therefore I say to you, the kingdom of God will be
taken from you and given to a nation bearing the fruits of it.
44And whoever falls on this stone will be broken; but on
whomever it falls, it will grind him to powder."
45Now when the chief priests and Pharisees heard His
parables, they perceived that He was speaking of them.
46But when they sought to lay hands on Him, they feared
the multitudes, because they took Him for a prophet.

CHAPTER 22

A Parable about a Rejected Invitation

1And Jesus answered and spoke to them again by parables
22:2–14 and said: 2"The kingdom of heaven is like
a certain king who arranged a marriage
for his son, 3and sent out his servants to call those who
were invited to the wedding; and they were not willing to
come. 4Again, he sent out other servants, saying, 'Tell those

21:42 [a]Psalm 118:22, 23

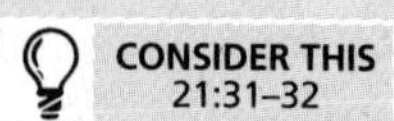

"HARLOTS ENTER THE KINGDOM"

Jesus' startling statement about prostitutes (vv. 31–32) was not an endorsement of that lifestyle but a condemnation of the self-righteousness and especially the unbelief of Israel's religious leaders. Faith was the key to the kingdom; yet even prostitutes were showing more faith in Christ than those who were viewed as "righteous."

Prostitution has been a part of religious rites since at least 3,000 B.C. In Babylon, Syria, Canaan, Arabia, and Phoenicia intercourse with a temple prostitute was believed to induce fertility among humans, animals, and crops. The historian Herodotus tells of a Babylonian custom that required every woman to sit in the temple of the goddess Ishtar until chosen by a stranger for sexual relations. A desirous man would toss a coin in a woman's lap. If she accepted the coin and his sexual advances, she would have paid her obligation to the goddess and be free to return to her normal life.

In Israel, however, ritual prostitution was forbidden (Deut. 23:17). Laws existed to prevent priests from marrying prostitutes (Lev. 21:7), and income from prostitution could not be used to pay vows in the temple (Deut. 23:18).

who are invited, "See, I have prepared my dinner; my oxen
and fatted cattle *are* killed, and all things *are* ready. Come to
the wedding." ' [5]But they made light of it and went their
ways, one to his own farm, another to his business. [6]And
the rest seized his servants, treated *them* spitefully, and
killed *them*. [7]But when the king heard *about it*, he was furi-
ous. And he sent out his armies, destroyed those murderers,
and burned up their city. [8]Then he said to his servants, 'The
wedding is ready, but those who were invited were not worthy. [9]Therefore go into the highways, and as many as you
find, invite to the wedding.' [10]So those servants went out
into the highways and gathered together all whom they
found, both bad and good. And the wedding *hall* was filled
with guests.

[11]"But when the king came in to see the guests, he saw a
man there who did not have on a wedding garment. [12]So he
said to him, 'Friend, how did you come in here without a
wedding garment?' And he was speechless. [13]Then the king
said to the servants, 'Bind him hand and foot, take him
away, and[a] cast *him* into outer darkness; there will be weeping and gnashing of teeth.'

[14]"For many are called, but few *are* chosen."

22:13 [a]NU-Text omits *take him away, and.*

◆ ◆ ◆ ◆ ◆ ◆ ◆ ◆ ◆ ◆ ◆ ◆ ◆ ◆ ◆ ◆

Nevertheless, commercial prostitutes practiced their trade rather freely in Hebrew society. They were easily recognizable by their hairstyle, head ornaments, or perhaps a special mark on their foreheads. Their clothing and jewelry signaled their availability, and like streetwalkers everywhere, they frequented particular locales well known as meeting spots. Payments were accepted in money, grain, wine, or livestock. It was even common to accept a pledge until the payment could be fulfilled.

In Jesus' day, prostitutes endured the particular condemnation of the religious elite, especially the Pharisees, who avoided all outward contact with such people. By contrast, Jesus became known as a friend of sinners who welcomed those in need of forgiveness (Matt. 11:19; Luke 7:36–50). His words on this occasion showed that people don't have to become religiously "proper" before they can believe. God responds to faith no matter how troubled one's personal life may be. What an encouragement to start now to put trust in Jesus and be among the first in the kingdom! ◆

WORSE THAN RUDE

CONSIDER THIS 22:2–14

Jesus' parable of the king's wedding feast for his son (vv. 2–14) turns on an important detail of Jewish marriage custom. Wedding hosts sent out two invitations for a wedding. The first was sent far in advance to let people know that a wedding was being prepared and they were invited. This was necessary because weddings were major events that could last as long as a week. Furthermore, it took time for the replies to come back.

When all the preparations were complete, messengers were sent out with a second invitation telling the guests that the feast was ready and it was time for the celebration to begin. To turn down that second invitation—which was the one the guests in the parable refused (v. 3)—was not merely bad manners. It was considered a rejection of the host family's hospitality and a complete insult to their dignity.

God had sent Israel an early "invitation" to His Son's wedding through the Old Testament Law and prophets. Now that Jesus had arrived, proclaiming the second invitation, the nation was rejecting Him—a perilous choice.

Trick Questions Foiled

CONSIDER THIS 22:23–33 **Have you ever seen someone try to manipulate someone else by asking for one thing in order to get another? Perhaps you've tried to outwit or embarrass someone with a less-than-direct approach.**

The Sadducees did precisely that when they tried to trap Jesus in front of a crowd (vv. 23–33). Using the subject of serial marriage relationships, they attempted to paint Him into a corner on His teaching about the resurrection, a belief that they rejected (v. 23).

Jesus confronted them on their thinly veiled pretext and at the same time affirmed the resurrection. He even used the very Scriptures they loved to quote: v. 32 is from Exodus 3:6. Jesus refused to let them get away with using subtle inferences to twist things to their own advantage. He cut to the heart of the matter.

There's nothing wrong with being discreet, using inference, or stating things subtly and diplomatically. Some situations call for planting seed ideas in someone else's thinking, then allowing time for the idea to take shape. Here, however, Jesus was challenging selfish manipulation and trickery which had no benefit for others.

Are you known as a speaker of truth among your peers? Are there ways you could be more forthright and helpful in your communications?

Speaking truth in love is one of the main characteristics of Christlike character. See Eph. 4:15.

Jesus Confounds His Challengers

15Then the Pharisees went and plotted how they might entangle Him in *His* talk. 16And they sent to Him their disciples with the Herodians, saying, "Teacher, we know that You are true, and teach the way of God in truth; nor do You care about anyone, for You do not regard the person of men. 17Tell us, therefore, what do You think? Is it lawful to pay taxes to Caesar, or not?"

18But Jesus perceived their wickedness, and said, "Why do you test Me, *you* hypocrites? 19Show Me the tax money."

So they brought Him a denarius.

20And He said to them, "Whose image and inscription *is* this?"

21They said to Him, "Caesar's."

And He said to them, "Render therefore to Caesar the things that are Caesar's, and to God the things that are God's." 22When they had heard *these words,* they marveled, and left Him and went their way.

22:23–33 23The same day the Sadducees, who say there is no resurrection, came to Him and asked Him, 24saying: "Teacher, Moses said that if a man dies, having no children, his brother shall marry his wife and raise up offspring for his brother. 25Now there were with us seven brothers. The first died after he had married, and having no offspring, left his wife to his brother. 26Likewise the second also, and the third, even to the seventh. 27Last of all the woman died also. 28Therefore, in the resurrection, whose wife of the seven will she be? For they all had her."

29Jesus answered and said to them, "You are mistaken, not knowing the Scriptures nor the power of God. 30For in the resurrection they neither marry nor are given in marriage, but are like angels of God[a] in heaven. 31But concerning the resurrection of the dead, have you not read what was spoken to you by God, saying, 32'I am the God of Abraham, the God of Isaac, and the God of Jacob'?[a] God is not the God of the dead, but of the living." 33And when the multitudes heard *this,* they were astonished at His teaching.

The Greatest of the Commandments

22:34–40 see pg. 98 34But when the Pharisees heard that He had silenced the Sadducees, they gathered together. 35Then one of them, a lawyer, asked *Him a question,* testing Him, and saying, 36"Teacher, which *is* the great commandment in the law?"

37Jesus said to him, " 'You shall love the LORD your God

22:30 [a]NU-Text omits *of God.* *22:32* [a]Exodus 3:6, 15

with all your heart, with all your soul, and with all your
mind.'[a] 38This is *the* first and great commandment. 39And
the second *is* like it: 'You shall love your neighbor as yourself.'[a] 40On these two commandments hang all the Law and
the Prophets."

Jesus Silences the Pharisees

41While the Pharisees were gathered together, Jesus asked
them, 42saying, "What do you think about the Christ?
Whose Son is He?"

They said to Him, "*The Son* of David."

43He said to them, "How then does David in the Spirit call
Him 'Lord,' saying:

44 'The LORD said to my Lord,
"Sit at My right hand,
Till I make Your enemies Your footstool" ' ?[a]

45If David then calls Him 'Lord,' how is He his Son?" 46And
no one was able to answer Him a word, nor from that day
on did anyone dare question Him anymore.

CHAPTER 23

Jesus Denounces the Scribes and Pharisees

23:1–30

1Then Jesus spoke to the multitudes
and to His disciples, 2saying: "The scribes
and the Pharisees sit in Moses' seat. 3Therefore whatever
they tell you to observe,[a] *that* observe and do, but do not do
according to their works; for they say, and do not do. 4For
they bind heavy burdens, hard to bear, and lay *them* on
men's shoulders; but they *themselves* will not move them
with one of their fingers. 5But all their works they do to be
seen by men. They make their phylacteries broad and en-
large the borders of their garments. 6They love the best
places at feasts, the best seats in the synagogues, 7greetings
in the marketplaces, and to be called by men, 'Rabbi,
Rabbi.' 8But you, do not be called 'Rabbi'; for One is your
Teacher, the Christ,[a] and you are all brethren. 9Do not call
anyone on earth your father; for One is your Father, He
who is in heaven. 10And do not be called teachers; for
One is your Teacher, the Christ. 11But he who is greatest
among you shall be your servant. 12And whoever exalts
himself will be humbled, and he who humbles himself will
be exalted.

22:37 [a]Deuteronomy 6:5 *22:39* [a]Leviticus 19:18 *22:44* [a]Psalm 110:1 *23:3* [a]NU-Text omits *to observe.* *23:8* [a]NU-Text omits *the Christ.*

QUOTE UNQUOTE

CONSIDER THIS 23:1–30 *Jesus denounced the Pharisees for their abuse of spiritual authority. Perhaps their daily contact with religion made them callous to it:*

Someone has said, "None are so unholy as those whose hands are cauterized with holy things"; sacred things may become profane by becoming matters of the job.

C.S. Lewis, Letter to Sheldon Vanauken, Jan. 5, 1951

Woe to the Scribes and Pharisees

[13]"But woe to you, scribes and Pharisees, hypocrites! For
you shut up the kingdom of heaven against men; for you
neither go in *yourselves,* nor do you allow those who are en-
23:14 tering to go in. [14]Woe to you, scribes and
Pharisees, hypocrites! For you devour
widows' houses, and for a pretense make long prayers.
Therefore you will receive greater condemnation.[a]

[15]"Woe to you, scribes and Pharisees, hypocrites! For you
travel land and sea to win one proselyte, and when he is
won, you make him twice as much a son of hell as yourselves.

[16]"Woe to you, blind guides, who say, 'Whoever swears by
the temple, it is nothing; but whoever swears by the gold of
the temple, he is obliged *to perform it.*' [17]Fools and blind!
For which is greater, the gold or the temple that sanctifies[a]
the gold? [18]And, 'Whoever swears by the altar, it is nothing;
but whoever swears by the gift that is on it, he is obliged *to*

23:14 [a]NU-Text omits this verse. *23:17* [a]NU-Text reads *sanctified.*

What Kind of Love Is This?

"Love" is a very confusing concept these days. People use the word "love" to describe very different relationships: people "love" their dog . . . a certain type of car . . . a brand of pizza . . . a sexually intimate partner . . . another person for whom they have deep feelings. What can "love" possibly mean if it applies equally well to dogs, machines, food, sex, or close companions?

The Bible is not confused or vague about the powerful concept it calls love. Greek, the international language of Jesus' day and the language in which the New Testament was written, had four distinct words for love, each with its own shade of meaning:

(1) Erōs *denoted the relationship between male and female, including physical desire, craving, and longing. That word for love is not used in the New Testament.*

(2) Stergos *described affection and was applied especially to the mutual love between family members. It is not used in the New Testament either.*

(3) Philos *reflected the care and concern that friends have for each other, what we would call brotherly love. Peter spoke of this kind of love when he and Jesus discussed his future task of serving others (John 21:15–17).*

perform it.' [19]Fools and blind! For which is greater, the gift
or the altar that sanctifies the gift? [20]Therefore he who
swears by the altar, swears by it and by all things on it. [21]He
who swears by the temple, swears by it and by Him who
dwells[a] in it. [22]And he who swears by heaven, swears by the
throne of God and by Him who sits on it.

23:23–24 see pg. 100

[23]"Woe to you, scribes and Pharisees,
hypocrites! For you pay tithe of mint and
anise and cummin, and have neglected the weightier *matters* of the law: justice and mercy and faith. These you
ought to have done, without leaving the others undone.
[24]Blind guides, who strain out a gnat and swallow a camel!

[25]"Woe to you, scribes and Pharisees, hypocrites! For you
cleanse the outside of the cup and dish, but inside they are
full of extortion and self-indulgence.[a] [26]Blind Pharisee, first
cleanse the inside of the cup and dish, that the outside of
them may be clean also.

(Bible text continued on page 101)

23:21 [a]M-Text reads *dwelt.* *23:25* [a]M-Text reads *unrighteousness.*

(4) Agapē *described a unique type of supreme love involving a conscious and deliberate choice to do good for another, a commitment based on the willful choice of the lover, not the qualities of the person receiving the love.* Agapē *love is perhaps best seen in God's love for the world (John 3:16) and in the love that God calls believers to display (1 Cor. 13:1–13).*

When Jesus recalled the greatest of the commandments, both of which had to do with love (Matt. 22:34–40), He was calling for agapē *love, a sustained and conscious choice to graciously serve God, neighbor, and self, expecting nothing in return. Followers of Christ learn this kind of love as God loves them first. He then commands us to live in the same way toward others (1 John 3:11–24). God's love empowers us to love by choice rather than just emotion or senses, and to sustain our love even in the face of hostility or rejection.*

*God wants to deliver a new kind of love—*agapē *love—to families, workplaces, and communities through His people. Who around you needs that kind of intentional touch of compassion and grace?* ◆

Growing Fat at the Poor's Expense

CONSIDER THIS 23:14

Jesus chastised the Pharisees for growing fat at the expense of widows (v. 14). Unfortunately, not much has changed from that day to this. We still see people with lots of power but few scruples grow rich by dislodging widows and other less powerful folks from what little they own.

Sadly, there are loan sharks and other flimflam artists who con the poor. But there are also more respectable businesspeople whose activities can hurt the powerless. For example, occasionally some "urban renewal projects" have driven the poor from one slum to another in a frantic search for housing that costs more than before.

Then there are those who buy, sell, close down, and bankrupt companies with little regard for the impact on workers or communities, whose only motive appears to be personal financial gain.

Jesus never condemned business or investment. But His stiff rebuke of the Pharisees challenges any of us involved in finance and deal-making to carefully weigh the ethics of our choices. Woe to us if we devour the resources of the disadvantaged.

Scripture has much more to say about our use and abuse of wealth. See "Christians and Money," 1 Tim. 1:6–19; and "Getting Yours," James 5:1–6.

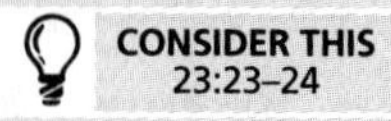

TITHING

J*esus' words to the Pharisees (v. 23) raise the issue of tithing. Should Christians today pay tithes? Or are we free from that practice?*

For that matter, what is a *tithe*? The word means "a tenth part." In the Old Testament, God commanded the Israelites to give tithes—one-tenth of their produce or income—for one of three reasons:

(1) To support the Levites, who were responsible for the tabernacle and worship (Num. 18:20–24).

(2) To support various feasts and sacrifices (Deut. 14:22–27), some of which lasted more than one or two days and were times of joyous celebration and thanksgiving.

(3) To establish a pool of resources to help the poor, orphans and widows, and strangers in the land (Deut. 14:28–29).

In the New Testament, neither Christ nor the apostles gave any explicit instructions about tithing. However, Jesus clearly endorsed it, as He did all the Law (v. 23; Matt. 5:17–20). He denounced the hypocritical way that the Pharisees ignored the "weightier matters" of the Law—justice, mercy, and faith. But those "heavy duty" issues by no means negated such "lightweight matters" as tithing.

So what is the place of tithing for believers today? Several principles might be considered:

(1) As Christians, our allegiance is not to the Old Testament Law, which was primarily given to Israel, but to Christ.

(2) Our giving needs to spring from a love of Christ, not a slavish obedience to a percentage standard. When Abraham gave the first tithe recorded in the Bible (Gen. 14:17–20), he did it as an expression of gratitude for God's deliverance of him in battle. Throughout Scripture, loving God and worshiping Him are at the heart of tithing.

(3) All of what we have ultimately comes from and belongs to God—not just what we give away, but also what we keep. So He has total claim on 100 percent of our income, not just 10 percent.

(4) Ten percent makes a great starting point for giving. However, studies indicate that as a group, Christians in the United States give nowhere near that much of their income away—to ministries or charities of any kind. In fact, while per capita income has increased, church members have actually *decreased* their contributions to churches.

(5) The New Testament is clear that vocational Christian workers have a right to financial support from those to whom they minister (1 Cor. 9:13–14; Gal. 6:6). Likewise, many churches and other ministries assist the poor, orphans and widows, and strangers. So it seems legitimate to expect believers to donate money to those causes.

(6) No matter how much we give or to whom, Matt. 23:23 indicates that our first priority should be to ensure that justice is carried out around us, that we show mercy to our "neighbors," and that we practice our faith and not just talk about it. In the end, it is through our obedience that Jesus increases our faith. ◆

23:27–28

[27]"Woe to you, scribes and Pharisees,
hypocrites! For you are like whitewashed
tombs which indeed appear beautiful outwardly, but inside
are full of dead *men's* bones and all uncleanness. [28]Even so
you also outwardly appear righteous to men, but inside you
are full of hypocrisy and lawlessness.
[29]"Woe to you, scribes and Pharisees, hypocrites! Because
you build the tombs of the prophets and adorn the monu-
ments of the righteous, [30]and say, 'If we had lived in the
days of our fathers, we would not have been partakers with
them in the blood of the prophets.'
[31]"Therefore you are witnesses against yourselves that you
are sons of those who murdered the prophets. [32]Fill up,
then, the measure of your fathers' *guilt*. [33]Serpents, brood of
vipers! How can you escape the condemnation of hell?
[34]Therefore, indeed, I send you prophets, wise men, and
scribes: *some* of them you will kill and crucify, and *some* of
them you will scourge in your synagogues and persecute
from city to city, [35]that on you may come all the righteous
blood shed on the earth, from the blood of righteous Abel
to the blood of Zechariah, son of Berechiah, whom you
murdered between the temple and the altar. [36]Assuredly, I
say to you, all these things will come upon this generation.

Jerusalem's Refusal

23:37 see pg. 102

[37]"O Jerusalem, Jerusalem, the one who
kills the prophets and stones those who
are sent to her! How often I wanted to gather your children
together, as a hen gathers her chicks under *her* wings, but
you were not willing! [38]See! Your house is left to you deso-

23:37–39

late; [39]for I say to you, you shall see Me
no more till you say, 'Blessed *is* He who
comes in the name of the LORD!' "[a]

CHAPTER 24

Jesus Predicts the Temple's Destruction

[1]Then Jesus went out and departed from the temple, and
His disciples came up to show Him the buildings of the
temple. [2]And Jesus said to them, "Do you not see all these
things? Assuredly, I say to you, not *one* stone shall be left
here upon another, that shall not be thrown down."

23:39 [a]Psalm 118:26

Whitewashed Tombs

CONSIDER THIS 23:27–28

Jesus drew upon a grim, arresting image in His denunciation of the self-righteous Pharisees (vv. 27–28). At the end of a Jewish funeral procession, which everyone was obliged to join, the body was placed on a rock shelf in a tomb. Once the flesh had decomposed, the bones would be collected and removed, allowing the shelf to be reused. Since Jews were made ritually unclean by touching graves (Num. 19:16), rocks used to seal tombs were whitewashed as a warning to stay away. The glaze gave the tombs a clean image on the outside—even though there were decomposing corpses on the inside.

Jesus Weeps for the Children

A CLOSER LOOK 23:37–39

Jesus wanted to gather together the lost children of Jerusalem (v. 37). Was He speaking only in spiritual terms? See "Good Men Cry," Luke 13:34.

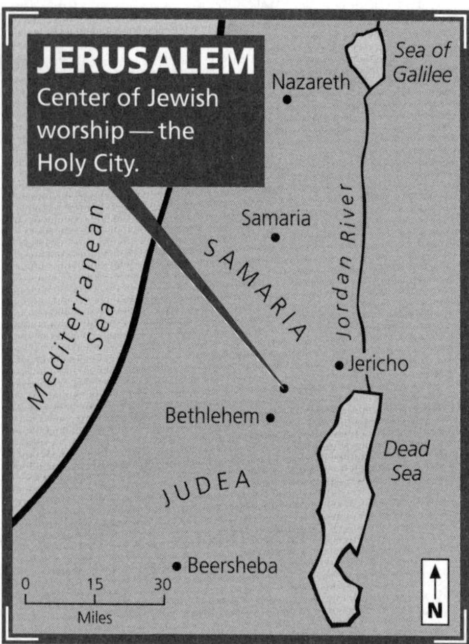

JERUSALEM

- **Main city of Palestine in biblical times.**
- **Well-situated for defense on two triangular ridges that converged to the south, bordered by the Kidron Valley on the east and the Valley of Hinnom on the west.**
- **Appears in the Bible as early as Abraham (Gen. 14:18), though the site had probably been inhabited for centuries before.**
- **Captured by David and made the capital of Israel.**
- **Site of Solomon's temple and, in the first century, Herod's temple.**
- **Estimated population in Jesus' day probably 60,000 to 70,000, though estimates range from 40,000 to 12 million.**
- **Besieged and destroyed by Rome in A.D. 70.**
- **Relatively small geographically, but a sizable metropolitan area with numerous suburban towns.**

(continued on next page)

3Now as He sat on the Mount of Olives, the disciples
came to Him privately, saying, "Tell us, when will these
things be? And what *will be* the sign of Your coming, and of
the end of the age?"
4And Jesus answered and said to them: "Take heed that
no one deceives you. 5For many will come in My name,
saying, 'I am the Christ,' and will deceive many. 6And you
will hear of wars and rumors of wars. See that you are not
troubled; for all[a] *these things* must come to pass, but the end
is not yet. 7For nation will rise against nation, and kingdom
against kingdom. And there will be famines, pestilences,[a]
and earthquakes in various places. 8All these *are* the beginning of sorrows.

Terrible Times to Come

9"Then they will deliver you up to tribulation and kill
you, and you will be hated by all nations for My name's
sake. 10And then many will be offended, will betray one another, and will hate one another. 11Then many false
prophets will rise up and deceive many. 12And because lawlessness will abound, the love of many will grow cold. 13But
he who endures to the end shall be saved. 14And this gospel
of the kingdom will be preached in all the world as a witness to all the nations, and then the end will come.
15"Therefore when you see the 'abomination of desolation,'[a] spoken of by Daniel the prophet, standing in the holy
place" (whoever reads, let him understand), 16"then let
those who are in Judea flee to the mountains. 17Let him
who is on the housetop not go down to take anything out
of his house. 18And let him who is in the field not go back
to get his clothes. 19But woe to those who are pregnant and
to those who are nursing babies in those days! 20And pray
that your flight may not be in winter or on the Sabbath.
21For then there will be great tribulation, such as has not
been since the beginning of the world until this time, no,
nor ever shall be. 22And unless those days were shortened,
no flesh would be saved; but for the elect's sake those days
will be shortened.
23"Then if anyone says to you, 'Look, here *is* the Christ!'
or 'There!' do not believe *it*. 24For false christs and false
prophets will rise and show great signs and wonders to deceive, if possible, even the elect. 25See, I have told you beforehand.
26"Therefore if they say to you, 'Look, He is in the desert!'
do not go out; *or* 'Look, *He is* in the inner rooms!' do not
believe *it*. 27For as the lightning comes from the east and
flashes to the west, so also will the coming of the Son of

24:6 [a]NU-Text omits *all*. *24:7* [a]NU-Text omits *pestilences*. *24:15* [a]Daniel 11:31; 12:11

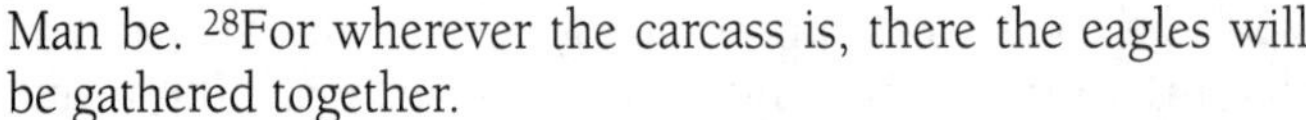

Man be. 28For wherever the carcass is, there the eagles will
be gathered together.
29"Immediately after the tribulation of those days the sun
will be darkened, and the moon will not give its light; the
stars will fall from heaven, and the powers of the heavens
will be shaken. 30Then the sign of the Son of Man will appear in heaven, and then all the tribes of the earth will
mourn, and they will see the Son of Man coming on the
clouds of heaven with power and great glory. 31And He will
send His angels with a great sound of a trumpet, and they
will gather together His elect from the four winds, from one
end of heaven to the other.
32"Now learn this parable from the fig tree: When its
branch has already become tender and puts forth leaves,
you know that summer *is* near. 33So you also, when you see
all these things, know that it[a] is near—at the doors! 34As-
suredly, I say to you, this generation will by no means pass
away till all these things take place. 35Heaven and earth will
pass away, but My words will by no means pass away.

Faithful and Foolish Living

36"But of that day and hour no one knows, not even the
angels of heaven,[a] but My Father only. 37But as the days of
Noah *were,* so also will the coming of the Son of Man be.
38For as in the days before the flood, they were eating and
drinking, marrying and giving in marriage, until the day
that Noah entered the ark, 39and did not know until the
flood came and took them all away, so also will the coming
of the Son of Man be. 40Then two *men* will be in the field:
one will be taken and the other left.
41Two *women will be* grinding at the mill:
one will be taken and the other left. 42Watch therefore, for
you do not know what hour[a] your Lord is coming. 43But
know this, that if the master of the house had known what
hour the thief would come, he would have watched and not
allowed his house to be broken into. 44Therefore you also
be ready, for the Son of Man is coming at an hour you do
not expect.
45"Who then is a faithful and wise servant, whom his
master made ruler over his household, to give them food in
due season? 46Blessed *is* that servant whom his master,

24:41

24:33 [a]Or *He* *24:36* [a]NU-Text adds *nor the Son.* *24:42* [a]NU-Text reads *day.*

(continued from previous page)

The Holy City

For centuries before and after Christ, Jerusalem has been viewed as more than just a city. It stands as a great symbol of the Bible and the Near East. As the center of Judaism and Hebrew culture, it bore the brunt of Jesus' dramatic cry of anguish over its rejection of Him (Matt. 23:37–38). He knew all too well that in a matter of years Jerusalem would indeed be left desolate by a myriad of Roman siege troops.

Jesus visited Jerusalem several times. Yet its population as a whole never did respond to the Son of God. Nor did it accept Christ's followers later when they tried to penetrate it with His message. Known as the Holy City (Matt. 4:5), Jerusalem nevertheless rejected the Holy One of Israel, the Messiah.

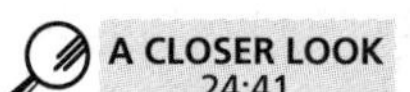

A CLOSER LOOK
24:41

An Everyday Task

Jesus promised that His return would burst into common, everyday life, as pictured in two women grinding grain (v. 41). See Luke 17:35.

The first headquarters of the early church was at Jerusalem, but the city's supremacy was short-lived. See "Jerusalem—Merely the Beginning," Acts 1:12–26.

when he comes, will find so doing. 47Assuredly, I say to you
that he will make him ruler over all his goods. 48But if that
evil servant says in his heart, 'My master is delaying his
coming,'[a] 49and begins to beat *his* fellow servants, and to
eat and drink with the drunkards, 50the master of that servant will come on a day when he is not looking for *him* and
at an hour that he is not aware of, 51and will cut him in two
and appoint *him* his portion with the hypocrites. There
shall be weeping and gnashing of teeth.

CHAPTER 25

A Parable about Ten Virgins

1"Then the kingdom of heaven shall be likened to ten virgins who took their lamps and went out to meet the bridegroom. 2Now five of them were wise, and five *were* foolish.
3Those who *were* foolish took their lamps and took no oil
with them, 4but the wise took oil in their vessels with their
lamps. 5But while the bridegroom was delayed, they all
slumbered and slept.

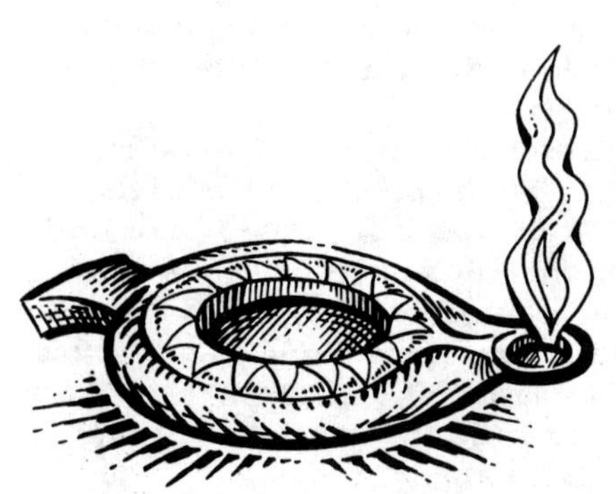

6"And at midnight a cry was *heard:* 'Behold, the bridegroom is coming;[a] go out to meet him!' 7Then all those virgins arose and trimmed their lamps. 8And the foolish said
to the wise, 'Give us *some* of your oil, for our lamps are going out.' 9But the wise answered, saying, '*No,* lest there
should not be enough for us and you; but go rather to those
who sell, and buy for yourselves.' 10And while they went to
buy, the bridegroom came, and those who were ready went
in with him to the wedding; and the door was shut.

11"Afterward the other virgins came also, saying, 'Lord,
Lord, open to us!' 12But he answered and said, 'Assuredly, I
say to you, I do not know you.'

13"Watch therefore, for you know neither the day nor the
hour[a] in which the Son of Man is coming.

A Parable about Investment

25:14–30

14"For *the kingdom of heaven is* like a
man traveling to a far country, *who* called
his own servants and delivered his goods to them. 15And to
one he gave five talents, to another two, and to another one,
to each according to his own ability; and immediately he
went on a journey. 16Then he who had received the five talents went and traded with them, and made another five talents. 17And likewise he who *had received* two gained two
more also. 18But he who had received one went and dug in
the ground, and hid his lord's money. 19After a long time the

24:48 [a]NU-Text omits *his coming.* *25:6* [a]NU-Text omits *is coming.* *25:13* [a]NU-Text omits the rest of this verse.

lord of those servants came and settled accounts with them.
20“So he who had received five talents came and brought
five other talents, saying, ‘Lord, you delivered to me five talents; look, I have gained five more talents besides them.’
21His lord said to him, ‘Well *done,* good and faithful servant;
you were faithful over a few things, I will make you ruler
over many things. Enter into the joy of your lord.’ 22He also
who had received two talents came and said, ‘Lord, you delivered to me two talents; look, I have gained two more talents besides them.’ 23His lord said to him, ‘Well *done,* good
and faithful servant; you have been faithful over a few
things, I will make you ruler over many things. Enter into
the joy of your lord.’
24“Then he who had received the one talent came and
said, ‘Lord, I knew you to be a hard man, reaping where
you have not sown, and gathering where you have not scattered seed. 25And I was afraid, and went and hid your talent
in the ground. Look, *there* you have *what is* yours.’
26“But his lord answered and said to him, ‘You wicked
and lazy servant, you knew that I reap where I have not
sown, and gather where I have not scattered seed. 27So you
ought to have deposited my money with the bankers, and
at my coming I would have received back my own with interest. 28Therefore take the talent from him, and give *it* to
him who has ten talents.
29‘For to everyone who has, more will be given, and he
will have abundance; but from him who does not have,
even what he has will be taken away. 30And cast the unprof-
itable servant into the outer darkness. There will be weeping and gnashing of teeth.’

Judgment of the Nations

25:31–46 see pg. 106

31“When the Son of Man comes in His
glory, and all the holy[a] angels with Him,
then He will sit on the throne of His glory. 32All the nations
will be gathered before Him, and He will separate them one
from another, as a shepherd divides *his* sheep from the
goats. 33And He will set the sheep on His right hand, but

25:34

the goats on the left. 34Then the King will
say to those on His right hand, ‘Come,
you blessed of My Father, inherit the kingdom prepared for
you from the foundation of the world: 35for I was hungry

25:31 [a]NU-Text omits *holy.*

TRUE SUCCESS MEANS FAITHFULNESS

CONSIDER THIS 25:14–30 **The story of the talents (vv. 14–30) is about the kingdom of heaven (v. 14), but it offers an important lesson about success. God measures our success not by what we have, but by what we do with what we have—for all that we have is a gift from Him. We are really only managers to whom He has entrusted resources and responsibilities.**

The key thing He looks for is *faithfulness* (vv. 21, 23), doing what we can to obey and honor Him with whatever He has given us. We may or may not be "successful" as our culture measures success, in terms of wealth, prestige, power, or fame. In the long run that hardly matters. What counts is whether we have faithfully served God with what He has entrusted to us. By all means we must avoid wasting our lives, the way the third servant wasted his talents, by failing to carry out our Master's business.

A talent was worth a lot of money. See "Seventy Times Seven—Still Not Enough," Matt. 18:21–35.

Jesus told a different version of this parable in Luke 19:15–27.

A CLOSER LOOK 25:34

Prepared for You

God's children will enjoy an inheritance that is beyond comprehension. See "What's In It for Me?" at Eph. 1:11.

The Final Exam

CONSIDER THIS 25:31–46 **Have you ever wondered whether God is going to give you a "final exam" when you stand before Him? If you pass you go to heaven, but if you fail . . . ? Fortunately, Jesus has already taken that exam for us—and passed (Eph. 2:4–10). Nevertheless, Matt. 25:31–46 reveals a final exam for the nations at Christ's return with one six-part question:**

Exam for the Nations		
Were you a friend of Jesus when He was *hungry*?	yes	no
Were you a friend of Jesus when He was *thirsty*?	yes	no
Were you a friend of Jesus when He was *a stranger*?	yes	no
Were you a friend of Jesus when He was *naked*?	yes	no
Were you a friend of Jesus when He was *sick*?	yes	no
Were you a friend of Jesus when He was *in prison*?	yes	no

The point is that those being examined at that time will have made certain choices: whether or not to feed the hungry, to give drink to the thirsty, to befriend the strangers, to clothe the naked, to heal the sick, to befriend the prisoners. Who ever said that life was a series of meaningless choices? And who can say that the evidence Christ will look for at His return is not the same evidence He wants to see in believers today? To love Jesus is to love all who need our care.

Who are those in need nearest you? See "Who Was the Neighbor?" Luke 10:37.

and you gave Me food; I was thirsty and you gave Me drink;
I was a stranger and you took Me in; 36I *was* naked and you
clothed Me; I was sick and you visited Me; I was in prison
and you came to Me.'
37"Then the righteous will answer Him, saying, 'Lord,
when did we see You hungry and feed *You,* or thirsty and
give *You* drink? 38When did we see You a stranger and take
You in, or naked and clothe *You?* 39Or when did we see You
sick, or in prison, and come to You?' 40And the King will
answer and say to them, 'Assuredly, I say to you, inasmuch
as you did *it* to one of the least of these My brethren, you
did *it* to Me.'
41"Then He will also say to those on the left hand, 'Depart
from Me, you cursed, into the everlasting fire prepared for
the devil and his angels: 42for I was hungry and you gave
Me no food; I was thirsty and you gave Me no drink; 43I was
a stranger and you did not take Me in, naked and you did
not clothe Me, sick and in prison and you did not visit Me.'
44"Then they also will answer Him,[a] saying, 'Lord, when
did we see You hungry or thirsty or a stranger or naked or
sick or in prison, and did not minister to You?' 45Then He
will answer them, saying, 'Assuredly, I say to you, inasmuch
as you did not do *it* to one of the least of these, you did not
do *it* to Me.' 46And these will go away into everlasting punishment, but the righteous into eternal life."

25:44 [a]NU-Text and M-Text omit *Him.*

Personality Profile: Caiaphas

Also known as: Joseph. His given name, Caiaphas, meant "a searcher."

Home: Jerusalem.

Occupation: High priest of Israel from A.D. 18 to 36.

Family: His father-in-law was Annas, also a high priest. Both father and son were Sadducees (see "Party Politics of Jesus' Day," Matt. 16:1) from aristocratic families in Israel.

Special interests: Maintaining the political and religious status quo.

Best known today as: The judge at the trial leading to Jesus' crucifixion.

CHAPTER 26

Leaders Plot to Kill Jesus

1Now it came to pass, when Jesus had finished all these
sayings, *that* He said to His disciples, 2"You know that after
two days is the Passover, and the Son of Man will be delivered up to be crucified."

26:3

26:3–5

3Then the chief priests, the scribes,[a]
and the elders of the people assembled at
the palace of the high priest, who was
called Caiaphas, 4and plotted to take Je-
sus by trickery and kill *Him.* 5But they said, "Not during the
feast, lest there be an uproar among the people."

26:3 [a]NU-Text omits *the scribes.*

FOR YOUR INFO 26:3–5

CAIAPHAS, THE RELIGIOUS POWER BROKER

As the high priest, Caiaphas was the most influential member of the Sanhedrin, or council, the highest ruling body and supreme court of the Jews (see "Stephen's Trial and Murder," Acts 6:12). However, while the position afforded him vast authority, it provided little job security. High priests served at the whim of Rome, and between 37 B.C. and A.D. 67, the empire appointed no fewer than 28 men to the position. The fact that Caiaphas held onto the job for 18 years is a tribute to his political savvy and, some felt, was evidence that he was in league with Rome.

There may be some truth to that, but if so, his concern was not to protect Rome's interests as much as Israel's. He feared lest the slightest civil disorder would mobilize Roman troops and lead to the nation's downfall. So when Jesus came, drawing the attention of vast numbers of the people and performing astounding miracles, especially the raising of Lazarus, Caiaphas determined that He would have to be destroyed (John 11:45–50).

This led to a well conceived plot in which Jesus was arrested, an illegal trial was held, and false evidence was brought against Him (Matt. 26:3–4, 57–68). By playing Pilate the Roman governor and Herod the Jewish king against each other, and by whipping up the people into a mob (Luke 22:66—23:25), Caiaphas triumphantly orchestrated Jesus' conviction leading to execution.

To Caiaphas' amazement, however, the sparks that he thought he had doused flamed up again with renewed power. The apostles began preaching the gospel in Jerusalem (and beyond) with great effect. And, like Jesus, they began performing miracles that not only drew the people's attention, but their response to the message about Christ (Acts 3:1—4:13). ◆

A Woman Anoints Jesus for Burial

26:6–13 [6]And when Jesus was in Bethany at the
house of Simon the leper, [7]a woman
came to Him having an alabaster flask of very costly fragrant oil, and she poured *it* on His head as He sat *at the*
26:8–9 *table.* [8]But when His disciples saw *it,* they
were indignant, saying, "Why this waste?
[9]For this fragrant oil might have been sold for much and
given to *the* poor."
[10]But when Jesus was aware of *it,* He said to them, "Why
do you trouble the woman? For she has done a good work
for Me. [11]For you have the poor with you always, but Me
you do not have always. [12]For in pouring this fragrant oil
on My body, she did *it* for My burial. [13]Assuredly, I say to
you, wherever this gospel is preached in the whole world,
what this woman has done will also be told as a memorial
to her."

Judas Sells Out

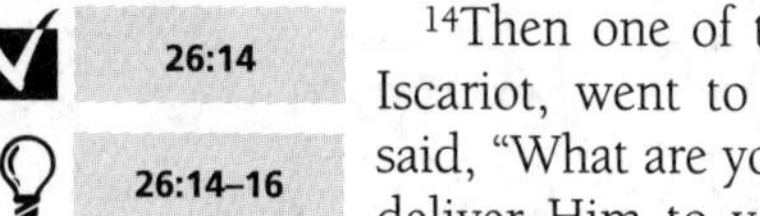

[14]Then one of the twelve, called Judas
Iscariot, went to the chief priests [15]and
said, "What are you willing to give me if I
deliver Him to you?" And they counted
out to him thirty pieces of silver. [16]So from that time he
sought opportunity to betray Him.

A Final Passover Meal

[17]Now on the first *day of the Feast* of Unleavened Bread
the disciples came to Jesus, saying to Him, "Where do You
want us to prepare for You to eat the Passover?"
[18]And He said, "Go into the city to a certain man, and say
to him, 'The Teacher says, "My time is at hand; I will keep
the Passover at your house with My disciples." ' "
[19]So the disciples did as Jesus had directed them; and
they prepared the Passover.
[20]When evening had come, He sat down with the twelve.

(Bible text continued on page 110)

Preparing Jesus for His Death

The woman who anointed Jesus turns out to have been Mary, Lazarus' sister. See "Funeral Preparations," John 12:1–8.

Squandering Wealth on Worship

A CLOSER LOOK 26:8–9

What the disciples saw as waste (vv. 8–9) the Lord saw as worship. The tension still exists. Is it right for a community of believers to spend millions on new church facilities when there are so many poor and homeless on the streets? Moreover, don't they, too, deserve the benefits of art and beauty? "A Parting Gift" (Mark 14:3–9) says more about this incident at Simon's home.

Personality Profile: Judas Iscariot

FOR YOUR INFO 26:14

Name meant: "Praise of the Lord."

Home: Probably Kerioth in southern Judah.

Family: His father was Simon Iscariot.

Occupation: Unknown, although he may have had some background in finance or accounting; he kept track of the money box for Jesus and the other disciples; John calls him a thief (John 12:6).

Best known then and now as: The disciple who betrayed Jesus to His enemies.

CONSIDER THIS 26:14–16

Judas Iscariot, the Betrayer

The New Testament never mentions Judas Iscariot without reminding the reader that he was the man who betrayed Jesus (for example, Matt. 10:4; Mark 3:19; John 12:4). Consequently, to this day the name Judas is a symbol of betrayal.

Why did he do it? His portrayal in the Gospels suggests that he had a keen interest in money. But the amount that the priests paid him—30 pieces of silver—was relatively small. Besides, he had access to the disciples' money box and apparently was known for helping himself to its contents (John 12:6).

Some have suggested that Judas thought that his betrayal would force Jesus into asserting His true power and overthrowing the Romans. Others have suggested that Judas became convinced that Jesus was a false Messiah and that the true Messiah was yet to come. Or perhaps he was upset over Jesus' seemingly casual attitude toward the Law in regard to associating with sinners and violating the Sabbath.

In the end, no one knows what Judas' exact motives were for turning against Jesus. He remains a shadowy figure in the Gospel accounts, unknown by his companions, unfaithful to his Lord, and unmourned in his death. ◆

Judas took his own life. Ironically, his death was memorialized in the purchase of a plot of ground for a cemetery. See "Field of Blood," Acts 1:19.

The New Testament mentions several other Judases. One was a brother of Jesus and probably the author of the book of Jude (Matt. 13:55). See the introduction to Jude.

21Now as they were eating, He said, "Assuredly, I say to you,
one of you will betray Me."
22And they were exceedingly sorrowful, and each of them
began to say to Him, "Lord, is it I?"
23He answered and said, "He who dipped *his* hand with
Me in the dish will betray Me. 24The Son of Man indeed
goes just as it is written of Him, but woe to that man by
whom the Son of Man is betrayed! It would have been good
for that man if he had not been born."
25Then Judas, who was betraying Him, answered and
said, "Rabbi, is it I?"
He said to him, "You have said it."
26And as they were eating, Jesus took bread, blessed[a] and
broke *it,* and gave *it* to the disciples and said, "Take, eat;
this is My body."
27Then He took the cup, and gave thanks, and gave *it* to
them, saying, "Drink from it, all of you. 28For this is My
blood of the new[a] covenant, which is shed for many for the
remission of sins. 29But I say to you, I will not drink of this
fruit of the vine from now on until that day when I drink it
new with you in My Father's kingdom."

26:26 [a]M-Text reads *gave thanks for.* ***26:28*** [a]NU-Text omits *new.*

CONSIDER THIS
26:35–74

Would You Choose These for Leaders?

Jesus was close to the end of His earthly ministry. His life was about to come to an agonizing end at the hands of bitter opponents. Shortly thereafter, those He had trained would be assuming the reins of His new movement.

That transition period would prove to be rather awkward. It didn't help that it was forced on the group by hostile outsiders. But the most troubling aspect was what happened to Jesus' associates, the ones who would have to carry His banner into the future. During those final days and hours, they began to fall apart:

- *Bravado caused them to overstate their commitment (v. 35). When the moment of truth came, they deserted the Lord (v. 56).*
- *Even though the Lord asked them to keep watch with Him during His final hours of freedom, they fell asleep twice (vv. 40, 43).*
- *At the very moment when Jesus was standing trial and enduring mockery and beatings, Peter, who had led the others in declaring their loyalty (v. 35), denied any association with Him (vv. 69–75).*

In short, the disciples hardly seem to have had the "right stuff" for continuing the important work that Jesus

30 And when they had sung a hymn, they went out to the
Mount of Olives.
31 Then Jesus said to them, "All of you will be made to
stumble because of Me this night, for it is written:

'I will strike the Shepherd,
And the sheep of the flock will be scattered.'[a]

32 But after I have been raised, I will go before you to
Galilee."
33 Peter answered and said to Him, "Even if all are made to
stumble because of You, I will never be made to stumble."
34 Jesus said to him, "Assuredly, I say to you that this
night, before the rooster crows, you will deny Me three
times."

26:35–74

35 Peter said to Him, "Even if I have to
die with You, I will not deny You!"
And so said all the disciples.

Jesus Prays in the Garden of Gethsemane

36 Then Jesus came with them to a place called Gethsemane, and said to the disciples, "Sit
here while I go and pray over there."

26:36

26:31 [a]Zechariah 13:7

began. Yet, even after all that He went through, Jesus returned to that very group of followers after His resurrection and declared that they were still His chosen representatives, the ones appointed to continue His work. He even affirmed His commitment to stick with them to the end (28:19–20).

Jesus' treatment of the disciples shows that failure is not the unforgivable act. In fact, it seems to be the crucible out of which character is formed. It is certainly not a sifting-out process to eliminate weak or useless people. Christ does not look for perfect people, but rather faithful people who can experience His forgiveness and grow.

Do you stick with people even though they stumble? Do you allow the shortcomings of your spouse, children, boss, coworkers, and neighbors to open up bright futures? Do you give yourself freedom to fail? ◆

The Twelve were all men. But women also played an important role in Jesus' life and ministry. See "The Women Who Followed Jesus," Luke 8:1–3.

God has always valued faithfulness over perfection when it comes to handing out acclaim. See "The Hall of Faithfulness," Heb. 11:1–40.

Praying in a Workplace

CONSIDER THIS 26:36

Jesus chose a familiar place of work in which to pray one of His final prayers (v. 36). The area around Jerusalem was rich with olive groves, and many people were employed at the commercial oil presses, or gethsemanes, to produce the city's only export product.

The particular garden mentioned here was a place to which Jesus often went alone or with His disciples for prayer or relaxation. As a result, Judas had no trouble finding Him when he led the party to arrest Him (John 18:1–2). The exact site of the garden is unknown, but it may have been located on the Mount of Olives, just east of Jerusalem across the Kidron Valley, opposite the temple (Mark 13:3; John 18:1).

37And He took with Him Peter and the two sons of Zebedee, and He began to be sorrowful and deeply distressed. 38Then He said to them, "My soul is exceedingly sorrowful, even to death. Stay here and watch with Me."

39He went a little farther and fell on His face, and prayed, saying, "O My Father, if it is possible, let this cup pass from Me; nevertheless, not as I will, but as You *will*."

40Then He came to the disciples and found them sleeping, and said to Peter, "What! Could you not watch with Me one hour? 41Watch and pray, lest you enter into temptation. The spirit indeed *is* willing, but the flesh *is* weak."

26:41

42Again, a second time, He went away and prayed, saying, "O My Father, if this cup cannot pass away from Me unless[a] I drink it, Your will be done." 43And He came and found them asleep again, for their eyes were heavy.

44So He left them, went away again, and prayed the third time, saying the same words. 45Then He came to His disciples and said to them, "Are *you* still sleeping and resting? Behold, the hour is at hand, and the Son of Man is being betrayed into the hands of sinners. 46Rise, let us be going. See, My betrayer is at hand."

"PUT YOUR SWORD IN ITS PLACE, FOR ALL WHO TAKE THE SWORD WILL PERISH BY THE SWORD."
—Matthew 26:52

Jesus Betrayed

47And while He was still speaking, behold, Judas, one of the twelve, with a great multitude with swords and clubs, came from the chief priests and elders of the people.

48Now His betrayer had given them a sign, saying, "Whomever I kiss, He is the One; seize Him." 49Immediately he went up to Jesus and said, "Greetings, Rabbi!" and kissed Him.

50But Jesus said to him, "Friend, why have you come?"

Then they came and laid hands on Jesus and took Him. 51And suddenly, one of those *who were* with Jesus stretched out *his* hand and drew his sword, struck the servant of the high priest, and cut off his ear.

52But Jesus said to him, "Put your sword in its place, for all who take the sword will perish[a] by the sword. 53Or do you think that I cannot now pray to My Father, and He will

26:42 [a]NU-Text reads *if this may not pass away unless.* *26:52* [a]M-Text reads *die.*

Lest You Enter into Temptation

A CLOSER LOOK 26:41 *Prayer is one of the most important strategies believers can use to avoid temptation (v. 41). Only by God's help can we resist. See "Pay Attention to Temptation!" at 1 Cor. 10:12–13.*

provide Me with more than twelve legions of angels? 54How
then could the Scriptures be fulfilled, that it must happen
thus?"
55In that hour Jesus said to the multitudes, "Have you
come out, as against a robber, with swords and clubs to take
Me? I sat daily with you, teaching in the temple, and you
did not seize Me. 56But all this was done that the Scriptures
of the prophets might be fulfilled."
Then all the disciples forsook Him and fled.

Jesus Is Brought Before the High Priest

57And those who had laid hold of Jesus led *Him* away to
Caiaphas the high priest, where the scribes and the elders
were assembled. 58But Peter followed Him at a distance to
the high priest's courtyard. And he went in and sat with the
servants to see the end.

26:59–68

59Now the chief priests, the elders,[a]
and all the council sought false testimony
against Jesus to put Him to death, 60but found none. Even
though many false witnesses came forward, they found
none.[a] But at last two false witnesses[b] came forward 61and
said, "This *fellow* said, 'I am able to destroy the temple of
God and to build it in three days.' "
62And the high priest arose and said to Him, "Do You answer nothing? What *is it* these men testify against You?"
63But Jesus kept silent. And the high priest answered and
said to Him, "I put You under oath by the living God: Tell
us if You are the Christ, the Son of God!"
64Jesus said to him, "*It is as* you said. Nevertheless, I say
to you, hereafter you will see the Son of Man sitting at the
right hand of the Power, and coming on the clouds of
heaven."
65Then the high priest tore his clothes, saying, "He has
spoken blasphemy! What further need do we have of witnesses? Look, now you have heard His blasphemy! 66What
do you think?"
They answered and said, "He is deserving of death."
67Then they spat in His face and beat Him; and others
struck *Him* with the palms of their hands, 68saying, "Prophesy to us, Christ! Who is the one who struck You?"

Peter Denies Knowing Jesus

69Now Peter sat outside in the courtyard. And a servant
girl came to him, saying, "You also were with Jesus of
Galilee."
70But he denied it before *them* all, saying, "I do not know
what you are saying."

26:59 [a]NU-Text omits *the elders.* *26:60* [a]NU-Text puts a comma after *but found none,* does not capitalize *Even,* and omits *they found none.* [b]NU-Text omits *false witnesses.*

No Right Answers

CONSIDER THIS 26:59–68 **Have you ever been trapped in a situation where there is no good alternative? Jesus faced that as He stood trial before Caiaphas and the Jewish elders (v. 59). They were determined to do away with Him by any means, even resorting to false witnesses (vv. 59–62). The situation was so distorted and malicious that there was no good response. So Jesus remained silent (v. 63).**

As their anger intensified, the high priest placed Jesus "under oath by the living God" (v. 63). This meant that Jesus was bound by Law to answer and answer truthfully. In effect, Caiaphas was coercing a response. Jesus rewarded him by giving the very response he expected and wanted—a claim to be "the Christ, the Son of God." This sent His accusers into a frenzy as it allowed them to impose their prearranged verdict (vv. 65–68).

Some situations cannot be salvaged. There is no way out and the worst happens. Like Jesus, however, believers can take hope that even in those moments, God remains in control. Ultimately, He will see that justice is done (Rom. 12:19).

TAINTED MONEY

CONSIDER THIS 27:3–10 **The chief priests knew that the coins tossed back at them by Judas were unacceptable to God (v. 6). It was blood money, money they had paid to apprehend their enemy, Jesus (26:14–16). Yet they turned around and used it to buy a cemetery for the poor—a good deed, yet hypocritical all the same.**

Do you ever present "tainted" money to the Lord—money not necessarily obtained through outright crime, but perhaps through deception, shady deal-making, or dirty politics? When we donate money to churches, missions, schools, ministries to the poor, and the like, we hide nothing from God. He knows all of our motives. He knows whether our gifts are from the first and best of what we've accumulated, or whether we're giving "leftovers." He knows whether our gifts cost us little or nothing (2 Sam. 24:21–24). And He certainly knows—and hates—whatever we have come by unjustly (Mal. 1:6–14). We deceive no one but ourselves if we pretend to honor God while giving Him the fruit of unrighteousness.

The early church found out just how much God disapproves of tainted money. See "Real Estate Deal Deadly," Acts 5:2–10.

71And when he had gone out to the gateway, another *girl* saw him and said to those *who were* there, "This *fellow* also was with Jesus of Nazareth."

72But again he denied with an oath, "I do not know the Man!"

73And a little later those who stood by came up and said to Peter, "Surely you also are *one* of them, for your speech betrays you."

74Then he began to curse and swear, *saying,* "I do not know the Man!"

Immediately a rooster crowed. 75And Peter remembered the word of Jesus who had said to him, "Before the rooster crows, you will deny Me three times." So he went out and wept bitterly.

CHAPTER 27

Jesus Is Taken to Pilate

1When morning came, all the chief priests and elders of the people plotted against Jesus to put Him to death. 2And when they had bound Him, they led Him away and delivered Him to Pontius[a] Pilate the governor.

Judas Hangs Himself

27:3–10 3Then Judas, His betrayer, seeing that He had been condemned, was remorseful and brought back the thirty pieces of silver to the chief priests and elders, 4saying, "I have sinned by betraying innocent blood."

And they said, "What *is that* to us? You see *to it!*"

5Then he threw down the pieces of silver in the temple and departed, and went and hanged himself.

6But the chief priests took the silver pieces and said, "It is not lawful to put them into the treasury, because they are the price of blood." 7And they consulted together and bought with them the potter's field, to bury strangers in. 8Therefore that field has been called the Field of Blood to this day.

9Then was fulfilled what was spoken by Jeremiah the prophet, saying, "And they took the thirty pieces of silver, the value of Him who was priced, whom they of the children of Israel priced, 10and gave them for the potter's field, as the LORD directed me."[a]

Jesus Before Pilate

11Now Jesus stood before the governor. And the governor asked Him, saying, "Are You the King of the Jews?"

27:2 [a]NU-Text omits *Pontius.* *27:10* [a]Jeremiah 32:6–9

Jesus said to him, "*It is as* you say." 12And while He was
being accused by the chief priests and elders, He answered
nothing.
13Then Pilate said to Him, "Do You not hear how many
things they testify against You?" 14But He answered him not
one word, so that the governor marveled greatly.
15Now at the feast the governor was accustomed to releas-
27:16 ing to the multitude one prisoner whom
they wished. 16And at that time they had
a notorious prisoner called Barabbas.[a] 17Therefore, when
they had gathered together, Pilate said to them, "Whom do
you want me to release to you? Barabbas, or Jesus who is
called Christ?" 18For he knew that they had handed Him
over because of envy.
19While he was sitting on the judgment seat, his wife sent
to him, saying, "Have nothing to do with that just Man, for
I have suffered many things today in a dream because of
Him."
20But the chief priests and elders persuaded the multitudes that they should ask for Barabbas and destroy Jesus.
21The governor answered and said to them, "Which of the
two do you want me to release to you?"
They said, "Barabbas!"
22Pilate said to them, "What then shall I do with Jesus
who is called Christ?"
They all said to him, "Let Him be crucified!"
23Then the governor said, "Why, what evil has He done?"
But they cried out all the more, saying, "Let Him be crucified!"
24When Pilate saw that he could not prevail at all, but
rather *that* a tumult was rising, he took water and washed
his hands before the multitude, saying, "I am innocent of
the blood of this just Person.[a] You see *to it.*"
25And all the people answered and said, "His blood *be* on
us and on our children."
26Then he released Barabbas to them; and when he had
scourged Jesus, he delivered *Him* to be crucified.

(Bible text continued on page 117)

27:16 [a]NU-Text reads *Jesus Barabbas.* *27:24* [a]NU-Text omits *just.*

BUT HE ANSWERED HIM NOT ONE WORD, SO THAT THE GOVERNOR MARVELED GREATLY.
—Matthew 27:14

The Prisoner Barabbas

A CLOSER LOOK 27:16

But for a remarkable set of circumstances, the "notorious prisoner called Barabbas" (v. 16) probably would have remained unknown to history. See "'Not This Man But Barabbas!'" Mark 15:7.

THE LITTLE PEOPLE AT JESUS' DEATH

ave you ever noticed that Jesus tended to surround Himself with or be surrounded by relatively average people of little social standing or influence?

At Jesus' birth, various kinds of "little people" were involved: a minor priest and his barren wife, a small town girl and a poor carpenter, shepherds, an elderly woman, and others. A similar cast appeared during Jesus' final days and hours, including Simon, who was compelled to carry His cross (v. 32). Many of these people showed curiosity about Christ, demonstrated understanding and loyalty, or provided needed services and acts of compassion. (See table below.)

Unlike many who rise to positions of prominence and leadership, Jesus never lost touch with the little people of society. He did not insulate Himself from difficulties by surrounding Himself with the powerful, the wealthy, and the privileged. His birth, life, and death involved countless ordinary folks who could perceive His message about true values and needs.

Are you in touch with the unnamed and unnoticed? How can you serve them? What can you learn from them? ◆

ORDINARY PEOPLE WHO SAW JESUS TO THE CROSS	
Simon the leper, who had been an untouchable outcast	Hosts Jesus as his house guest (Matt. 26:6)
An unnamed woman (probably Mary of Bethany; see John 11:2; compare 12:1–8)	Uses expensive ointment to anoint Jesus' head (26:7)
An unnamed homeowner in Jerusalem	Opens his home to Jesus and the Twelve for their last meal together (26:18)
The disciples, Jesus' chosen successors from rural Galilee	Overstate their faith (26:35); join Jesus in a garden during the final hours before His arrest (26:40, 43, 56)
An unnamed servant girl	Asks Peter about his association with Jesus (26:69)
Another girl in the crowd	Also asks Peter about his association with Jesus (26:71)
Unnamed crowd members	Also enquire about Peter's association with Jesus (26:71)
Judas	Betrays Christ; later breaks down with guilt and commits suicide (27:3–5)
Barabbas, a convicted criminal	Is freed instead of Jesus due to a mob's demands (27:16, 26)
Simon of Cyrene, a man in the watching crowd	Is conscripted to carry Jesus' cross (27:32)
Two dying robbers	Are executed with Jesus (27:38, 44)
An unnamed crowd member	Offers Jesus a drink as He is in His death throes (27:48)
An unnamed Roman centurion	Observes that Jesus must be the Son of God (27:54)
Some loyal women from Galilee	Look on from afar (27:55–56)

Soldiers Mock Jesus

27Then the soldiers of the governor took Jesus into the
Praetorium and gathered the whole garrison around Him.
28And they stripped Him and put a scarlet robe on Him.
29When they had twisted a crown of thorns, they put *it* on
His head, and a reed in His right hand. And they bowed the
knee before Him and mocked Him, saying, "Hail, King of
the Jews!" 30Then they spat on Him, and took the reed and
struck Him on the head. 31And when they had mocked
Him, they took the robe off Him, put His *own* clothes on
Him, and led Him away to be crucified.

The Crucifixion

27:32

32Now as they came out, they found a
man of Cyrene, Simon by name. Him
they compelled to bear His cross. 33And when they had
come to a place called Golgotha, that is to say, Place of a
Skull, 34they gave Him sour[a] wine mingled with gall to
drink. But when He had tasted *it,* He would not drink.
35Then they crucified Him, and divided His garments,
casting lots,[a] that it might be fulfilled which was spoken by
the prophet:

> "They divided My garments among them,
> And for My clothing they cast lots."[b]

36Sitting down, they kept watch over Him there. 37And they
put up over His head the accusation written against Him:

THIS IS JESUS THE KING OF THE JEWS.

38Then two robbers were crucified with Him, one on the
right and another on the left.
39And those who passed by blasphemed Him, wagging
their heads 40and saying, "You who destroy the temple and
build *it* in three days, save Yourself! If You are the Son of
God, come down from the cross."
41Likewise the chief priests also, mocking with the scribes
and elders,[a] said, 42"He saved others; Himself He cannot
save. If He is the King of Israel,[a] let Him now come down
from the cross, and we will believe Him.[b] 43He trusted in
God; let Him deliver Him now if He will have Him; for He
said, 'I am the Son of God.' "
44Even the robbers who were crucified with Him reviled
Him with the same thing.

(Bible text continued on page 119)

27:34 [a]NU-Text omits *sour.* *27:35* [a]NU-Text and M-Text omit the rest of this verse. [b]Psalm 22:18 *27:41* [a]M-Text reads *with the scribes, the Pharisees, and the elders.* *27:42* [a]NU-Text reads *He is the King of Israel!* [b]NU-Text and M-Text read *we will believe in Him.*

AND THEY BOWED THE KNEE BEFORE HIM AND MOCKED HIM.
—Matthew 27:29

FOR YOUR INFO
27:57

WEALTHY PEOPLE IN THE NEW TESTAMENT

Most of Jesus' followers were not wealthy, but a few notable ones, like Joseph of Arimathea (v. 57), were. We can learn a great deal from the wealthy people recorded in the New Testament, about the dangers and the disciplines of money.

Persons	What They Did With Their Wealth	Lessons To Be Learned
Zacchaeus the tax collector (Luke 19:1–10)	• Before faith, cheated citizens and abused the poor. • After faith, repented and made restitution.	(1) Ill-gotten gain must be repaid. (2) God saves and changes us—all the way down to our pocketbooks.
Joseph of Arimathea (Matt. 27:57–61; Mark 15:42–46; Luke 23:50–53)	• Pre-paid his own funeral. • Donated his tomb for the burial of Jesus.	(3) Forsaking treasures on earth for the kingdom will be rewarded.
Women supporters of Christ (Luke 8:3*; Luke 23:55–24:10; Mark 15:40; 16:1)	• Supported Jesus' work. • Assisted in His burial (probably donated expensive perfume).	(4) Generosity characterizes those who follow Jesus.
Roman centurion who believed (Matt. 8:5–13; Luke 7:5)	• Showed kindness toward the Jews. • Paid for the building of a synagogue. • Showed compassion for his ill servant.	(5) When we love people it shows in the things we do and the projects we support.
Rich young ruler (Matt. 19:16–30; Mark 10:17–31; Luke 18:18–30)	• Unwilling to part with his wealth when tested by Jesus.	(6) Those who cling to wealth have difficulty getting into the kingdom. (7) Righteousness cannot be earned, but must be received as a gift. (8) "Many who are first will be last, and the last first."
Philemon (Philem. 1*)	• Owned slaves and other property. • Forgave a runaway slave, both morally and financially.	(9) People are more valuable than property.
Joseph, called Barnabas (Acts 4:36–37*)	• Sold land and gave the proceeds to believers.	(10) Partnership in the gospel may mean putting your money where believers hurt.
Ananias and Sapphira (Acts 5:1–11*)	• Sold land and tried to deceive the church about the proceeds to gain a reputation.	(11) God is not fooled by gracious appearances but sees the heart and acts accordingly.
Rich Christians written about by James (James 2:1–7)	• Exploited the tendency of some to cater to them because of their wealth. • Dragged other believers into court and slandered Jesus' name.	(12) God favors those who are rich in faith; they will inherit the kingdom.
Lydia (Acts 16:13–15*, 40)	• Hosted the first church in Europe in her home.	(13) We should use our resources and homes to accomplish God's purposes.
Cornelius the centurion (Acts 10:1–48*)	• Generous to the poor. • Sought out Peter concerning the faith.	(14) Fear of God should prompt us to admit our own need for a Savior.
The Ethiopian treasurer (Acts 8:26–40)	• Nurtured his belief in God by traveling to Jerusalem. • Invited Philip to explain more about the faith.	(15) Stewardship of money and study of Scripture go hand in hand—as do business trips and worship services.
Simon the Sorcerer (Acts 8:9–25)	• Longed for spiritual power and thought it could be bottled and sold.	(16) The gifts of God cannot be bought.

Your checkbook is a diary of your values. God calls believers to be compassionate, merciful, and just to all. Does your checkbook reflect such values? Does it show a pattern of godly concern for people?

***See profiles of these people at the texts indicated.**

Wealth is a major topic in the New Testament. Jesus often warned about its dangers. See Matt. 6:24; Mark 10:17–31; and Luke 12:13–21. Likewise, Paul challenged believers to use their resources in a Christlike way. See "Christians and Money," 1 Tim. 6:6–19.

45Now from the sixth hour until the ninth hour there was darkness over all the land. 46And about the ninth hour Jesus cried out with a loud voice, saying, "Eli, Eli, lama sabachthani?" that is, "My God, My God, why have You forsaken Me?"[a]

47Some of those who stood there, when they heard *that,* said, "This Man is calling for Elijah!" 48Immediately one of them ran and took a sponge, filled *it* with sour wine and put *it* on a reed, and offered it to Him to drink.

49The rest said, "Let Him alone; let us see if Elijah will come to save Him."

50And Jesus cried out again with a loud voice, and yielded up His spirit.

51Then, behold, the veil of the temple was torn in two from top to bottom; and the earth quaked, and the rocks were split, 52and the graves were opened; and many bodies of the saints who had fallen asleep were raised; 53and coming out of the graves after His resurrection, they went into the holy city and appeared to many.

54So when the centurion and those with him, who were guarding Jesus, saw the earthquake and the things that had happened, they feared greatly, saying, "Truly this was the Son of God!"

55And many women who followed Jesus from Galilee, ministering to Him, were there looking on

27:56

from afar, 56among whom were Mary Magdalene, Mary the mother of James and Joses,[a] and the mother of Zebedee's sons.

Jesus Is Buried in a Borrowed Tomb

27:57

57Now when evening had come, there came a rich man from Arimathea, named Joseph, who himself had

27:58–61

also become a disciple of Jesus. 58This man went to Pilate and asked for the body of Jesus. Then Pilate com-

27:59–60

manded the body to be given to him. 59When Joseph had taken the body, he wrapped it in a clean linen cloth, 60and laid it in his new tomb which he had hewn out of the rock; and he rolled a large stone against the door of the tomb, and departed. 61And Mary Magdalene was there, and the other Mary, sitting opposite the tomb.

62On the next day, which followed the Day of Preparation, the chief priests and Pharisees gathered together to Pilate, 63saying, "Sir, we remember, while He was still alive, how that deceiver said, 'After three days I will rise.' 64Therefore command that the tomb be made secure until the third day, lest His disciples come by night[a] and steal Him *away,* and say to the people, 'He has risen from the dead.' So the last deception will be worse than the first."

65Pilate said to them, "You have a guard; go your way, make *it* as secure as you know how." 66So they went and made the tomb secure, sealing the stone and setting the guard.

CHAPTER 28

The Resurrection

28:1–10 see pg. 120

1Now after the Sabbath, as the first *day* of the week began to dawn, Mary Magdalene and the other Mary came

(Bible text continued on page 121)

27:46 [a]Psalm 22:1 *27:56* [a]NU-Text reads *Joseph.* *27:64* [a]NU-Text omits *by night.*

Mary—A Common Name for Some Uncommon Women

A CLOSER LOOK 27:56 *At least six Marys are mentioned in the New Testament. Why was the name so common? See "Why So Many Marys?" Mark 15:40.*

For a listing of other women who followed Jesus, see Luke 8:1.

A Borrowed Tomb

A CLOSER LOOK 27:58–61 *Just as God provided for Jesus' needs at His birth (see "A Poor Family Comes into Wealth," Matt. 2:11), He provided for His needs in death (27:57–61). "A Burial Fit for a King" at Mark 15:42—16:1 talks about the gift of a borrowed tomb.*

Expensive Funerals

A CLOSER LOOK 27:59–60 *It is common for people to spend a great deal on funerals, sometimes more than they should. See "A Burial Fit for a King," Mark 15:42—16:1, for more on honoring the dead without breaking the bank.*

CONSIDER THIS
28:1–10

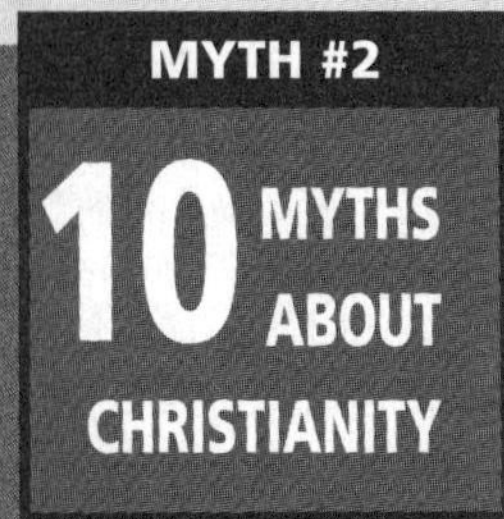

MYTH: THERE IS NO EVIDENCE THAT JESUS ROSE FROM THE DEAD

Many people today accept a number of myths about Christianity, with the result that they never respond to Jesus as He really is. This is one of ten articles that speak to some of those misconceptions. For a list of all ten, see 1 Tim. 1:3–4.

All four Gospels give an account of Jesus' resurrection (vv. 1–10; Mark 16:1–18; Luke 24:1–12; John 20:1–29). Moreover, the rest of the New Testament speaks with a tremendous sense of confidence about an empty tomb and the triumph of Christ over death.

And no wonder. If true, the resurrection is the most amazing news the world has ever heard. It means there is a God after all. It means that Jesus really is God's Son. It means that Christ is alive—today—and we can know Him and be touched by His life and power. It means that we need not fear death the way we once did; we are not destined to oblivion but to spend eternity with God. It also means that knowing God is of the utmost importance right now, while we can.

These are important implications, so the question of whether Jesus actually rose from the dead is crucial. At least four lines of evidence indicate that He did:

(1) *Jesus really was dead.* Every source we have indicates that Jesus was publicly executed before large crowds. He was certified as dead by both a centurion in charge of the execution—a professional whose job it was to determine that death had taken place—and by the regional governor, Pilate, who sent to have the matter checked. This is an important point because some skeptics claim that Jesus was not really dead, that He was only near death but revived in the cool of the tomb.

(2) *The tomb was found empty.* Jesus was buried in a new tomb, one that had never before been used (John 19:41). That means it was in perfect condition and would have been easy to locate. But when Jesus' friends arrived on the second morning after His death, His body was gone. All the accounts agree on this.

The empty tomb was no less astonishing to Jesus' enemies than it was to His friends. His enemies had been working for years to see Him dead and buried. Having accomplished their goal, they took pains to post a guard and seal the tomb with an enormous boulder. Nevertheless, on Easter morning the tomb was found empty.

Who emptied it? Either men or God. If men, which ones? Jesus' enemies would have been the least likely to have stolen the body. Even if they had, they would certainly have produced it later to refute the claims of the disciples that Jesus was alive. What about Jesus' friends? Unlikely, since the accounts show them to have been very demoralized after the crucifixion. Nor would they have willingly suffered persecution and death for what they knew to be a lie.

(3) *Jesus appeared after His death to many witnesses.* In a garden, on a road, in an upstairs room, by a lake—each of the Gospels recounts Jesus' post-resurrection appearances to His fearful, doubting followers over a period of forty days. Were these hallucinations? That seems implausible, since they happened to too many people, among them hardheaded fishermen, steadfast women, civil servants, and the ultimate skeptic, Thomas.

(4) *Countless people have encountered the living Jesus and been changed by Him.* The resurrection is not simply a matter of intellectual curiosity or theological argument, but of personal experience. From the first century to today there have been innumer-

(continued on next page)

to see the tomb. [2]And behold, there was a great earthquake;
for an angel of the Lord descended from heaven, and came
and rolled back the stone from the door,[a] and sat on it. [3]His
countenance was like lightning, and his clothing as white as
snow. [4]And the guards shook for fear of him, and became
like dead *men.*

[5]But the angel answered and said to the women, "Do not
be afraid, for I know that you seek Jesus who was crucified.

28:6 [6]He is not here; for He is risen, as He
said. Come, see the place where the Lord
lay. [7]And go quickly and tell His disciples that He is risen
from the dead, and indeed He is going before you into
Galilee; there you will see Him. Behold, I have told you."

[8]So they went out quickly from the tomb with fear and
great joy, and ran to bring His disciples word.

(Bible text continued on page 123)

28:2 [a]NU-Text omits *from the door.*

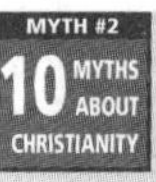

(continued from previous page)

able people who have turned from being totally opposed or indifferent to Christianity to being utterly convinced that it is true. What changed them? They met the living Jesus. He has invited them to respond to Him in faith and challenged them to live according to His way. Jesus is as alive now as He was that first Easter morning. He still invites people to know Him today. ◆

CONSIDER THIS 28:6

DON'T MISS GOD'S HELP

Do you feel uneasy when it comes to religion and spirituality? Do issues of faith and morality create fear? The women who went to the tomb on the first Easter Sunday were terribly frightened by what they found—or rather, by what they didn't *find, for the tomb was empty (v. 6)!*

Fortunately, God understands when spiritual matters invade the safety of our world. He offers help to overcome our fears and deal with whatever has come our way. For Mary and Mary Magdalene, He sent an angel to comfort and enlighten them about the reality of Christ's resurrection. He also sent an angel to Joseph, the earthly father of Jesus, when he was troubled by his fiancée's miraculous pregnancy (1:18–25).

So it was for many others in Scripture, who were no less troubled by spiritual events and truths than many of us are today. In addition to angels, God's help has included other people, dramatic and even miraculous demonstrations of His power, direct promises, and the enormous comfort of His Word. These helps show that God appreciates the impact of spiritual light suddenly shining in a dark world. He helps us overcome the shock not only of what *He has spoken, but* that *He has spoken.*

The question remains, will we respond to His message? No matter how awkward we may feel about matters of faith, we dare not avoid them. God opens up these scary places in our lives only because He wants to restore us to Himself. ◆

To All the Nations

Jesus sent His followers to make disciples of all the nations (ethnē, *"peoples"; v. 19). That mandate may seem obvious to us today. After all, we live at the end of 2,000 years of Christian outreach based on this and similar passages. Christianity now is an overwhelmingly Gentile religion subscribed to by roughly one-third of the world's population. And with modern technology, it appears to be a relatively simple task to expand that outreach even further.*

Yet in many ways we are just like Jesus' original disciples. They wanted a local hero, a Messiah just for Israel, one who would follow their customs and confirm their prejudices. So they were no doubt stunned by the scope and far-reaching implications of the global, cross-cultural vision that Jesus now presented. He was turning out to be more than the King of the Jews; He was the international Christ, the Savior of the entire world.

Actually, Jesus had been showing them this since the beginning of His ministry. Matthew recorded again and again His work among the Gentiles (Matt. 8:10; 15:24). The writer even cited Isaiah 42:1–4, that Jesus would "declare justice to the Gentiles [nations] . . . and in His name Gentiles will trust" (12:14–21). Yet the disciples had a hard time believing it. Could their Lord really be interested in "all the nations"? They certainly weren't.

(continued on next page)

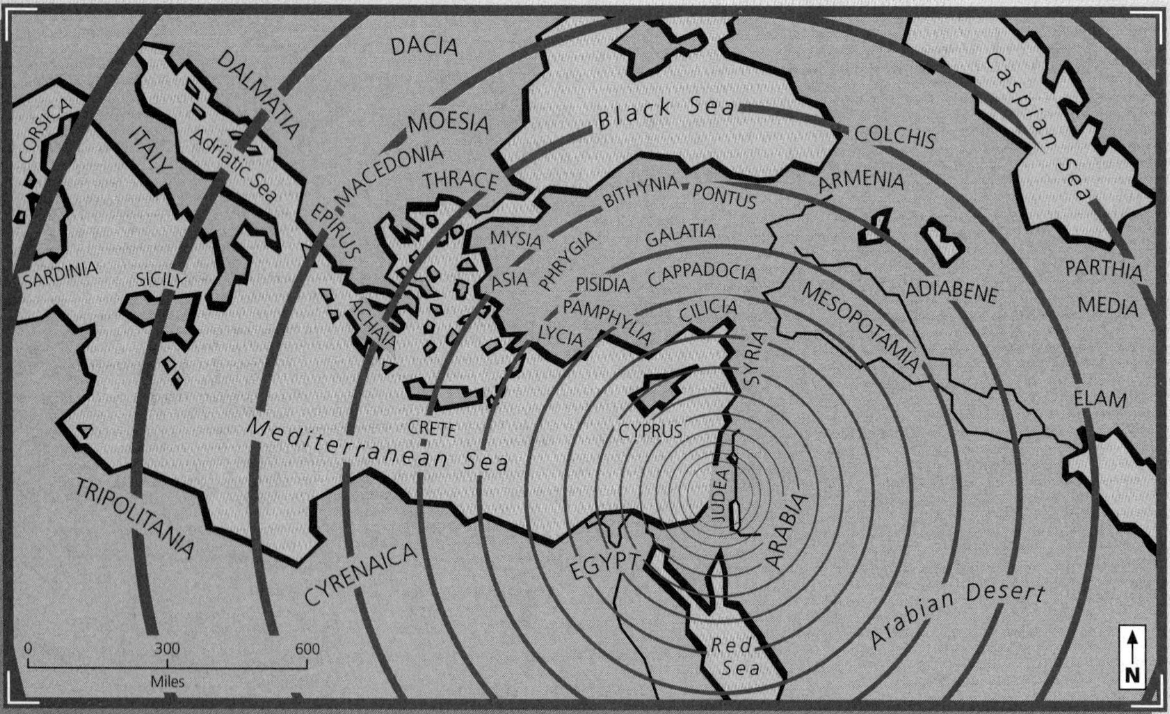

"To All the Nations"

9And as they went to tell His disciples,[a] behold, Jesus met
them, saying, "Rejoice!" So they came and held Him by the
feet and worshiped Him. 10Then Jesus said to them, "Do not
be afraid. Go *and* tell My brethren to go to Galilee, and
there they will see Me."

The Guards Are Bribed

11Now while they were going, behold, some of the guard
came into the city and reported to the chief priests all the
things that had happened. 12When they had assembled with
the elders and consulted together, they gave a large sum of
money to the soldiers, 13saying, "Tell them, 'His disciples
came at night and stole Him *away* while we slept.' 14And if
this comes to the governor's ears, we will appease him and
make you secure." 15So they took the money and did as
they were instructed; and this saying is commonly reported
among the Jews until this day.

Jesus Sends His Followers into the World

16Then the eleven disciples went away into Galilee, to the
mountain which Jesus had appointed for them. 17When
they saw Him, they worshiped Him; but some doubted.

28:18

28:19

18And Jesus came and spoke to them,
saying, "All authority has been given to
Me in heaven and on earth. 19Go therefore[a] and make disciples of all the na-
tions, baptizing them in the name of the Father and of the
Son and of the Holy Spirit, 20teaching them to observe all
things that I have commanded you; and lo, I am with you
always, *even* to the end of the age." Amen.[a]

28:19 [a]M-Text omits *therefore*. *28:20* [a]NU-Text omits *Amen*.

Jesus' Power

The power that gave Jesus authority and that He promised to His followers (vv. 18–19) was not the power of force or political authority. It was an ability to accomplish a very specific task. See "Power," Acts 1:8.

(continued from previous page)

Are we? It's easy to pay lip service to the idea that Jesus cares for the whole world. But isn't it easier to follow a Christ that fits comfortably into our own culture?

Culture, after all, is the key. Jesus told His Galilean followers to "make disciples," and they did—*Jewish* disciples. But they experienced profound culture-shock when the Holy Spirit brought new groups into the fellowship, including Hellenist disciples (Acts 6:1–7), Samaritan disciples (8:4–25), and eventually even Gentile disciples of all kinds (10:1—11:18; 15:1–21).

Today the bulk of new disciples are non-white and non-Western. Not surprisingly, they bring very different cultural perspectives into the church. So one of the greatest challenges believers will face in the coming years is the same one that the original disciples faced at the inauguration of the movement: to not only believe but to *accept* that Jesus really is for all the nations. ◆

One of the key people responsible for helping communicate the message about Christ throughout the Roman world was "Luke, the Gentile Author." Find out more about him at the introduction to Luke.

The spread of the gospel to "all the nations" began in an explosive way just a few days after Jesus' words in Matthew 28. See "A Surprising First Fulfillment of Acts 1:8," Acts 2:8–11.

As the gospel spread to people of different cultures, there was always the danger of believers going their separate ways. That's why Paul challenged Christians to pursue unity in the body of Christ and charity among the peoples of the world. See "Are We One People?" Rom. 11:13–24.

THEMES TO STUDY

Matthew's Gospel speaks to numerous practical themes, as shown below. Studying the texts associated with a given issue will help you apply God's Word to your experience. To study a theme, refer to the articles listed for that theme. Within the articles you'll find references to additional helps, Bible texts, and related themes.

THE CHURCH

What does "church" mean? Is it a building? An institution? A community of believers? Is there an "ideal church"? We can learn much from the New Testament about what God wants the church to be. Reading the Matthew articles listed below and their related texts will get you started:

To Be Like Jesus Means to Commit to Other Believers (Matt. 3:1–17)
The King Declares His Kingdom (Matt. 4:17)
To Be Like Jesus Means to Serve Others (Matt. 8:1—9:38)
To Be Like Jesus Means to Affirm Other Leaders (Matt. 10:1–42)
The Twelve (Matt. 10:2)
"The Gates of Hell" (Matt. 16:18)
Would You Choose These for Leaders? (Matt. 26:35–74)
To All the Nations (Matt. 28:19)

ETHICS AND CHARACTER

God calls His people to integrity and compassion. But because all of us are sinners who have rebelled against God and come into bondage to our own self-interests, following God's calling does not come naturally. Instead we find in ourselves agendas and patterns of behavior that fall far short of Christ's example of goodness and humane treatment of others.

How can we change? How can born sinners develop into ethical people? To find out, start by studying the categories, articles, and passages below:

Behavior on the Job
Sulfa Drugs and Street Lights (Matt. 5:13–16)
The Public Side of Faith (Matt. 14:13–14)

Christlike Character
Being Like Jesus (series, Matt. 10:25)

Decision Making
Judge Not! (Matt. 7:1–5)
Trick Questions Foiled (Matt. 22:23–33)

Humility
The Power of Humility (Matt. 3:11)
The Way Up Is Down (Matt. 5:3)

Integrity
Is Evasion Ethical? (Matt. 21:24–27)
Trick Questions Foiled (Matt. 22:23–33)

Justice
An Eye for an Eye (Matt. 5:38–42)
Judge Not! (Matt. 7:1–5)
No Forgiveness! (Matt. 12:31–32)
Seventy Times Seven—Still Not Enough! (Matt. 18:21–35)
Jesus and Unjust Pay (Matt. 20:1–16)
The Final Exam (Matt. 25:31–46)

Love
What Kind of Love Is This? (Matt. 22:34–40)

Money and Wealth
Living Within Your Limits (Matt. 16:22–23)
Jesus and Unjust Pay (Matt. 20:1–16)
Tainted Money (Matt. 27:3–10)

Morality
The Morality of Christ (Matt. 5:17–48)
What About Old Testament Law? (Matt. 5:19)
An Eye for an Eye (Matt. 5:38–42)

Power and Authority
To Be Like Jesus Means to Serve Others (Matt. 8:1—9:38)
Under Authority (Matt. 8:5–13)
The Power of Forgiveness (Matt. 9:4–8)
Servant-Leaders (Matt. 20:25–28)
A New Style of Fame (Matt. 21:8–11)
Would You Choose These for Leaders? (Matt. 26:35–74)

Public Ethics
Sulfa Drugs and Street Lights (Matt. 5:13–16)
The Public Side of Faith (Matt. 14:13–14)
Jesus and Taxation (Matt. 17:24–27)

Right and Wrong
The Morality of Christ (Matt. 5:17–48)

Success
True Success Means Faithfulness (Matt. 25:14–30)

Temptation
Wealth's Temptation (Matt. 4:8–10)

Miscellaneous
City Kids Die over Adult Matters (Matt. 2:16–18)

THE FAMILY

There is great confusion in today's society about the family. Some have high expectations for the family; some do not. For some families, the usual experience is tension, conflict, pain, and loss, when it ought to be love, commitment, pleasure, and security. Scripture has a lot to teach about the nature of the family. The articles listed below will help you to begin your study:

Jesus' Family
Jesus' Roots (Matt. 1:1–16)
The Women in Jesus' Genealogy (Matt. 1:3–6)

Asian-born Jesus Becomes a Refugee in Africa (Matt. 2:13–15)
Jesus—A Homeless Man? (Matt. 8:20)

Families of the New Testament

A Poor Family Comes into Wealth (Matt. 2:11)
A Surprise in Peter's Household (Matt. 8:14–15)
Hateful Herodias (Matt. 14:3)
A Pushy Mother (Matt. 20:20–23)

Family Backgrounds

Jesus' Roots (Matt. 1:1–16)
To Be Like Jesus Means to Accept Our Roots (Matt. 1:1–17)
The Women in Jesus' Genealogy (Matt. 1:3–6)

Family Life Issues

Family Loyalty (Matt. 12:46–50)
Children and Childcare (Matt. 19:14)

Other

A Poor Family Comes into Wealth (Matt. 2:11)
City Kids Die over Adult Matters (Matt. 2:16–18)
Jesus Weeps for the Children (Matt. 23:37–39)

Getting to Know Jesus

Jesus Christ is the center around which Christianity and all of Scripture revolve. He invites everyone to know Him, and Matthew's Gospel helps us do that by recording Jesus' life, work, teaching, death, and resurrection. To know Him is to know God. It is also the way to know what God intended us to be like, before sin began its terrible work on us. The articles listed below will help you get started in learning about the Son of God:

Being Like Jesus

A good place to begin your study would be to read the series of articles under the heading, "Being Like Jesus." The main article can be found at Matt. 10:25.

The Life and Work of Jesus

Jesus' Roots (Matt. 1:1–16)
Asian-born Jesus Becomes a Refugee in Africa (Matt. 2:13–15)
Jesus' Galilean Ministry (map; Matt. 4:25)
Jesus—A City Preacher (Matt. 9:35)

Jesus' Nature and Character

Ten Myths about Christianity, Myth #1: Jesus Christ Was Only a Great Moral Teacher (Matt. 13:34–35)
The Names of Jesus (Matt. 17:5)

Jesus and People

Jesus' Roots (Matt. 1:1–16)
Jesus' Global Connections (Matt. 8:10)
Jews, Gentiles, and Jesus (Matt. 15:24)

Jesus Our Example

Jesus—A Homeless Man? (Matt. 8:20)
Jesus—A City Preacher (Matt. 9:35)
Jesus and Taxation (Matt. 17:24–27)
Jesus and Unjust Pay (Matt. 20:1–16)
Trick Questions Foiled (Matt. 22:23–33)
Jesus Weeps for the Children (Matt. 23:37–39)

Laity

When we examine the New Testament's description of the early church, we find that pastors, teachers, and other leaders functioned "for the equipping of the saints for the work of ministry" (Eph. 4:12). Ministry also belonged to the ordinary believers, or laity, who lived and worked in the everyday world. The articles below speak to the value, calling, and work of laypeople:

The Twelve (Matt. 10:2)
Being Like Jesus (series, Matt. 10:25)
A Prayer of the Laity (Matt. 10:7–10)
Work-World Stories Describe the Kingdom (Matt. 13:1)
Would You Choose These for Leaders? (Matt. 26:35–74)
Wealthy People in the New Testament (Matt. 27:57)

Men

What does it mean to be male? How can a man live with Christlike character? By studying the men of the New Testament and the passages that speak to masculine concerns, we can begin to learn what God intends for a man, and how men can grow and serve Christ in every area of life:

The Man Jesus

Jesus' Roots (Matt. 1:1–16)
Jesus: A Homeless Man (Matt. 8:20)

Men in the New Testament

Matthew, the Social Outcast (Introduction to Matthew)
A Rich Man Enters the Kingdom (Matt. 9:9–13)
The Twelve (Matt. 10:2)
Caiaphas, the Religious Power Broker (Matt. 26:3)
Judas Iscariot, the Betrayer (Matt. 26:14)

A Man's Character

See the list of articles under "Ethics and Character" in this section.

Other

A New Respect for Women (Matt. 5:32)

People to Know

Scripture provides many things to many people, such as doctrine, comfort, guidance, and principles for day-to-day life. Another treasure in God's Word is a host of people who lived and worked in public and private places. Their stories are told so we can learn from their examples (whether good or bad), as we see how they struggled with issues of faith and life:

Matthew, the Social Outcast (Introduction to Matthew)
The Women in Jesus' Genealogy (Matt. 1:3–6)
A Rich Man Enters the Kingdom (Matt. 9:9–13)
The Hemorrhaging Woman (Matt. 9:20–22)
The Twelve (Matt. 10:2)
A Pushy Mother (Matt. 20:20–23)
Judas Iscariot, the Betrayer (Matt. 26:14)
Would You Choose These for Leaders? (Matt. 26:35–74)
Wealthy People in the New Testament (Matt. 27:57)

Race and Ethnicity

No matter who we are, our family histories have shaped us profoundly. Sometimes we misunderstand people from other backgrounds. But God values everyone in the world and seeks to bring all people into His eternal family. Scripture teaches us about the riches of ethnic diversity. See the following articles in Matthew:

Jesus' Roots (Matt. 1:1–16)
To Be Like Jesus Means to Accept Our Roots (Matt. 1:1–17)

Asian-born Jesus Becomes a Refugee in Africa (Matt. 2:13–15)
Jesus' Global Connections (Matt. 8:10)
The Twelve (Matt. 10:2)
Jews, Gentiles, and Jesus (Matt. 15:24)
To All the Nations (Matt. 28:19)

Urban Life

Soon, more of the world's people will live in cities than outside of them, and technology will continue to bring the values of the city to the countryside. Matthew's Gospel has much to say about the impact of urban society on believers—and vice versa:

To Be Like Jesus Means to Engage the World's Pain (Matt. 1:18—2:23)
City Kids Die over Adult Matters (Matt. 2:16–18)
Can a Noisy, Dirty, Smelly City Also Be Holy? (Matt. 4:5)
The King Declares His Kingdom (Matt. 4:17)
Sulfa Drugs and Street Lights (Matt. 5:13–16)
Jesus' Global Connections (Matt. 8:10)
Jesus—A Homeless Man? (Matt. 8:20)
The Public Side of Faith (Matt. 14:13–14)
Party Politics of Jesus' Day (Matt. 16:1)
Jesus and Taxation (Matt. 17:24–27)
The Holy City (Matt. 23:37)
The Final Exam (Matt. 25:31–46)

Wealth and Poverty

By worldwide standards, anyone is "rich" who has choices in life. Poverty means having no options about where to live, what to eat, or whom to be with. In Scripture, wealth and poverty are major topics. In fact, more of Jesus' words about money have been preserved than about heaven. You might want to discuss the following articles with other believers or coworkers:

Wealthy People
A Rich Man Enters the Kingdom (Matt. 9:9–13)
Who Were Those Tax Collectors? (Matt. 9:10)
Wealthy People in the New Testament (Matt. 27:57)

Words to the Wealthy
Growing Fat at the Poor's Expense (Matt. 23:14)
True Success Means Faithfulness (Matt. 25:14–30)

Poor People
A Poor Family Comes into Wealth (Matt. 2:11)
Jesus—A Homeless Man? (Matt. 8:20)

Words Concerning the Poor
Growing Fat at the Poor's Expense (Matt. 23:14)

The Challenge of Wealth
Wealth's Temptation (Matt. 4:8–10)
Living Within Your Limits (Matt. 16:22–23)
Tainted Money (Matt. 27:3–10)

Charitable Contributions
Anonymous Donors (Matt. 6:1–4)

Taxes
Jesus and Taxation (Matt. 17:24–27)

Other
Some Surprising Evidence (Matt. 11:2–6)
Jesus and Unjust Pay (Matt. 20:1–16)

Witness and Evangelism

What does it mean to "be a witness" for Christ? What is evangelism all about? How can believers influence others to consider and accept the message about Jesus? Study the following articles in Matthew and their related passages to start learning more about sharing the Christian faith:

The Example of Jesus
Being Like Jesus (series, Matt. 10:25)
Jews, Gentiles, and Jesus (Matt. 15:24)

The Church's Mandate
The Public Side of Our Faith (Matt. 14:13–14)
To All the Nations (Matt. 28:19)

Women

The New Testament was written in an age when women faced very different roles and expectations than they experience today. Nevertheless, Jesus took women seriously. He enjoyed important friendships with a number of women and affirmed their value and significance. Here are some articles to study as you consider what Scripture has to say about women and subjects that pertain to them:

Jesus and Women
The Women in Jesus' Genealogy (Matt. 1:3–6)
A New Respect for Women (Matt. 5:32)
Family Loyalty (Matt. 12:46–50)
Persistence Pays Off (Matt. 15:21–28)

Women in New Testament Times
The Women in Jesus' Genealogy (Matt. 1:3–6)
The Hemorrhaging Woman (Matt. 9:20–22)
Hateful Herodias (Matt. 14:3)
Persistence Pays Off (Matt. 15:21–28)
Children and Childcare (Matt. 19:14)
A Pushy Mother (Matt. 20:20–23)
"Harlots Enter the Kingdom" (Matt. 21:31–32)

A Woman's Character
See the list of articles under "Ethics and Character" in this section.

Other
The Way Up Is Down (Matt. 5:3)
A New Respect for Women (Matt. 5:32)
Children and Childcare (Matt. 19:14)

Work

In today's world some people see their work as a long, dark tunnel between leisurely weekends, others as a passion bordering on addiction; some as a curse from God, others as a divine calling. What does Matthew's Gospel say about this crucial area that so dominates day-to-day life? Begin finding out by studying the articles listed below:

The Nature and Value of Work
Our Daily Bread (Matt. 6:11)

Communicating the Gospel in the Workplace
Sulfa Drugs and Street Lights (Matt. 5:13–16)
The Public Side of Our Faith (Matt. 14:13–14)

Money and Profits

Jesus and Unjust Pay (Matt. 20:1–16)
Growing Fat at the Poor's Expense (Matt. 23:14)

Success and Significance

True Success Means Faithfulness (Matt. 25:14–30)

Work and the Church

A Prayer of the Laity (Matt. 10:7–10)
Work World Stories Describe the Kingdom (Matt. 13:1)

Work and Workers in the New Testament

Who Were Those Tax Collectors? (Matt. 9:10)
See also the list of articles under "Ethics" in this section.

LARGE ARTICLES

The Women in Jesus' Genealogy (Matt. 1:3–6)
The King Declares His Kingdom (Matt. 4:17)
The Sermon on the Mount (Matt. 5:2)
The Morality of Christ (Matt. 5:17–48)
An Eye for an Eye (Matt. 5:38–42)
A Rich Man Enters the Kingdom (Matt. 9:9–13)
Jesus—A City Preacher (Matt. 9:35)
A Prayer of the Laity (Matt. 10:7–10)
Ten Myths about Christianity, Myth #1: Jesus Christ Was Only a Great Moral Teacher (Matt. 13:34–35)
Treasures New and Old (Matt. 13:52)
Jews, Gentiles, and Jesus (Matt. 15:24)
Party Politics of Jesus' Day (Matt. 16:1)
"The Gates of Hell" (Matt. 16:18)
Tithing (Matt. 23:23–24)
Ten Myths about Christianity, Myth #2: There Is No Evidence That Jesus Rose from the Dead (Matt. 28:1–10)

Also see the book introduction.

MAPS

A number of maps help you put the events of Matthew's Gospel into geographical perspective:

The Land of the Gospels (Introduction to Matthew)
To Egypt and Back (Matt. 2:13–15)
Jerusalem (Matt. 4:5)
Jesus' Galilean Ministry (Matt. 4:25)
Cities of Palestine in Christ's Time (Matt. 9:35)
Jesus' Entry (Matt. 21:1)
"To All the Nations" (Matt. 28:19)

Locator Maps

A locator map shows where a certain place is with reference to the surrounding area. The following are locator maps in Matthew:

Chorazin (Matt. 11:21)
Magdala (Matt. 15:39)
Jerusalem (Matt. 23:37)

CITY AND REGIONAL PROFILES

The world of the Bible was far more urban than many modern readers realize. Jesus, Paul, and others in the first century grew up and carried out most of their work among the cities of the Roman Empire. Three of them are profiled in Matthew's Gospel:

Chorazin (Matt. 11:21)
Magdala (Matt. 15:39)
Jerusalem (Matt. 23:37)

PERSONALITY PROFILES

The Bible provides believers today with many illustrations of people responding to God in one way or another. By studying the Personality Profiles below and reading the related texts in Matthew, you can learn much (both positive and negative) about these individuals whose lives the Holy Spirit chose to record in Scripture for our benefit:

Caiaphas (Matt. 26:3)
Judas Iscariot (Matt. 26:14)
Matthew (Introduction to Matthew)

TABLES AND DIAGRAMS

Jesus' Global Connections (Matt. 8:10)
The Twelve (Matt. 10:2)
Work World Stories Describe the Kingdom (Matt. 13:1)
Telling Time (Matt. 14:25)
Party Politics of Jesus' Day (Matt. 16:1)
The Names of Jesus (Matt. 17:5)
The Little People at Jesus' Death (Matt. 27:32)
Wealthy People in the New Testament (Matt. 27:57)

Index to Key Passages in Matthew

The following index provides access to selected passages from Matthew's Gospel that speak most directly to practical concerns in today's world. Use this index along with the other helps and annotations to see quickly what Matthew says about each subject.

(Passages are listed alphabetically by brief content summaries. The words 'a' and 'the' are ignored in the alphabetizing.)

Accountability
(*see* Duty; Responsibility)

Anger
Anger without cause . . . . . Matt. 5:22
Of Herod, at wise men . . . . . Matt. 2:16
Of Jesus, directed against evil . . . . . Matt. 21:12–13

Authority
Binding and loosing . . . . . Matt. 18:18
In heaven and earth . . . . . Matt. 28:18
Jesus taught with authority . . . . . Matt. 7:29

Boldness
Joseph of Arimathea with Pilate . . . . . Matt. 27:57–58
Peter bold to defend Jesus . . . . . Matt. 26:33–35, 51
Whom to fear and to fear not . . . . . Matt. 10:26–31

Career/Calling
Jesus calls His first disciples . . . . . Matt. 4:18–22
Laborers called to their work . . . . . Matt. 20:1–16
Improvement of God's gifts . . . . . Matt. 25:14–30

Children
(*see* Youth)

Christlikeness
A disciple is like his teacher . . . . . Matt. 10:25
Jesus says to follow him . . . . . Matt. 4:19; 8:22; 9:9
Take up the cross . . . . . Matt. 16:24
Relinquish possessions . . . . . Matt. 19:21

Cities
Capernaum "Jesus' own city" . . . . . Matt. 9:1
The city of the great king . . . . . Matt. 5:35
A divided city cannot stand . . . . . Matt. 12:25
Jesus brought up in a city . . . . . Matt. 2:23
Jesus preached in the cities . . . . . Matt. 9:35; 11:1
Some cities rebuked by Jesus . . . . . Matt. 11:20–24

Competition
Be a servant to be great . . . . . Matt. 20:20–28
Blessed are the meek . . . . . Matt. 5:5
Many of the first shall be last . . . . . Matt. 19:30; 20:16

Conscience
Clear it by seeking forgiveness . . . . . Matt. 5:23–24

Crime and Punishment
Better to settle out of court . . . . . Matt. 5:25–26
Do not resist the perpetrator . . . . . Matt. 5:38–39
Keep the commandments . . . . . Matt. 19:17–19
Property is subject to theft . . . . . Matt. 6:19–20

Duty
Duty to the government . . . . . Matt. 17:27; 22:21
Duty toward enemies . . . . . Matt. 5:44
Help the destitute . . . . . Matt. 25:34–40
Obey the will of God . . . . . Matt. 12:50
(*see also* Government)

Education
Disciples to teach all nations . . . . . Matt. 28:19–20
Jesus taught the multitudes . . . . . Matt. 5:1–2
Teaching illustrated from nature . . . . . Matt. 6:25–30

Enmity
An enemy, the devil, sowed tares . . . . Matt. 13:24–28, 39
Love your enemies . . . . . Matt. 5:43–48

Environment
God's care for His creation . . . . . Matt. 6:26–30
Stewards expected to be faithful . . . . . Matt. 25:14–30

Envy
The evil eye of jealousy . . . . . Matt. 6:23; 20:15
Priests and elders envied Jesus . . . . . Matt. 27:18

Evangelism
Disciples sent out to preach . . . . . Matt. 10:5–20
Go to the nations . . . . . Matt. 28:19–20

Evil
Do not resist evil . . . . . Matt. 5:38–39
Evil tree produces evil fruit . . . . . Matt. 7:17
Sun rises on evil and good . . . . . Matt. 5:45

Faith
Faith made a person whole . . . . . Matt. 9:22
Great faith found . . . . . Matt. 8:10; 15:28
Little faith produces doubt . . . . . Matt. 16:8
A weighty matter of the law . . . . . Matt. 23:23

Family
Forsaking family for Jesus' sake . . . . . Matt. 19:29
The gospel overrides family ties . . . . . Matt. 12:48–50
The gospel will disrupt families . . . . . Matt. 10:35–37
Jesus had an earthly family . . . . . Matt. 13:55
Marriage is God-ordained . . . . . Matt. 19:4–6

Fellowship
All believers are brethren . . . . . Matt. 23:8
Gathered in Jesus' name . . . . . Matt. 18:20
Jesus with three disciples . . . . . Matt. 17:1–4
Where two or three are gathered . . . . . Matt. 18:20
With the wicked forbidden . . . . . Matt. 18:17

Matthew: Index to Key Passages

Friendship
False friendship shown . . . Matt. 26:48–49
Jesus a friend of sinners . . . Matt. 11:19
Women befriended Jesus . . . Matt. 27:55–56

Government
Give to Caesar what is his . . . Matt. 22:17–21
Jesus will rule Israel . . . Matt. 2:6
A king and his servants . . . Matt. 18:23–35
Misrule by kings . . . Matt. 2:3–16; 14:1–11
Pilate sentences Jesus . . . Matt. 27:11–26

Gratitude
Grace at meals . . . Matt. 14:19
Jesus set us an example . . . Matt. 11:25; 26:27

Greed
Treasures in heaven . . . Matt. 6:19–21, 33
What profit is gain? . . . Matt. 16:26

Hatred
Being hated for Jesus' sake . . . Matt. 10:22
Love your enemies . . . Matt. 5:43–44

Holiness
Angels are holy . . . Matt. 25:31
Don't give what is holy to dogs . . . Matt. 7:6
Jerusalem the holy city . . . Matt. 4:5; 27:53

Honesty
Jesus praised for telling truth . . . Matt. 22:16
Known by one's words . . . Matt. 12:33–37

Honor
Honor parents . . . Matt. 15:4
Honoring Jesus with lip service . . . Matt. 15:8
A prophet not honored at home . . . Matt. 13:57

Humility
Be humble as a child . . . Matt. 18:4
The humble will be exalted . . . Matt. 23:12

Immortality
Eternal life by following Jesus . . . Matt. 19:21, 29
Eternal life or punishment . . . Matt. 25:46

Inclusiveness
The gospel for all nations . . . Matt. 28:19–20

Justice
God sends rain on just and unjust . . . Matt. 5:45
Joseph's justice toward Mary . . . Matt. 1:18–25
Justice declared to Gentiles . . . Matt. 12:18–21
Pilate and wife called Jesus just . . . Matt. 27:19, 24
A weighty matter of the law . . . Matt. 23:23
Wicked and just to be separated . . . Matt. 13:49–50

Knowledge
The future is known to God . . . Matt. 24:36
God knows all things . . . Matt. 6:8, 32
Jesus knows our thoughts . . . Matt. 9:4
Knowledge of the Father and Son . . . Matt. 11:27
Kingdom mysteries made known . . . Matt. 13:11

Laziness
Parable of the talents . . . Matt. 25:14–30

Leadership
Be a servant-leader . . . Matt. 20:26
The blind cannot lead the blind . . . Matt. 15:14

Love
Love Christ more than family . . . Matt. 10:37
Love the Lord God . . . Matt. 22:37
The love of many will grow cold . . . Matt. 24:12
Love toward one's neighbor . . . Matt. 19:19; 22:39
Love toward enemies . . . Matt. 5:43–46

Lust
Lust for a woman is adultery . . . Matt. 5:28
Proceeds out of the heart . . . Matt. 15:19

Men
Beware of men; trust the Spirit . . . Matt. 10:17–22
A generous father . . . Matt. 7:9–11
A man and his wife are united . . . Matt. 19:3
A man under authority . . . Matt. 8:8–10
A rich young man . . . Matt. 19:16–24

Mercy
Blessed are the merciful . . . Matt. 5:7
Healing flows from mercy . . . Matt. 20:30–34
Mercy preferred over sacrifice . . . Matt. 9:13; 12:7
A weighty matter of the law . . . Matt. 23:23

Money and Finances
Forsaking all for Christ . . . Matt. 19:29
Hard for rich to enter kingdom . . . Matt. 19:23–24
Moneychangers driven from temple . . . Matt. 21:12–13
Parable of the Talents . . . Matt. 25:14–30
Payment of taxes . . . Matt. 17:24–27; 22:16–21
A rich man buried Jesus . . . Matt. 27:57
Riches are deceitful . . . Matt. 13:22
Worry is unnecessary . . . Matt. 6:25–34
(*see also* Greed)

Poverty
Blessed are the poor . . . Matt. 5:3
Give to the poor . . . Matt. 19:21
The gospel preached to the poor . . . Matt. 11:4–6
The poor are with us always . . . Matt. 26:11

Power
God's is the power forever . . . Matt. 6:13
Jesus has power to forgive sins . . . Matt. 9:6–8
Power over unclean spirits . . . Matt. 10:1
Sadducees knew not God's power . . . Matt. 22:29
Son of Man to return with power . . . Matt. 24:30

Pride
Avoid the pride of Pharisees . . . Matt. 23:1–8
Be a servant . . . Matt. 20:26–27
Position sought for sons . . . Matt. 20:20–23
The self-exalted will be abased . . . Matt. 23:12

Religion
The law summarized . . . Matt. 22:36–40
Not saying, "Lord, Lord" . . . Matt. 7:21–23
Some are religious hypocrites . . . Matt. 23:13–33
True religion: Sermon on Mount . . . Matt. 5:1—7:29

Repentance
Involves a change of behavior . . . Matt. 3:8
Jesus preached it . . . Matt. 4:17
John the Baptist preached it . . . Matt. 3:2
Ninevites repented . . . Matt. 12:41
Unrepentant cities rebuked . . . Matt. 11:20–21

Responsibility
Toward those who wrong us. . . . . Matt. 18:15–17, 21–22
Use God-given talents . . . . Matt. 25:14–30

Rest and Leisure
Jesus gives rest for the soul. . . . . Matt. 11:28–30
Jesus relaxed with friends . . . . Matt. 9:10–15; 11:19
Jesus slept during a storm . . . . Matt. 8:24

Righteousness
Exceed scribes' and Pharisees' . . . . Matt. 5:20
First seek God's righteousness . . . . Matt. 6:33
Jesus was baptized to fulfill it . . . . Matt. 3:15
Those persecuted for its sake . . . . Matt. 5:10
Those who thirst for it blessed . . . . Matt. 5:6
Righteous not called but sinners. . . . . Matt. 9:13
Will shine like sun in kingdom . . . . Matt. 13:43

Salvation
Desire to lose life and find it. . . . . Matt. 10:25
He who endures to the end saved . . . . Matt. 10:22; 24:13
Jesus will save His people. . . . . Matt. 1:21
Son of Man came to seek and save . . . . Matt. 18:11

Sin
Blood shed for sin's remission . . . . Matt. 26:28
Do not cause a child to sin . . . . Matt. 18:6
If a brother sins against you . . . . Matt. 18:15
Jesus forgave sins . . . . Matt. 9:2
Sinners called upon to repent. . . . . Matt. 9:13
Those baptized confessed sins . . . . Matt. 3:6

Speech
Jesus spoke words to heal. . . . . Matt. 8:8–13, 16
Live by every word from God. . . . . Matt. 4:4
The Spirit gives words to speak . . . . Matt. 10:18–20
Vain repetition in prayer. . . . . Matt. 6:7–8
Will give account of idle words . . . . Matt. 12:36
Words justify and condemn . . . . Matt. 12:32–37

Suffering
Jesus alleviated suffering . . . . . . Matt. 9:20–22; 17:15–18
Jesus had to suffer for us . . . . Matt. 16:21; 17:12

Temptation
Jesus was tempted by the devil. . . . . Matt. 4:1–10
Pray to avoid temptation . . . . Matt. 26:41

Urban Life
(*see* Cities)

Wealth
(*see* Money and Finances)

Wisdom
Be wise as serpents but harmless . . . . Matt. 10:16
Things of God hidden from wise . . . . Matt. 11:25
Wisdom justified by her children. . . . . Matt. 11:19
A wise man builds on rock. . . . . Matt. 7:24
Wise men honored Jesus . . . . Matt. 2:1–16
Wise virgins were ready . . . . Matt. 25:1–13

Women
Women anointed Jesus for burial . . . . Matt. 26:6–13
Women followed Jesus. . . . . Matt. 27:55–56
Women got John beheaded . . . . Matt. 14:3–11
Women were healed by Jesus . . Matt. 9:18–26; 15:22–28
Women witnessed the resurrection. . . . . Matt. 28:1, 5–10

Work
All who labor can come to Jesus. . . . . Matt. 11:28–30
Laborers needed for the gospel. . . . . Matt. 9:37–38
The landowner and his laborers . . . . Matt. 20:1–16
Two sons asked to work . . . . Matt. 21:28–32
Work for treasures in heaven . . . . Matt. 6:19–34
(*see also* Career/Calling; Laziness)

Worship
Hypocrites worship in vain . . . . Matt. 15:9
Jesus accepted worship . . . . Matt. 8:2; 9:18; 14:33
Worship and serve God only . . . . Matt. 4:10

Youth
Become like children in spirit. . . . . Matt. 18:1–4
Childish behavior rebuked. . . . . Matt. 11:16
Children worshiped Jesus . . . . Matt. 21:15
Let children come to Jesus . . . . Matt. 19:13–14
The rich young ruler . . . . Matt. 19:16–22